MORE PRAISE FOR LETTING GO

"As deans and college parents, we have found *Letting Go* an invaluable resource in providing perspective and thoughtful advice on the ups and downs, joys and trials of college life and parenting college students. We will continue to recommend it to Smith parents and to use it ourselves!"

> —*Merry Farnum, Assistant Dean for Student Affairs, and Tom Riddell, Dean of the First-Year Class, Smith College*

"*Letting Go* has been the consummate resource for parents (and college administrators working with parents) in attempting to understand the transitions of college students during the undergraduate years. This new edition combines the timeless wisdom of past editions with updated social research and the implications of the 'information age' on student behavior and performance. *Letting Go* is an important work and continues to be the most comprehensive publication available for all concerned with making sense of what are the inevitable yet often bewildering changes students in college will experience."

> —*Thomas C. Shandley, Ph.D., Vice President for Student Life, Davidson College*

"Sensible, thorough, comforting. The authors offer a wealth of helpful information to guide parents through an important family transition."

> —*Parker J. Beverage, Dean of Admissions and Financial Aid, Colby College*

"*Letting Go* unscrambles the exhilarating, confusing, and anxiety-producing experience of launching a child in the world of higher education. With sensitivity, humor, and wisdom, Karen Coburn and

Madge Treeger provide sound advice, good counsel, and practical strategies to help parents navigate the experience. We refer to *Letting Go* in our orientation sessions with parents every year, and always get excellent comments and responses."

—*Sheila Murphy, Dean for Student Life, Simmons College*

"When I agreed to read a preview copy of the new edition of *Letting Go*, I did not realize just how extensive the revisions would be. I could not be more pleased, not only because of the many relevant additions (and improvements) but also because the authors have preserved their very personal and accessible style. As someone who works with stressed-out high school seniors and their anxious parents, I especially appreciate their honesty about, and their obvious affection for, the complexities of college life. The book is not only extremely informative and timely; it is also warmly reassuring. I think it belongs on the bookshelves of parents, teachers, and college counselors alike."

—*James Alan Astman, Ph.D., Headmaster, Oakwood School, Los Angeles*

"I have admired the previous editions and this one maintains the themes with up-to-date examples and language. Definitely a 'guidebook for the 90's.' Mesdames Coburn and Treeger are both realistic and reassuring—not an easy balance to strike in a time when contemporary culture seems bent on cynicism as a way of thinking about youth. We will recommend this book to our parents because of its forthright optimism, good advice, and good humor."

—*Edes Gilbert, Headmistress, Spence School, New York*

"No other book so accurately describes this important developmental stage and significant rite of passage. I recommend it to all parents at every senior parent night and know it has provided support to hundreds of parents. Of the many books available today on college admissions, this one should be required reading for all parents. It is guaranteed to reduce the stress that surrounds the process."

—Judy B. Pietsch, *Director of College Counseling, Punahou School, Honolulu*

"This is certainly the best treatment I have read on this subject. It is intelligent, thorough, and researched with great professionalism and care. The discussion of the impact of technology is superb."

—Stephen Singer, *Horace Mann School, New York*

"A delightful blend of the humorous and the profound. . . . In a day when 'how to get in' books flood the market, it is refreshing to see someone address the question, 'now what?'"

—Keith E. Shahan, *Headmaster, John Burroughs School, St. Louis*

"A thoughtful, well written and comprehensive guide for parents. [It describes] in understandable terms the major changes that have taken place on the American college campus over the last twenty to thirty years. Even though I have lived continuously on a campus during that time, I would have found this guide useful when my oldest son went to college."

—Lattie F. Coor, *President, Arizona State University*

"Very practical, with lots of nuts-and-bolts illustrations of how to deal with concrete situations that arise for freshman college students."

—John N. Gardner, *National Center for the Study of the Freshman Year Experience, University of South Carolina*

"After more than a dozen years as a dean of first year students, of routinely advising parents on how to 'let go,' I sent my own first child off to college, as nervous and tearful as my 'lay' friends. My own professional experience proved less-than-useful; *Letting Go* helped to assure and reassure me. A practical reference tool, it kept me on track in the challenging and complex transition to being the parent of a college student."

—*Dorothy Denburg, Dean of College, Barnard College*

"Whether you are a parent taking your first child, last child, or only child away to college, this book is for you. The book superbly guides parents through the many difficult waters of parenting a college student."

—*Frances Lucas-Tauchar, Vice President and Dean for Campus Life, Emory University*

"This is definitely the book for students entering any post-secondary institution and their parents as we move into the twenty-first century. I will refer to it as the *"Letting Go Bible"* starting at grade nine. It will be our top reference book for students and parents."

—*Dorothy T. Swann, Guidance Counselor, Benjamin Mays High School, Atlanta*

"Marvelously reassuring reading for parents of undergraduates or those who are about to be."

—*Bruce Donovan, Associate Dean, Brown University*

LETTING
GO

A Parents' Guide to Understanding the College Years

Karen Levin Coburn
& Madge Lawrence Treeger

HarperPerennial
A Division of HarperCollins*Publishers*

*To our loving partners, Stephen
and Tom . . . and Alison, Andrew, Anne, and
Jennie, who continue to teach us about
letting go.*

HarperCollins books may be purchased for educational, business, or sales promotional use. For information please write: Special Markets Department, HarperCollins Publishers, Inc., 10 East 53rd Street, New York, NY 10022.

First HarperPerennial edition published 1997.

Designed by Elina D. Nudelman

Library of Congress Cataloging-in-Publication Data

Coburn, Karen Levin, 1941–
    Letting go : a parents' guide to understanding the college years / Karen Levin Cobun and Madge Lawrence Treeger. — 1st HarperPerennial ed.
     p. cm.
    Includes bibliographical references and index.
    ISBN 0-06-095244-X
    1. College students—United States—Psychology. 2. Parenting—United States. 3. Parent and child—United States. 4. Universities and colleges—United States. I. Treeger, Madge Lawrence, 1934– .
II. Title.
LA229.C53   1997
378.1'98—dc21   97-5901

00 01 ❖/RRD 20

C O N T E N T S
■ ■ ■

ACKNOWLEDGMENTS

WE ARE DEEPLY GRATEFUL TO ALL THE STUDENTS, parents, and college faculty and administrators who have shared their insights and experiences with us. We have changed some of the identifying information to protect anonymity, but you are the heart of this book.

In addition, we would like to thank the following friends and colleagues who have listened, questioned, critiqued, and continued to give us their support: Shirley Baker, John Berg, Beth Binns, Justin Carroll, Alyse Dampf, Robert Easton, Sara Epstein, Heather Feuerhahn, Rosemary Garagnani, Peggy Guest, Meg Jacobs, Julie Jones, Delores Kennedy, Helen Kornblum, Ellen Krout-Levine, Marylen Mann, Marny Muir, Harry Ratliff, Susan Rava, Paul Scheffel, Jane Schoenfeld, Linda Skrainka, Stephen Skrainka, Bob Sortland, Sally Lorber Stein.

Thank you also to Jonathan Cohen and Carla Loon, our research assistants, who checked facts, organized files, and helped us navigate the World Wide Web.

We appreciate the active interest of our initial publishers, Esthy and Jim Adler, and our current publisher, HarperCollins. Our editor, Kate Ekrem of HarperCollins, has contributed her intelligence, talent, and energy to this expanded third edition. And finally we give special thanks to our agent, Elizabeth Kaplan of Ellen Levine Literary Agency, Inc., who saw this project through from the kernel of an idea to its completion. She has been a constant source of good advice, enthusiasm, and encouragement.

PREFACE TO THE THIRD EDITION

FOR US, RETURNING TO LETTING GO WAS LIKE opening an old family photo album—full of nostalgia, with warm memories of the time when our own children were venturing forth on this college journey and we were immersed in writing the first edition. We remember beginning our research and writing in 1986 with pads of yellow lined paper . . . yes, yellow lined paper . . . but we soon conquered our computer phobia and embraced the word processor. We met nightly, after our daytime jobs, on the third floor of Karen's house; often ours was the only light still shining, well beyond midnight, on this quiet residential street. We talked together, separated to write, and came together to talk some more; we cut and pasted and found the rhythm of our partnership.

When we decided last year to do a comprehensive revision for the third edition and joined forces with HarperCollins, we hoped we could recapture the energetic and unusual collaboration that we had enjoyed earlier. Madge had left Washington University four years before to enter a private psychotherapy practice. Karen was working at a stimulating, but increasingly demanding, position as Associate Dean of Students. And so much had happened to university life in the four years since we had written the second edition. We knew this would be a major undertaking.

Once again, with a sense of déjà vu, we found ourselves in front of a computer, but this one had color and graphics and e-mail and the Internet. We made our headquarters Karen's office at Washington University, a practical decision based on access to resources and equipment. But working evenings and weekends at this location proved to have a surprising and auspicious impact on our work. We were constantly surrounded by the sounds, sights, and interactions of university life.

Karen's office sits in a building that is a hub of activity, housing the student affairs staff, sorority suites, a formal lounge for academic and social gatherings, and a drama and dance studio. As we wrote about diversity and multiculturalism, we experienced its campus presence firsthand. We listened night after night to the haunting songs and intense sounds of students in the studio across the hall rehearsing *The Dybbuk*, a play sponsored by the performing arts department in conjunction with Hillel's fiftieth anniversary. One night, as rehearsal was letting out, we spotted a tall, slender Asian-American student wearing a yarmulke and singing "Hava Tequila" (an irreverent and playful college student's variation on the traditional Jewish song "Hava Nagila"). Another evening, the first night of the Black Arts and Sciences Festival, joyous sounds of gospel singing and clapping resounded from the chapel. The fireworks bursting in the sky to celebrate the Indian festival Diwali brought color and sound to our nightly ritual on still another evening. And as we were putting the finishing touches on the manuscript one cold, bleak night during finals, gentle sounds of traditional Chinese music drew us across the hall to the dance studio, where a dozen Chinese students clad in jeans and T-shirts and holding fuchsia flutter fans were rehearsing a graceful dance for the upcoming Chinese New Year Festival.

Each day or night was different, all reverberating to the college scene: sounds of cheering over the PA system during a football game across the campus; the hypnotic beat of drums from an African dance class across the hall; polite applause from the Formal Lounge after a poetry reading by a writer-in-residence. Taking a break for dinner one night, we ate Chinese stir-fry in the food court as several visiting a cappella singing groups practiced before a concert. We didn't have to imagine the heartbeat of campus life; we felt it.

■

One of our major goals for this new edition is to capture the transformative impact of rapidly emerging technologies. Through the process of updating the book, we became aware of how far-reaching these changes are. In 1986, we traveled around the country interviewing students, parents, and administrators for their perceptions and points of view; in 1996, we supplemented our in-person interviews and campus visits with lively on-line communication via the click of an electronic mouse. Our research took us on nightly journeys to Web sites and links all over the country. We took virtual tours of campuses; explored their student services and activities; read their catalogs and syllabi for specific courses; "met" students on their Web pages and interviewed them by e-mail or phone. We discovered with delight the ease of finding a student in a campus directory, writing a note to him or her via e-mail, and within hours getting a reply. Our senses became heightened to the blinking light of our voice mail, the beep signaling the arrival of e-mail, and the whirring of the fax machine, bringing communications from hither and yon.

Determined to stay steadily on task, we found that the vibrancy and richness of the collegiate world surrounding us made a constant bid for our attention. The scenarios ranged from the comic to the poignant to the sobering. On Parents' Weekend, when a parent in the student center innocently touched the screen of a computer kiosk looking for the campus calendar and brought up instead an erotic Web page (the work of a student "cyber-prankster"), we had evidence of one unexpected consequence of this new technology right before our eyes. On the same weekend, when parents and their daughter sauntered by the office and poked their heads in, curious about our working on a Saturday at midnight, we had the privilege and pleasure of sharing a spontaneous conversation and basking in the warm glow of their clearly wonderful evening together.

Karen's life as dean, of course, spilled over into our evenings of work on the book: a visit and follow-up phone call from a father worried that his daughter might be involved in a cult; an e-mail message from a mother concerned about her homesick freshman son; a late-night call from a frantic student advisee, lamenting that she had been shut out of a psychology course, then shrieking with relief as she checked the on-line registration system from her room and found she had been taken off the waiting list; an e-mail from a prospective exchange student in Sweden wanting to know what activities the Washington University Outing Club has; students wandering in the door, one requesting a recommendation for an internship in Japan, another reporting both on a great speaker she had heard at an architecture symposium and her "dorky" Friday night date . . . all in a day's work.

■

We complete our project full of stimulation and renewed enthusiasm for our topic. As you will see throughout the book, there is much in today's college experience that has a distinctly new flavor. The rate of change in many dimensions of college life has accelerated dramatically; today's college scene is surprisingly different from the one we originally described only ten years ago. But much of what we wrote in the original edition of Letting Go remains the same; it is the soul of our book—the ongoing but changing relationship between parent and student during the college years.

Karen Levin Coburn and Madge Lawrence Treeger
St. Louis, Missouri 1997

Part I

THE COLLEGE EXPERIENCE

1
LETTING GO

"I'M NOT GETTING OUT."

I sat behind the wheel of the car; Jennie sat beside me with her tattered stuffed teddy bear at her side, and we looked out at the line of young men and women laughing and chatting as they waited for the doors of the freshman dormitory to open.

"I'm not getting out," she repeated.

I panicked. My mind flashed back to the first day of nursery school. "Don't leave me," were her words then.

"But you wanted to get here early to get the best bed," I reminded her.

"I've changed my mind," she replied. That was evident.

We had just traveled for seventeen hours, over two days. Jennie was beginning her freshman year at college—our first child to leave home. Was I going to have to turn around and go back to St. Louis with her still beside me?

"Suppose we get out and just stand next to the car." She agreed reluctantly. I was relieved to see her leave the teddy bear in the car.

Jennie made it to the line of seemingly relaxed, happy freshmen—and was swept along by an overanxious young woman who handled her anxiety by hyperactivity instead of shyness. I looked

3

over and saw Jennie blending in and looking just as relaxed as the others and let out a sigh of relief.

Within a half hour, I was excess baggage. Now it was my turn to separate. "Why don't you wander around campus and stop back in a few hours," Jennie suggested diplomatically. (What about all my fantasies of helping you fix up your room, chat with your roommates a bit, and see what coed living looks like? Of course, I kept these thoughts to myself.)

I smiled diplomatically in return, said good-bye, and began a somewhat aimless tour of the campus, passing other parents along the way who looked as lost as I felt. When I returned to the dorm, I found out Jennie had arranged for me to have dinner with another parent since she already had plans. I graciously bowed out, returned to the motel, and had a good cry.

Two days earlier, as a part of freshman orientation at Washington University, I had stood on a stage before approximately three hundred parents who had come to hear my professional words of wisdom as a member of the Student Counseling Service. The topic was "Letting Go."

And now I had begun.

■

The process of "letting go" actually starts in the first years of life. As parents, we can remember the struggles of the early years, especially between the ages of 1½ and 3, when our children seesawed back and forth between acts of independence—a toddling strut accompanied by a "world is my oyster" smile—and clinging, whining periods of hanging on. Although this separation process continues throughout our children's growing years, it is especially evident as they move through adolescence and begin to leave home, when we once again see their ambivalence acted out in puzzling ways. We were often more patient and understanding of the process when our children were small. We were also better informed. The "terrible twos" may not have been pleasant, but we all knew they were coming, and we knew they would end. Information and reassurance were readily available if we felt uncertain about our children's development or our roles as parents. But when we send our sons and daughters off to college, there are no Dr. Spocks to reassure us, no guidelines for moving through this time of transition.

Some parents don't see this as a time of transition at all. It is simply the end of childrearing for them and of childhood for their sons and daughters. "You're an adult now; start acting like one," they admonish. Others have trouble giving up their role. They still see themselves as necessary protectors and their sons and daughters as immature children rather than self-reliant young adults. "Don't you worry about it, dear. I'll call your dean and take care of it for you."

Most of us flounder somewhere in between. We send our children off with a mixture of anticipation and anxiety, a sense of loneliness and freedom, fantasy and reality. Our childrearing days are ending. Our children are launched. We anticipate dealing with our own reactions to their leaving—time on our hands, financial belt-tightening, a quiet house—but we are caught off guard by the continuing demands and concerns that we discover as each week and month goes by *after* the launching. As they struggle to be independent and separate once again, as in their toddler years, they venture forth with bravado and periods of newfound confidence and wisdom, only to retreat into times of anxiety and hanging on. They want Mom or Dad to be there *when* they want them. They call and pour out fears and hurts, hoping to be understood, or they withdraw into silence; advice and parental concerns become intrusions.

We shift gears constantly as we meet our offspring in an elusive dance of change. We find ourselves relentlessly retracing old patterns one week and discovering new ways of getting along the next. The temptation to tell our children *how* to be independent is a compelling one. The contradictory, but all too familiar, parental message is "It's about time you were grown up and on your own, so follow my advice." Translated, this painfully becomes "It's time for you to be independent, but I don't trust your judgment."

As our sons and daughters enter these college years, we have to come to terms with their strengths *and* their limitations. At the same time we realize that we too are at a watershed, entering into a new phase of our lives—growing older. We may find ourselves taking a new look at our marriage or career—our own limitations. And so as they struggle with a turmoil of conflicting emotions about leaving, we often are flooded with conflicting feelings of our own about being left.

It is common for parents who were eager to see their children leave, to lament their departure later. "Somehow there must be a biological process at work; my son is so impossible this year it makes it easy to see him go—in fact, "I can't wait" becomes, three months later, "It's so quiet in the house; I have to hold back from wanting to call him and find out how his day went"—the same parents wanting to stay connected and wanting to let go.

Another parent, whose daughter had struggled through several rebellious years in high school and emerged at 17 as a delightful young woman and close companion to her mother, confessed, "I dreaded her leaving; we had just begun to enjoy each other again. But now that she's gone, I have to admit I love the simplicity and freedom of living as a couple again."

We all know intellectually that this is a time for our children to separate and assert their independence. But long after they have become taller or stronger than we are, our primal protective feelings are easily unleashed. We carry images in our heads of the curly haired toddler, the gap-toothed 6-year-old, and times when a caress or a hug could make their world all better. As they get older the problems they face have increasingly greater consequences. The stakes get higher. The mature, rational part of us wants them to solve their own problems and believes they can, but another part of us wants to stay connected, be in control, feel needed, and protect them from the pain we know they will have to face.

We tend to see the years of college as the calm before the storm—a time within a safe bastion of learning that will provide a protected environment for our children as they prepare for the "real world." Though college provides a unique opportunity for learning, the college years are no more a calm than all the years that follow are necessarily a storm. College students are confronted with a host of the pressures and societal constraints that are part of the *ongoing* process of human experience.

Your style. Now showing.

We have hundreds of new frame styles, including designer brands like Lauren Hutton,™ Champion™ and Oscar. Chic, elegant, classic or trendy, we have it all at Sears Optical. Now more than ever, you'll find lots of new ways to look great. Come visit us soon.

$99⁹⁹ Eyeglasses

SEARS

See our great new frame selection
at www.searsoptical.com

Protect your sight.

You wouldn't think of letting years go by without regular medical and dental checkups, but how long has it been since you had an eye exam? A regular eye exam with a Doctor of Optometry is your first line of protection for the only pair of eyes you'll ever have. The over 700 independent Doctors of Optometry located in or next to Sears locations all over the country are here to make sure you get the care you need. See the eye doctor at Sears! Convenient weekend and evening appointments are available.

New at Sears Optical

Titanium Frames

- **Lighter and more durable than stainless steel**

- **Corrosion resistant**

Come to Sears Optical now for the best selection of designer looks in titanium.

SEARS Optical

Our expectations of college life are often large-scale and grandiose. They are born of many factors: our own hopes and dreams, images from the media, a need to justify the large financial investment we are making. The fire is fanned by the big buildup—years of planning and positioning so that our children can compete in the furor of "getting in." We are courted with a marketing blitz from the institutions themselves, all promising dreams fulfilled, horizons waiting to be discovered, unencumbered bliss. The effect of all this is to raise the college years to a larger-than-life once-in-a-lifetime opportunity that will make or break our children's future. Both parents and students feel the pressure and push to make this myth their reality.

Most of us have the same hopes and goals for our children as they have for themselves. We want them to be happy and successful, self-confident and self-reliant. The trouble is that the specific notion of what constitutes success or self-reliance is often very different for a parent than it is for his or her offspring. Although independence is valued as a goal, actual steps toward independence are likely to make parents nervous. Intellectual exploration tends to threaten established family values and ideas about life's meaning. Sudden shifts in behavior and ideas are confusing, and sometimes exasperating, to even the most patient, understanding parents. Too often, parents inhibit their children's growth without realizing how their good intentions are backfiring. It doesn't have to be that way, but as educators, we've seen it happen again and again, and as parents, we have felt this dilemma ourselves.

Students talk to us about their parents—about pressures and misunderstandings and their longing to be accepted by their parents as separate adults. We listen, we probe, we empathize, and then we recall conversations with our own college-age children who recited variations on the same themes. Except that with them, *we* were the ones who didn't understand, who were putting on too much pressure, who were overprotective or not around when we were needed. Our experience as parents broadened our perspectives and brought new insights to our professional work.

We have both spent much of our adult lives working on college and university campuses. We have listened to countless students as they have struggled with the disparity between their parents' expectations and their own; with broken romances and disappointing grades; with the excitement and confusion of expanding intellectual horizons and new values. As we look out our windows at the ivy-covered Gothic buildings and the Frisbee game in the quad, all may look idyllic, but when we listen to what students have to say, it is clear that their lives are complex and often unsettling. No matter how fraught with complications and responsibilities our own adult lives may seem, we can't simply retreat to the "good old college days" refrain sung by many of our peers. Our students give us daily reminders that youth is not synonymous with simplicity or freedom from responsibility.

The college years are a time of transition for young people and their parents. There is no way to move through such an important passage without some feelings of dislocation and loss. But information and insight can help parents negotiate this significant and often neglected phase of their children's lives.

As professionals immersed in the daily routine of life on the college campus, we hope to offer a realistic view of the many facets of this experience—one that reflects the trials and tribulations as well as the excitement, opportunity, and promise of these years. We will focus on the experience of traditional-age college students who go to school away from home, but much of the material will be relevant to parents of commuter students as well.

Part I of this book, "The College Experience," begins with information about late adolescent development, so that our children's behavior can be viewed in the broader context of normal growth. We will explain how *all* college students struggle with developing a sense of their own identity, with becoming independent, and with establishing intimacy. Each young person finds his or her own way to express these struggles, often to the consternation and confusion of concerned parents. But knowing that a certain amount of experimenting and exploring is, in fact, healthy can be reassuring. Insight into normal development enables parents to discriminate between the universal problems of college students and those that require parental or professional intervention. With this understanding, parents can respond more appropriately and with more assurance to the signals their children send them.

We will look also at the changes in the larger contemporary society, and at its campus reflections in high-tech classrooms, multicultural activities and courses, complex security systems, and a proliferation of choices. Although we all went through our own versions of young adult confusion and self-discovery, the world in which we grew up was clearly different from the one our children are grappling with today. Perhaps nowhere is that more evident than on college campuses.

This chapter opened with the story of Jennie, clutching her childhood teddy bear. Her tenuous approach to the freshman dormitory and subsequent dismissal of her mother a few hours later was not an unusual sequence of events. What she needed most at that point was nothing more than her mother's willingness to let go.

Other freshmen find different ways to begin. One departs from his hometown airport, guitar slung casually over his shoulder, barely stopping to wave good-bye as he walks out to the plane. Then he calls his mother every night for two weeks. What does he need? Probably just a reassuring adult voice on the other end of the line, someone who understands and tolerates his temporary need to return to familiar territory while he adjusts to an alien one. A flashback to his toddler years as he rushed off with gusto only to check back and make contact will help us to understand—he is still in the ongoing process of separating.

Another young woman drives off to college only a few hours from home. She doesn't call or come home for weeks. Her parents worry and feel hurt. She too is separating; perhaps she needs to "go cold turkey"—to sever the ties abruptly, at least for a while—so that she isn't pulled back to the close, secure home that is so easily accessible.

The theme of separation is the same for all these young people. The variations are uniquely their own. An understanding of separation, the thematic cornerstone of every chapter of this book, enables parents to engage in that process more productively.

Part II, "A Parents' Guide: From Start to Finish," provides a chronological guide to the college experience from senior year in high school through college graduation. We'll look at the way the separation process evolves, and the predictable rhythm it takes throughout the first academic year and the years that follow. Above all, we will listen to what college students and their parents have to say as they move through this exciting, sometimes turbulent phase of life. They will tell us what has worked for them and what hasn't.

Understanding what we and our children are going through reduces our fear and validates our reality. It opens our eyes so that we can see what our children's world is like; it allows us to listen and communicate more effectively. It frees us to help our children become themselves.

2

SOME THINGS NEVER CHANGE

The Search for Identity, Independence, and Intimacy

"WHO AM I, APART FROM MY FAMILY, MY CHURCH, my school?" This question is what young people ask themselves over and over again. It is a question replayed by every generation, each in its own context. We, their parents, struggled with the same question years ago as we tried to find our own way on the road to adulthood. The context may have changed, the choices may be different, but the theme is the same—the theme of self-definition. This is the curriculum not spelled out in college catalogs, and yet much of the college experience is devoted to it.

I'm going to let my hair grow; I'm going to cut out drinking and smoking and be quiet and subdued—the way I was when I came here. They say a girl can't be like that and "get by," but I always loathed the typical college girl anyway. The main trouble is that whenever I am or claim to be different, I'm accused of posing—people can't conceive of how anyone can have any individualism. Damn it all, I'm going to change and be me.

JOURNAL ENTRY, SOPHOMORE, SMITH COLLEGE, 1924

I feel like I can't be myself. I try to pretend everything's fine, but who am I kidding? I feel lonely and isolated even from my family and best friends at home. Part of that's my fault, because every time I try to write a letter or talk on the phone, I catch myself trying to impress people with how great things are. I don't want to admit to anyone that I'm having problems adjusting, so I try to overcompensate and act as if everything's wonderful and then I sound fake and I feel fake. I can't be natural—I'm not even sure what that is.

JOURNAL ENTRY, SOPHOMORE, UNIVERSITY OF VERMONT, 1984

Sixty years passed between the journal entries of this contemporary college student and her grandmother, and yet both of these women are grappling with issues of identity, with who they are and how to integrate this sense of themselves with the world in which they live.

Becoming a unique and individual person doesn't happen at any one particular time. Hallmark has yet to design a card for the universal celebration of "being an adult." Graduation days, 18th birthdays, bar mitzvahs, all have been adopted as dates to mark entry into so-called adulthood. The fact that one ritual takes place at 13, another at 18 or 21 tells us that our notion of what adulthood is varies by religion, culture, and individual family.

Many young men and women leave their homes to work, marry, or go away to college. But to become separate in a psychological sense is a lifelong process of becoming—continually building on, reaffirming, and refining a sense of self. This process begins in the first months of life.

Although the seeds of their own identity exist from the start, infants are totally dependent on the person who cares for them, usually their mother. Before they can discover their separateness, they must establish the boundaries between their mothers and themselves. Understanding the complexities of that earlier time helps put in perspective the often puzzling transitions of the college years.

SEPARATION IN EARLY CHILDHOOD AND ADOLESCENCE

The separation that begins in the first year of life is a prototype for later separations, in particular for the turbulent years of adolescence and young adulthood. Separation is not isolation from others but is instead a bridge that helps us cross from dependence to interdependence. Parents' memories and photograph albums carry images of their children's early attempts at separation: a baby tugging on his mother's nose, yanking at her hair, peering out from behind chubby spread fingers to play peekaboo; a 7-month-old creeping across the floor, pausing to glance back at her mother before scurrying on; a toddler walking like a drunken sailor, building up speed as he giggles exuberantly, running away from his mother; the same toddler, as his mood shifts, waddling along, thumb in mouth, dragging a blanket behind him; a 2-year-old throwing herself on the floor in the supermarket, screaming "no" furiously, her face red with rage and frustration, wanting to do it herself one minute and whiningly asking for help the next—all of these are the images of young children struggling with the confusion and ambivalence of separation.[1]

The images of separation in adolescence are as vivid and familiar to all parents as those of our children's early days. They are new images, reminiscent of old struggles: the teenager chafing at his parents' simplest words of advice; the 17-year-old, heady with a sense of her own high school success, flying off to college unaccompanied and secure, coming home six weeks later for refueling, her wings clipped with the discovery that she is no longer special; the 19-year-old, calling home depressed and frightened; an anxious high school senior asking her parents for advice one day and snapping "It's my life" the next. All of these efforts to move away echo earlier times from our children's first three years of life. And they reawaken our own ambivalence about separation and may make it more difficult for us to let go.[2]

IDENTITY

To separate psychologically is to know oneself. The core of identity, of one's uniqueness, is what makes it possible to tolerate the inevitable feeling of aloneness that we all experience. Despite moving across the country or the world, despite dramatic changes in emotions or physical feelings or interactions with a variety of people, we develop a sense of continuity, a consistent sense of who we are. It is this self-knowledge that makes it possible to move into truly intimate relationships with others without the fear of losing oneself or one's own integrity. Indeed, this search for a cohesive and integrated self is one of the major tasks of the college student.

Why now? Why does the concern for identity become so all-consuming during the college years? We know that our children have had distinct personalities for as long as we can remember. We speak of them in phrases that encapsulate characteristics that are uniquely theirs. "Ellen's our organizer. She's been organized since she was a toddler." Or "Peter's very easygoing; he's always marched to the beat of a different drummer." Our children have been building since birth an inner core that is exclusively theirs, identifying with significant people in their lives, developing talents, internalizing notions of right and wrong.

But puberty arrives and shakes their foundations; bodies shift so that their tall and rounded selves no longer reflect their inner image of themselves as a small and fragile child. Tenors turn into basses and with the change may lose a special singing talent. The "braininess" that was scorned at 8 is valued at 16, but the feeling of being an outsider—the one who was picked last for the kickball game—lingers. Sexual yearnings are new and unpredictable. With the onslaught of puberty, our children lose the sense of continuity that they had; confusion sets in; change becomes the norm. The spontaneity and creativity of childhood become the self-conscious inhibition of early adolescence.

To assure stability and some illusion of identity, adolescent boys and girls often attach themselves to a group or an idol to show the world who they are—"a jock," "a punk," "a geek," "a deadhead." And somewhere in the process of discovering who they are, they leave for college. Not all will have reached the same developmental point at the same time or with the same intensity. All the variables that influence development—genetic factors, cultural heritage, gender, societal influences, personal experiences—are brought to bear.

For some, the transition to college is a smooth and gradual one; it may be the time for consolidation after a rocky adolescence. For others, the distance in miles that the freshman travels may represent the *only* separation that takes place as the student holds on tightly and brings his parents with him, in spirit if not in body. Their identity is his; he defines himself according to their guidelines. Still another freshman may plunge headfirst into the new environment, cutting loose from ties in an impulsive and sometimes desperate manner, attaching herself quickly in a mutually dependent romance, jumping into a new lifestyle, or running frantically from one new activity to another. She may join the rugby club one day, the literary society the next, and hang out in the alternative coffee houses on the weekends, bouncing back and forth between groups, searching for a new identity in this new place.[3]

Often students find themselves burdened with guilt, wanting to remain loyal to their families' traditional values but also wanting to chart their own courses. The young man who is still tied to home and places his parents in the center of his thoughts and decisions, who says, "I can't major in art history; my parents would be so disappointed in me," is struggling with the same dependency as the scientifically talented but belligerent young woman who proclaims, "I wouldn't consider medicine if it were the last profession on earth. I've had it shoved down my throat all my life. I wouldn't give them the satisfaction." Both are having trouble letting go, unable to make choices of their own.

As our children move through the college years, most of them will be wrestling with the question "Who am I?" They will be trying to integrate what they've learned about themselves in earlier stages with the demands of the adult world. Some will defer to those demands so completely that they will conform to expectations of family and society at the expense of a sense of self. For others, their identity is so precious that they will ignore social norms entirely and become alienated from the mainstream.

In late adolescence, the time is ripe to focus on self-definition; our children are ready physically, cognitively, and socially. Colleges and universities offer a breather after the dependency of childhood and before the commitments of adulthood. During this time, students may explore, take risks, test and "try on" new ways of being, and make mistakes without drastic consequences. Many of us look back to our own youth and recall such times of uncertainty, excitement, and turmoil.

When our children cast about in search of this sometimes elusive identity, their behavior is often misunderstood. At times, in their exuberant discovery of new worlds, they test extremes and hang on tight to them for a while as their fragile sense of self regains enough equilibrium to settle on a more balanced view. The tighter the psychological knot that ties them to their parents, the more abrasive and rebellious the testing may be. A perplexed mother from New Jersey describes her daughter on her first visit home from college:

> Cindy—she's asked us to call her by her full name, Cynthia—has the most beautiful hair. She's always worn it long to show off its natural thickness and shininess. It was her badge, her emblem. Her motions, the way she would peek out from that wavy raven mop, the way she would toss it around—a sort of exclamation point to emphasize whatever she was saying—it would be both irritating and ingratiating. And now it's gone, at least on one side of her head. She's practically shaved one side and the other is cut in a severe line which falls over one eye—only she doesn't toss it anymore. It just sort of hangs there. I'm not sure how she sees, and I'm not sure what it means.

Another exasperated parent from a conservative midwestern community lamented, "I'm still trying to explain to myself, and to other people, why Brian came home from his first year of college wearing an earring."

One thing their parents can be sure of, Brian and Cindy are trying on a new identity, one that may or may not fit. They cling to their new looks, which may be quite different from the conservative wardrobe they left for school with. Does this mean Brian is gay? Is this the beginning of a permanent punk look for Cindy? Perhaps they're both on drugs. The mind of a worried parent knows no bounds. Parental imagination may run rampant to explain a new hairstyle or a tiny dot of gold in a son's ear. But it is best if parents refrain from jumping in and creating a chasm between themselves and their experimenting offspring. They might do well to recall themselves or their peers at 18 or 19 as bell-bottomed encounter-group aficionados of the '70s or peace-loving flower children of the '60s. One mother commented with amusement:

> Every time Maggie came home to visit she had a new persona. We sent her off freshman year in the proverbial polo shirt and conservative matching shorts. She prided herself on her neatness, never a hair out of place. We used to laugh about how long she spent taking showers and joked about finally being able to use the bathroom again when she went to college. Her first trip home, we barely recognized her at the airport. She was wearing a thrift-shop version of a Garbo hat, and a lot of somebody else's much-too-large and very dirty clothes. She explained that she hadn't done laundry during finals. Actually, a bigger shock came in the spring when she was wearing men's boxer shorts, and wasn't it wonderful how much money we would save because they were so cheap and she could wear her father's! Our trips to pick her up at the airport became filled with "what next" jokes between John and me. She never failed to surprise us.

But these are just the external signs of exploration. Young men and women during their college years are defining everything from their sexual orientation to their place in the world of work. They wrestle with the same questions—What do I want to be like as a sexual being? How do I want to define myself as a man or woman? How does my racial, ethnic, or religious heritage fit into who I am? What do I believe in? What will I fight for? What do I want to do with my life?

INTELLECTUAL DEVELOPMENT: NEW WAYS OF THINKING

How do students go about making these important decisions? Along with the dramatic onslaught of hormonal and physical changes, adolescents undergo a more subtle but equally important intellectual growth. During their college years, students develop the capacity to engage in more complex and abstract thinking.[4]

At the time they enter college, many students see the world in black-and-white, clear-cut, and often rigid terms—a dichotomous view in which answers are simply right or wrong. They view their professors as the source of right answers and assume that their own role is to learn and retain these right answers. For the student who sees the world in this way, absolute truths prevail outside of the classroom as well—right or wrong answers to moral dilemmas, to career choices—and as a result they are often seeking *the* right answer and are impatient and judgmental of compromises: "All jocks are zeros"; "My dad sold out when he became a banker"; "I can't seem to find the right career for me."

As students become exposed to the diversity of ideas and people at college, their world no longer looks quite so simple. They gradually move from their clearly defined black-and-white view of the world to one of stimulating, but often blinding, color—a kaleidoscope of possibilities. Absolute truths no longer prevail. Many points of view seem to have equal value.

From the day they arrive at their dormitory, they are confronted by the diverse population of their fellow students. Students who have been brought up in homogeneous environments—whether in small towns revolving around a single church or political point of view or sheltered segments of a larger city bound by social and economic norms—are often overwhelmed and confused by the variety of people, values, and ideas they encounter in the first months on a college campus.

An 18-year-old freshman from the Bible Belt exclaimed:

> I had never met anyone Jewish before. I always felt kind of sorry for them, because they hadn't accepted Jesus and were sinners in our church. My roommate's a really obser-

vant Jew, and we've talked for hours late at night. He believes in his religion as much as I do and he's a really great guy. It confusing; it's a whole new world here.

In their classrooms, too, professors encourage varying opinions and ideas. Revered professors disagree with each other. Students see more than one "authority" with opposing viewpoints. Doing research in the library, students find sources with different credible answers to the same question. They can no longer rely simply on the dogma of an authority. Numerous possibilities become evident. For many, this is unsettling and often overwhelming. So many choices may lead to a kind of paralysis. "If all opinions have validity, how do I decide?" "How do I make sense of my world?" Sophomores, suitably named from the Greek roots for *wise* and *fool*, often find themselves at this precarious point, recognizing the complexity of the world and their vulnerability in it.

As they move through their four years, students are increasingly expected to analyze and give evidence to support their opinions, and gradually most of them begin to understand that truth is often relative and depends on the context in which it is viewed. Students are challenged by professors to back up their opinions with cogent arguments and relevant data. The same professor who might have been seen as arbitrary and confusing by a freshman may be valued as a catalyst for individual critical thinking by a junior or senior who has begun to wrestle with the complexity of making personal and intellectual commitments.

Intellectual growth often fosters a new sense of community, as students share ideas in exhilarating late-night debates with friends who hold divergent opinions. The lens that was focused so narrowly when students saw the world in dualistic terms, and then became wide-angled and expansive, begins to focus again. But this time, the so-called authorities are the students themselves. As they see that many dilemmas can't be reduced to simple right or wrong answers, they weigh each situation, let go of the lesser alternatives, and take a personal stance.

Many students leave college before they have made sustained

choices of life direction, values, and relationships. Most don't change evenly in their intellectual growth. Some, in fact, pause or retreat or may choose to avoid responsibility altogether by letting the chips fall where they may. But most students will not leave college without making impressive strides in their ability to think critically.

For many parents, the commitments that they made as young adults have become so familiar and so much a part of them that their beliefs begin to look rigid and arbitrary to their children. The questions that arise when their children challenge their values often unsettle, even threaten, parents of college students. Parents are forced to look at their earlier decisions in today's context—decisions that may range from the place of sex in relationships to the value of intensive hard work. Through their college years, students confront their parents' values, lifestyle, and relationships. A student's developing identity brings his or her parents face-to-face with their own.

None of this maturing exists in a vacuum, of course. Growth is nourished by an environment that is both supportive and challenging. Colleges and universities offer students opportunities to stretch themselves, but within safe boundaries. Parents can join university personnel as partners in encouraging their children to explore and take those risks, to discover their multifaceted world, and in so doing to discover themselves.

INDEPENDENCE

Talk about our children's identity formation or intellectual development is not part of our common parlance. We do talk often, however, about their growing independence. Independence is part of our children's vernacular as well, a word bandied about among friends and family. What does it really mean? Probably different things to them than to us, at least initially. For many of our children, it means "I can do it by myself, thank you very much!"—an updated version of earlier attempts at tying shoelaces, crossing streets, and the like. It is the badge of separateness. In high school, the car was the symbol of independence for many students. "I can get away from you—take charge of where I'm going." A car is freedom; it provides an opportunity to explore and experiment with time and space away from home. It is associated with control and power. "I don't need you to drive me" is a metaphor for "I don't need to depend on you anymore."

In addition to the car, many high school students have access to a new financial freedom as they earn their own money working after school or during the summers. Ironically, for those who go away to college to live, these symbols of independence become less accessible. Cars are not permitted for freshmen on many college campuses, and the prohibitive costs of a college education often place students in a dependency bind—reconnected to parents through a powerful monetary umbilical cord.

College students do learn to take care of themselves in important new ways, however. Handling the humdrum details of everyday life that many of us take for granted is an important step on the road to a growing independence. They have to do laundry, to get themselves up in the morning, to decide when to come home at night or if they will come home at all; they manage their money; decide where and if to study, when and what to eat; they take care of their contact lenses, their acne, and their stomach flu. As they move on to become upperclassmen, they may have a car to take care of or may move off-campus and assume the added responsibility of apartment living. To care for themselves as their parents have cared for them brings feelings of confidence and strength, a self-reliance that can't be taught, only learned through experience.

Management of money often becomes an arena for the independence struggle. The reality is that for most students, financial dependence of some sort is a fact of life. In relationships with mutual respect, the conflict should be minimal. But most parents worry about the return on the huge financial investment they have made in college. The cost seems preposterous. Will it enable their child to become a successful professional, financially solvent, able to live comfortably on his or her own? Will their investment be worth it? As their worry grows and their resources dwindle, even the most well-intentioned parents may feel the need to take control as they would with any other investment. They may try to direct, to point out how to do it better, to orchestrate their children's college years—which courses to take, how to spend their time, and perhaps even with whom to spend it. In doing so, of course, they deprive their children of the most long-lasting knowledge they can gain: the knowledge of how to live independently, form their own opinions, make their own decisions and mistakes, and ultimately make their own commitments to personal and political values, a vocation, and another human being.

The freedom that students enjoy with this sense of independence is often coupled with fears, especially about the change in their relationship with their parents. "Will my parents still care *about* me if they're not caring *for* me?" "Will they still love me even though they don't approve of my choices?" "Will I be abandoning them if I don't need them anymore?" They fear the responsibility inherent in their new self-reliance. The buck stops here.

Part of their discomfort comes from the false notion that independence means never asking for help. Many students, intent on asserting their autonomy, do so with a bravado and insistence that belies the feeling of tenuousness underneath. Teetering on the edge of separation, they turn away help and advice, fearing that they will be pulled back into the safety of the fold. One poised young woman, a Middlebury sophomore from Illinois, looks back at her freshman year:

> I had always prided myself on my independence, so I went to school alone. That was dumb. I was so unfamiliar with the area. I lost all perspective those first few weeks.
>
> I wasn't nervous at all when I went. I took a cab from Burlington—shared a ride with a guy who was also a freshman. I was very friendly, and he was very cold. That started it. People seemed cold in general. The more people seemed turned off to me, the more uptight I became. Then people were really turned off by me. I was very intimidated. I had never had problems meeting people before. I began to think, it must be because I'm from the Midwest. I'm not cool. I'd try to talk to people, but I felt so self-conscious and got more and more withdrawn and nervous. People didn't want to be with me. I didn't blame them. I didn't want to be with me either.

My parents didn't know too much about how miserable I was those first few months. I think I was always fighting dependence on my parents, so I didn't say much. The one time I really broke down and called about ten times in one week, my father got angry. For me to be weak was hard for them to see. They counted on me to be strong and independent.

Balancing autonomy and closeness to parents and others is an ongoing theme that intertwines with a developing sense of self. In the comings and goings of vacations and summers during their college years, students often describe a gradual change—a redefinition of their relationship with their parents. One senior at Rice recalls a shift in perspective:

It was winter break of my junior year. I was exhausted from some all-nighters to finish up papers and study for finals. In the past, I had often felt mixed emotions about going home. I was usually looking forward to it—anything after the craziness of the end-of-semester crunch—but shortly after I got there, my mom and I would be at it, and I'd just want to get away someplace where I wouldn't be treated like a kid.

But this year was different. I remember saying on the way home from the airport, "I'm really exhausted; I just want to be pampered and taken care of." And I was! My parents were great. I could never let myself admit that was what I wanted before, but somehow now I felt different. I knew that I wasn't going to become a baby just because I wanted a little tender loving care. I wasn't fighting it anymore, because I guess I just felt generally more in charge of things.

INTIMACY

The issues of identity and intimacy are bound together in a dynamic interplay that encourages the growth of each.[5] Throughout their college years, young men and women experiment with a variety of relationships. These may include intense new friendships with the same or the opposite sex, sexual play and exploration, and for many, falling in love. As students continue to refine aspects of their identity through these relationships, they become more self-confident and allow themselves the vulnerability to enter into increasingly open and mature partnerships. Over and over again, students describe their relationships with friends and lovers as critical to the learning and growth that takes place during the college years.

A young woman in her final year at Washington University traces the evolution of her developing sexual identity and her increasing capacity to enter into close relationships:

> Freshman year, I developed some very close friends. We really played a lot. It's kind of hard to describe. Maybe it's easier to describe what it wasn't. I wasn't going out on dates or to parties. It was just two guys and another girl, and we spent a lot of time hanging out talking, going to the zoo and the park. It was a very happy time.
>
> I had a really close relationship with one of the guys. We were together all the time. We even slept in the same room a lot, but it was never sexual. He had a girlfriend at home, and even after I started going with someone, we still spent a lot of time together. This was a big change for me. I wasn't even allowed to have guys come upstairs at home.
>
> Second semester, I started going out with Jim. Our first date was the spring formal. Until then, he was just a guy I knew in the dorm. It was my first real relationship, and it definitely was his. It was a very intense relationship—symbiotic, actually.
>
> We spent about a third of the summer together. He was my life; I was his life—for a whole year. My parents were kind of cool about it. My dad just said it wouldn't last, and my mom didn't say much of anything—or if she did, I don't remember.
>
> We spent most of our sophomore year together. We

were with each other all the time—slept in each other's rooms. That was never any problem. Our roommates were very flexible. We always worked it out easily. We weren't like the kids who kick their roommates out or leave secret codes on the door that mean "stay out."

We took a couple of classes together, but mostly we were together outside of classes. It was real good for both of us. We both grew a lot and became a lot more confident. We each began to see each other through the other person's eyes, which I know did incredible things for my self-image, and it did for his also. And it's funny that the basic reason we broke up was that we both needed to spend time with other people, and we couldn't adjust our relationship to do that. We were used to having each other available when-ever we wanted. We ended up spending September to March of junior year breaking up and getting together over and over again. When I think of college, junior year was spent breaking up with Jim. Without us becoming aware of it, we had come to expect total availability of the other person. We were an incredible support system to each other. But we just couldn't make the transition to staying together while moving out to be with other people also.

It was a time of separation from my mother. Up till then, my mom knew everything that happened to me that had any significance, but last summer I decided I didn't want to tell her everything. I didn't want her to know all about us.

My relationship with Jim was an important time of my life; it affects how I am now too. I'm more open. I'm more conscious of what's going on in my relationships, of taking risks and making commitments.

Throughout the college years, the pendulum continues to swing back and forth between separateness and union. Many relationships during these years of learning and experimentation will have the look of intimacy but may be well-disguised attempts at fulfilling other needs. Often during the freshman year, especially in the first semester, students pair up, substituting new dependent relationships for old ones. As the Washington University senior above related, even though there are difficulties with such a relationship, this kind of bond may serve to help students grow, reassuring them of their self-worth as they discover their sexuality, learn to be open, and separate from close, perhaps too close, families.

Some students substitute sexual relationships for emotional closeness, a pseudointimacy that provides temporary release but often a gnawing sense of emptiness and isolation as well. Others who open up and trust before they have a sense of their own identity may become frightened as they begin to feel themselves engulfed by another's demands.

Mutual trust is essential—trust that one's friend or partner will respect and appreciate one's separateness, trust in one's own capacity to "let go" temporarily and remain intact. To be intimate is to expose one's vulnerabilities to another. To be intimate is to balance one's own needs with someone else's and to resolve conflict together. Students learn that to give is not to give in—compromise is part of the partnership.

CHANGE

There is no way to predict exactly how our children will move through the continuing ebb and flow of growth and development during their college years. For a number of students, college prolongs adolescence and is just the beginning of their search for identity, independence, and intimacy. For others, the progress in these arenas from freshman to senior year is staggering. We *can* predict, however, that change will occur, that it is an inevitable byproduct of the college experience. With change, even positive change, adjustment is necessary and stress unavoidable. For most students, many of the disruptions will lead to opportunities for growth, and they will continue to learn how to think more critically and to take responsibility for their own opinions and actions. For these same students, there will be times of stagnation and regression.

Along the way, the road is often a rocky one for parents as well as children. The inconsistencies of a student's behavior may leave parents breathless. How could someone who acted with such mature deliberation one day resort to such ill-conceived impulsiveness the next? Should we respond with amusement or concern?

One mother of a Bates freshman, her first child to go to college, offers a familiar refrain:

> When he was a toddler, I used to worry that Eric would never give up his bottle. I remember my pediatrician telling me with a wry smile to stop worrying, that he would not go to college with it. Now I worry that he will never be organized enough to hold a responsible job. And when I worry, I start barging in on his life and try to tell him once more what he already knows. Won't I ever learn that my perspective as a 45-year-old is not his at 19? I keep thinking that I will have really matured when I can get that wry smile on *my* face, and stop worrying.

Understanding some of the underpinnings of normal development may alleviate parents' anxiety. It is easier to be supportive when we can see the broader view. Our children may rebuff our advice, but they will appreciate our acknowledgment of their distress—a listening ear that doesn't judge even if we disagree, a sense of confidence that doesn't crumble when they do, an adult anchor who provides perspective on the predictable but often painful changes that they are bound to go through.

3

SOME THINGS DO CHANGE

College Life Today

STROLLING ONTO A COLLEGE CAMPUS, WE ARE struck by a sense of history and continuity. Who walked these paths before? Who will walk them in the years to come? For some of us there is a dizzying nostalgia. For almost all of us there are feelings of respect, even awe.

Imposing rectangular structures of red granite or limestone, Georgian brick residences with symmetrical columns, ivy-covered Gothic lecture halls with leaded windows and vaulted archways announce that this place commands attention. Our eyes glance past the modern glass and steel additions, lighting on the older, more traditional centers, the quadrangles, the plazas, the courtyards. Giant oaks and elms attest to the passing of time. Latin phrases over doorways remind us of the scholarship that is carried on here. This oasis of learning, separated from the cacophony of the workaday world just beyond its gates, lulls us into tranquillity, perhaps even reverie.

So it is with a jolt that we come upon a bulletin board layered with recent posters and notices askew—a collage of ink and paper—a jarring reminder that time has not stood still: "Bulimia Support Group," "Gay, Lesbian, and Bisexual Alliance," "Hindi Film Club," "Net Surfer Volunteers," "Adult Children of Alcoholics Group,"

"Wanted: Roommate to share apartment. Male or female, non-smoker, no drugs," "AIDS Symposium," "Take Back the Night March," "Women on Wall Street: Alumnae Panel."

Sandwiched between these announcements are notices of recitals and colloquia on more orthodox scholarly topics; of art exhibits and plays and poetry readings; of pep rallies and tailgate parties. But these traditional cultural and social events of the campus scene are overshadowed by the contemporary reflections of today's world.

The social transformations of the past thirty years, which have touched all of our lives, have invaded the seemingly tranquil campus as well. Changes in technology, curriculum, institutional policies, extracurricular offerings—even the very makeup of the student population—confirm that today's college is neither rarefied nor unaffected by the rapidly changing society of which it is a part.

WHO ARE TODAY'S STUDENTS AND
WHAT DO THEY BELIEVE?

Impressionistic portraits of today's students range from conservative, hardworking Babbitts to materialistic, freewheeling Gatsbys—from uncaring, self-involved careerists to statement-making demonstrators—from '40s-style ballroom dancers to proud and active supporters of gay rights. Personal impressions such as these are important to keep in mind as a backdrop for the profile drawn by specific data and statistics. Both contribute to our understanding of today's college students.

Perhaps the most comprehensive storehouse of information about college freshmen is *The American Freshman: National Norms,* an ongoing survey of representative samples of college freshmen conducted annually since 1966 by the Cooperative Institutional Research Program and sponsored by the American Council on Education and the University of California at Los Angeles. Edited by Alexander Astin and his colleagues, these reports present a vivid picture of changes in the "characteristics, attitudes, values, educational achievements, and future goals of students who enter college in the United States."[1] The data that follow are culled from this important research project.

No longer the elite bastion of affluent white 18- to 22-year-olds, today's college campus is home to students from an increasing diversity of backgrounds. In 1960, 94 percent of college students were white, and 63 percent were men. Colleges and universities first opened their doors to a wider spectrum of students in the '60s and early '70s. The percentage of minorities in entering freshman classes nearly doubled between the mid-1960s and mid-1970s, and these students became a notable presence on campuses that had formerly excluded them. In 1995, more than 21 percent of college freshmen were students of color.

The women's movement has also influenced campus demographics. After a steady increase in women's enrollments throughout the '70s, there are now more women than men in college. And with the decline in the number of single-sex institutions, women have become an integral part of the most prestigious, formerly all-male Ivys and their small, elite counterparts.

The number of international students enrolling in American colleges and universities has reached an all-time high. According to the Institute of International Education, in 1995 there were close to 500,000 international students enrolled on U.S. campuses—more than thirteen times as many as there were in the mid-1950s. And the "graying" of the campus has become a common phenomenon, particularly at community and other commuter colleges that court older students.

Today's students come from a broad range of economic backgrounds. An increasing number of them are concerned about having adequate funds for college. Most students have to help finance their education; they spend their college years trying to maintain a delicate balance among part-time jobs, academic demands, extracurricular activities, and time with friends. And as the availability of scholarship and grant money has diminished and college costs have continued to rise, the number of students who will graduate with extensive loans to pay off has increased substantially. According to the American Council on Education, the number of students borrowing money for college and the size of the loans they take out are both continuing to soar.

Financial aid officers try to educate students, both when they arrive as freshmen and before they graduate, about the realities of taking on huge debt from loans and the implications it may have for their career options when they graduate.

The economic polarities on campus are striking. Students whose financial worries are part of their daily consciousness live side by side with those who arrive on campus with a sense of entitlement and an alphabet soup of expensive equipment—TVs, PCs, CD players, and VCRs.

Reflecting changing family patterns nationwide, more students are coming to college from divorced, single-parent, and so-called blended families formed through remarriage. In 1955, 60 percent of American households were of the "Leave It to Beaver" genre— working father, stay-at-home mother, and two or more school-age children. By 1985, only 7 percent of the population belonged to this type of family unit, although many people and institutions still regard it as the norm.

The American family is in flux, and a substantial number of today's college students have paid the price. Many come from families that provided them with little structure while they were growing up. It is common to hear students lament the loss of their childhood as they describe taking on the role of friend and confidant to a distraught parent, or the role of surrogate parent to a needy younger sibling. University personnel are concerned about the high percentage of students who come from families with an alcoholic member. And campus psychologists and counselors serve an increasing number of students who report incidents of childhood physical and sexual abuse.

Some students have struggled with alcohol problems of their own and have participated in residential treatment programs while still in high school. Some arrive on campus with a substantial drug habit or an eating disorder, such as anorexia or bulimia. Many of these students are unable to deal with the stress in their lives; they resort to destructive coping mechanisms that temporarily relieve their pain or provide them with the illusion of control that they desperately seek.

Others enter college with well-developed, constructive coping skills. Many of today's freshmen have a healthy respect for exercise, and they are intent upon enhancing both their physical and emotional well-being. They bike, jog, and rollerblade, lift weights, and join aerobics classes; they participate in intramural sports, practice tai chi, or take dance to keep in shape. These health-conscious students are concerned about eating well and favor vegetarian and pasta dishes over Big Macs and fries.

Today's students enter college with higher high school grades and lower basic skills than ever before. As a result of grade inflation, many are optimistic about their academic performance but ill-equipped to succeed. They come to college expecting a great deal of themselves, the institution, and the whole academic enterprise.

One way to better appreciate and understand this generation of college students is to view them within the context of the world that has shaped them. To these young men and women, John F. Kennedy and Martin Luther King, Jr. are names in history books, and the Vietnam War is the subject of period films. Though the civil rights and women's movements have profoundly affected their expectations and opportunities, they remain relatively detached from them as impassioned causes. For most of today's students, these are the obsessions of another era. Their realities are the threats of environmental devastation and AIDS, worldwide economic and political upheaval, and national and international terrorism.

There is no doubt that these young people have been affected by the economic and political uncertainties of their formative years. With constant reminders from the media that theirs may be the first college generation to face a world of fewer opportunities than their parents had, many of them are seeking a safe route that will lead them to the diminishing number of career slots that provide high compensation and a sense of security. More and more of them have seen their parents in traditionally secure professions face downsizing or uncertainty about their future. Whether or not this generation actually will have fewer opportunities for success and career fulfillment remains to be seen. However, students appear to be making decisions about their majors and their futures based on this assumption.

According to Astin's study, the percentage of freshmen who said they intended to major in business increased steadily throughout the '70s and most of the '80s, peaking in 1987 at 25 percent. Interest in business majors and careers dropped by almost half between 1987 and 1992 but increased for the first time in eight years in 1995. The 1995 Astin report showed the highest level of interest in careers in education in over twenty years, while interest in engineering and the law reached an all-time low for the thirty years during which the report has been published.

Majors in the humanities, the fine and performing arts, and the social sciences witnessed dramatic declines through the '70s and early '80s. Recently, however, numerous universities have reported a trend toward increased enrollments in the liberal arts.

In 1995, more than 72 percent of freshmen in the UCLA study said that a very important reason for going to college was "to make more money" and 77 percent said "to get a better job." They placed considerably less value than their predecessors had on "developing a philosophy of life." Those committed to "keeping up to date with political affairs" dropped to an all-time low of 28.5 percent, compared with 42.4 percent in 1990 and 57.8 percent in 1966. Since 1992, the report shows a drop in freshmen interested in "influencing social values," "cleaning up the environment," "influencing the political structure," "promoting racial understanding," and "participating in a community action program." Not surprisingly, the percentage of these students who believed that "an individual can do little to change society" reached a ten-year high of 33.6 percent. This contrasts dramatically with Astin's remarks in the summary of his 1990 survey, when he declared that the trends suggested "a rapidly expanding number of American college students who are dissatisfied with the status quo and who want to become personally involved in bringing about change in American society."[2] There seems to be a growing disillusionment about the possibility of effecting political and social change. Paradoxically, record numbers of college students are actually devoting time to community service.

Fund-raising and volunteer service projects are part of the tradition of the fraternities and sororities that are a strong presence on many campuses. Community service organizations such as Phillips Brooks House at Harvard and Student Volunteers Council at Princeton are thriving. In 1986, 125 college presidents, including those from Georgetown, Brown, and Stanford, formed a consortium, Campus Compact, to promote community service. By 1995, the number of member institutions had increased to well over 500, reflecting the growing campus interest. Campus Compact has joined with other advocates in exploring the notion of "service-learning," linking the curriculum with community concerns and bringing the concept of community service into the mainstream of the academy.

The majority of today's students describe themselves as "middle-of-the-road" politically. The percentage of freshmen who identify their general political position as liberal declined from 33.5 percent in 1970 to 21.1 percent in 1995. However, the data from the UCLA survey indicate that students still show strong endorsement of a number of liberal social and political issues, such as national health insurance, gun control, and gay rights. Although the majority of college students support legalized abortion, the support declined from a high of 64.9 percent in 1990 to 58.4 percent in 1995. Occasionally, issues such as American military involvement in foreign conflicts, reproductive rights, or affirmative action stir up small but vocal groups of students. Concerns closer to home—an admired professor being turned down for tenure or rising tuition costs—are more likely to mobilize students, even those typically uninterested in political affairs.

There is, however, a widening rift between the far left and the far right. Isolated ugly incidents shatter an image of harmony on usually peaceful campuses: the president of the Jewish Student Alliance receives a barrage of Nazi slogans and hate messages via e-mail; a poster announcing a program sponsored by the university's gay, lesbian, and bisexual coalition is defaced with obscenities; the African-American students' center is spray painted with graffiti.

Student attitudes toward the roles of men and women have changed dramatically over the last twenty-five years. When asked whether they supported the traditional notion that "the activities of married women are best confined to the home and family," 30.3 percent of today's male freshmen in the Astin study answered yes, as opposed to 66.5 percent in 1970. The support for this view among young women in the freshman class declined from 44.3 percent to 19.3 percent in the same time period. About 33 percent of freshmen women approve of sex between two people who have known each other a short while; 56.1 percent of men approve.

The media have labeled today's youth as materialistic, careerist, and conservative, yet many have also been characterized as self-indulgent, drifting, and reluctant to make commitments. This generation was introduced to education via *Sesame Street*'s 30-second segments and to problem solving through popular sitcoms that resolve conflicts in 30 minutes. Many of their teachers comment that they are used to constant stimulation and want to be entertained. They want simple answers to complex questions and often seek formulas for success rather than opportunities for exploration and risk taking. A favorite phrase is "I want to keep my options open."

Larry Moneta, Associate Vice Provost for University Life at the University of Pennsylvania, expresses a view that's echoed by many of today's educators:

> These students may be the true MTV generation and they exhibit many of the MTV characteristics: short attention span, hectic pace, intensity, and materialism. They've also been influenced by a growing distrust in public officials and have a relativistic attitude toward rules and laws. Speed limits are relative; alcohol consumption laws are relative; and academic integrity is relative. On the other hand, they also recognize a need to engage in service and do so in record numbers. They are family oriented and seem to have more positive relationships with parents and extended families than has been true for a while. Religion's cool for many, and they expect value for the dollar they're spending.

Sylvia Hoffert, Professor of History and Women's Studies at the University of North Carolina, offers another point of view:

My students are interested in social issues, particularly those relating to changing gender roles. Most of them work hard in class. Many of them are involved in community service projects and some of them have jobs as well. They're earnest, and they want to make connections between what they're studying and their own lives. But there are other students who are not particularly focused on either education or service. They make poor judgments about their social life, immersing themselves in the party and drinking culture. Unfortunately, they're the ones that get all of the media attention.

Paul Ginsberg, former Dean of Students at the University of Wisconsin, bristles at the media's disparaging throw-away descriptions of today's students, about whom he speaks with respect and affection:

When the media call this an apathetic generation, they misread the lack of marching crowds, protests, and social activism and assume that there is a return to the apathy of the '50s. This is not an apathetic generation, but the energy level is going toward issues of survival and of academic competency. These young men and women are dealing with options never available to generations of students before, and these choices create tensions and anxieties. They are scared—not uncaring people. They feel they need to taste every morsel on the table of life because the table may not be there in a few years. This is a generation more tuned in to survival, that is true. But this is not a basis for condemnation.

Listening to faculty and administrators share their perceptions of this generation reminds us that in spite of broad-scale studies and statistical reports of trends, students differ from campus to campus, as well as within each school. As one dean from a midwestern university puts it:

For every professional yuppie on campus, there are other students who still volunteer to tutor in the ghetto. Student populations, after all, are a lot like real communities; they have their doers and their loafers, their leaders and their followers, their heroes and their low-lifes.

In her book, *Campus Life,* historian Helen Lefkowitz Horowitz challenges her readers to look beyond the stereotypes that characterize each generation of college students:

> In any decade since 1920, single images of collegians have dominated the public consciousness; it is implicitly assumed that no other kinds of students have existed. Thus all students in the 1920s are seen to wear raccoon coats and carry hip flasks, while those of the 1930s march in demonstrations against war. The problem has been the failure to recognize that undergraduates have been divided into contending cultures. In any one era, one of these appears to be dominant and catches the public eye.[3]

Horowitz describes the students that dominate today's campuses as "grim professionals," cramming for tests, more interested in grades than in learning, and driven by a desire for success and security. But sharing the campus with them are political activists, carefree hedonists, and the students she calls "the quiet rebels," who see college not as a preprofessional hurdle but as a time to experiment, to struggle with new ideas and take intellectual risks.

WHAT IS HAPPENING ON TODAY'S CAMPUS?

Colleges and universities have come under scrutiny recently for everything from athletic scandals and questions about indirect costs and price fixing to debate about the academic canon and the tyranny of the "politically correct." But colleges and universities have always been works in progress, and campus dialogue about the future of education has never been more lively. The hot topics on most campuses include: internationalization of the university and preparing students to live in a global society; enhancement of undergraduate education with special attention to advising, residential life, and a core curriculum; commitment to a unified sense of community and personal contact within an increasingly technologically informed campus.

High-Tech Ivy: The Wired Campus

As faculty and administrators move into the 21st century, they are grappling with the challenges of maintaining the best of scholarly tradition and university life, while attending to the ever-accelerating pace of change at the brink of a technological revolution. Technology has transformed today's campuses, affecting all aspects of life from admissions and registration to classroom methodology and the very concept of community. The access to instant information on-line is exciting and seductive, but this transformation raises profound questions about the nature of the university as we have known it.

Although the ultimate benefits of these emerging technologies are beyond the scope of our imaginations, they have already significantly influenced the academic enterprise and methods of scholarly research. On many campuses, the library of yesteryear has been enhanced by a sophisticated central information retrieval network, with an electronic catalog and links throughout the campus and the world. Students can sit in their residence hall room and browse the on-line catalog of their university library as well as connect to libraries around the world. Students at a computer terminal in Boston can compare the same page of two different editions of Proust—one from a library in Paris and another from the University of Virginia.

In multimedia classrooms, professors supplement traditional texts with a rich array of computer graphics, virtual tours, and links to worldwide resources, bringing an astounding depth and breadth to any subject. Many lectures are taped or broadcast by university cable TV, allowing students to make up or review classes. Teleconferences make possible interactive lectures or panel discussions; students from around the country can participate by calling in with questions or comments.

With today's computer technology, learning extends beyond the formal classroom in new ways. Students communicate on-line at all hours and across time zones, debating and questioning their professors and other students in small electronic discussion groups, study groups, and one-on-one conversations. Some undergraduates say that they have more student-professor contact in cyberspace than they did in a traditional classroom bound by the limits of the lectern and the clock.

These new modes of communication encourage students to be active participants in the learning process, not just passive listeners and note-takers. Through technology, faculty can foster vibrant interaction and collaboration; they can create an environment that encourages thoughtful questions, reasoned debate, and problem solving. And they can now expand the notion of community beyond the bricks and mortar of their campus buildings to include a worldwide virtual community of students actively engaged in discourse about a common intellectual pursuit.

A vision of future creative possibilities, the Media Union at the University of Michigan is a 250,000-square-foot state-of-the-art radically new environment for learning, teaching and performing. Open 24 hours a day, 7 days a week, the center houses traditional and digital libraries, virtual reality labs, performance and design studios, and interactive multimedia classrooms. The building offers a vivid glimpse into the world of emerging technologies with a lively mix of artists, architects, engineers, and scholars. On any particular day, a visitor might find architecture students, faculty, and a representative from a leading design manufacturer exploring new forms of learning and work environments; local school children enjoying a digital music ensemble performance; and scholars in a video conference room working on a project with their colleagues in Taipei.

But universities are steeped in tradition, and radical change brings with it fears of technology run amok. How do we discriminate between the useful and the trivial with this barrage of information? It's easy to waste time surfing the Net, and our systems for sorting out and organizing the data are still crude and inadequate. With the growth of distance learning, will campuses of the 21st century be virtual universities without the need for a physical plant? How much will all of this cost, and how will this shift the allocation of financial resources? And what about the human element? How can faculty use these new resources to enhance the dialogue between professor and student?

Neil Rudenstine, President of Harvard University, devoted his entire 1996 commencement speech to the enormous transformation that is now underway in higher education as a result of the development of the Internet. He described the fast-paced and far-reaching changes in information processing as the most significant since the latter part of the 19th century. At that time, university research libraries came into their own, and the explosion of information-processing caused cries of concern—cries that have a familiar ring among today's technology dissidents. President Rudenstine related former Harvard President Charles Eliot's musings on information overload in 1876:

> What was to prevent students (and even faculty) from disappearing into the stacks for days on end pursuing a subject from book to book, shelf to shelf, unable to discriminate easily among the limited number of volumes, or to absorb more than a small fraction of the information available on a given topic? And what could possibly prevent less industrious students from simply browsing their lives away in sweet procrastination?

Rudenstine continued to put today's accelerated changes into an historical context:

> Some of these fears were not completely new. As early as the 18th century, Diderot remarked that "a time will come when . . . the printing press, which never rests, [will fill] huge buildings with books [in which readers] will not do very much reading . . . . [Eventually] the world of learning . . . our world . . . will drown in books."

President Rudenstine also referred to a 1795 German treatise on public health, which warned people that too much reading might lead to a long list of physical maladies and, most troublesome of all, replace human contact. Some of today's educators have the same concerns; to lose the human contact is to lose the soul of the university. As they struggle with these issues, however, most faculty and administrators, President Rudenstine included, applaud the uses of these new technologies as opportunities to supplement and enrich the traditional academic experience, not to replace it.

In the September 1996 *American Association for Higher Education Bulletin*, Barbara Leigh Smith, Provost at The Evergreen State College, writes of the need to use technology thoughtfully:

> I have certain apprehensions about the effectiveness of some forms of learning with technology. But, I must admit that I'm impressed with how far we've come in the last decade. I've seen faculty and students come alive with the creative opportunities emerging technologies can provide. . . . What's really important, I think, is having clear educational values to guide the use of technology and a clear sense of purpose.

Technology's impact outside of the classroom is evident in everyday scenes along the campus pathways and in the student centers, images that are a far cry from those a mere ten years ago. Occasional students reach into their backpacks, check their pocket electronic datebooks, and pull out a cellular phone. Others gather around computer kiosks where, at the touch of a screen, they peruse the local entertainment, watch a music video, or check the campus calendar. They may stop in at a cyber-café for a cappuccino and an interlude on the Web or check their e-mail at a terminal in the library.

Electronic mail has changed communication patterns in ways we are only beginning to understand. Students can write to parents or friends and have a response within minutes. Some love "talking" to parents on their own time, at three in the morning if that's when the spirit moves them. Many say they're likely to be more communicative on-line, when there are no interruptions or nuances of changing tone—those subtle triggers that may lead to defensiveness or misunderstanding. Students "chat" electronically with friends across campus, across the country, or even across the world. Some reserve this mode of communication for quick exchanges of information but prefer the telephone for more intimate conversation. Others actually develop relationships on-line, and carry on long-distance romances via electronic mail.

Technology has transformed the hidden administrative processes of many universities as well. Frustrated students used to stand in long lines hoping to get the appropriate signature so they could register for a popular course. Many of today's students register on-line from their rooms, some even from their homes before arriving. They find it hard to believe that most of their older brothers and sisters did it all with pencil and paper. They take for granted easy access to course listings and requirements, their grades and grade point averages (GPAs), financial aid information and their financial statements, all available from public terminals. With the aid of their personal identification number, they can check their status and carry on business with speed and confidentiality.

The access and convenience that technology brings are not without their problems and challenges. Educators are trying to deal with issues of privacy and plagiarism, and e-mail adds a whole new dimension to harassment. The Net provides endless distractions for procrastinators, and counseling services report increasing numbers of students who suffer from Internet addiction. Though a wired campus has the potential to form new kinds of community, it can also isolate students, especially those who are introverted or depressed.

"Finding the funds and personnel to support this rapidly changing technology is a real challenge to universities today," says Shirley K. Baker, Vice Chancellor for Information Technology and Dean of University Libraries at Washington University. This problem hits home for parents when their children call to complain:

- I have to stand in line to get access to my e-mail.
- The machines in my dorm don't have Netscape 3.
- I start writing a paper in the library—then I go back to the dorm to finish, but oops—it has a newer version of Word, and I can't continue—so it's back to the library.

Baker explains, "Universities need to budget for a replacement cycle for technology. Many institutions haven't learned to do that yet. They also need to factor in support costs. Technology is cheap compared to the cost of human beings who provide support."

In these early stages of this high-tech revolution, the sophistication of technology varies widely among America's thousands of campuses. All schools, however, are planning for an ever-increasing demand for technological equipment and services from each new entering class of students.

Academic Life

Academics remain at the core of the college experience. But the world of scholarly pursuits has a whole new look.

"Race, Class, and Gender in American Science Fiction? Feminism in Turkish Literature?" queried a puzzled father after his daughter called home to report on the classes she planned to take. Like many parents, he was more than a little suspicious of courses with such esoteric titles, courses he wouldn't have found in a college catalog when he was his daughter's age.

The course listings in contemporary catalogs include a legacy from the '60s and '70s, when universities opened their doors to diverse populations and the civil rights and women's movements made their mark. "At that time colleges and universities began to give students a variety of lenses through which to view a problem," comments Professor Thomas Ehrlich of Stanford University. He adds:

> Western Civilization courses, which were equated with the history of great men, were dropped. We began to ask, "What about women and minorities?" The structure of the curriculum became more open, and courses began to cut across disciplines. We developed a much more variegated academic set of inquiries.

The influence of black and women's studies programs, which were created more than twenty years ago, reaches beyond departmental boundaries. Feminist theory and research have changed the face of contemporary psychology, and history departments have incorporated scholarship on women and blacks into the curriculum. Most English departments no longer divide their courses simply by centuries and literary periods. "Women Writers in Medieval France" and "Native American Expressive Traditions" join the more traditional fare of "Chaucer" and "Elizabethan Poetry."

In recent years, there's been a movement toward interdisciplinary studies. Faculty in psychology, neuroscience, and philosophy are working together to explore and study the brain. Environmental Studies brings together biologists, anthropologists, economists, and political scientists. And many educators stress the importance of integrating new technology and the social sciences. The Values and Science/Technology (VAST) courses at Lafayette College are interdisciplinary seminars challenging students to address the values issues of our technological age, with titles such as "The Printing Press and the Computer: Technology and the Historical Imagination." At Haverford, students can study "Freud and the Web: Culture and Personality in Cyberspace."

Some courses have made their way into the contemporary curriculum because they meet new marketplace demands—courses such as "Telecommunications," "Computer Assisted Design," and "Negotiation and Conflict Resolution." Others reflect a growing interest in international affairs and an increasing awareness on the part of the faculty that we are truly members of a global village. Along with an increased interest in Latin American Studies and Asian and Near Eastern Studies, students are taking courses with titles such as "Global Cooperation" and "Arms Control and Global Security."

The decline in foreign language studies that occurred in the '60s now appears to be reversed. Foreign language courses are in ascendancy, and the number of institutions that require course work in a foreign language for completion of an undergraduate degree has increased markedly during the last fifteen years. In many schools today, the language laboratories are high-tech wonders. Students use interactive programs to help them improve their pronunciation, and

TV shows via satellite allow them to watch news and entertainment in the language they are studying. The majority of colleges and universities offer opportunities for study abroad; many encourage all students to participate in some kind of international experience during their undergraduate years.

Even in schools that don't require foreign language study, students are flocking back to these courses. A recent survey of 2700 colleges and universities revealed that the number of students enrolled in Chinese, Arabic, and Spanish increased dramatically between 1990 and 1995. At the same time, French, German, and Russian have waned in popularity. Language study often takes a vocational slant, as students sign up for classes entitled "Legal and Business Japanese" and "Spanish in Medicine."

In an attempt to understand the culture spawned by the '60s, students gravitate to courses about that era. Some courses, such as "The Impact of the Vietnam War on American Values," at the University of California at Santa Barbara, deal not just with the war itself, but with the cultural and political movements that grew out of that era. There are now more than three hundred such courses on campuses across the country.

Although enrollment in the liberal arts dropped precipitously in the '70s, there is evidence that the pendulum is swinging back. In the late '80s, applications to liberal arts colleges increased at a greater rate than applications to universities and technical schools. Selective, small liberal arts schools, such as Amherst and Pomona, report that competition for admissions has been particularly keen in recent years.

The word is out that employers are interested in liberal arts students. They are sending messages that they value critical thinking and writing skills and the ability to be flexible—that technical training is outdated quickly, and today's workforce, above all, has to be adaptable to change. Moreover, students enrolled in undergraduate professional programs such as business and engineering are taking more liberal arts courses than they used to. MIT has broadened its engineering program to include more course work in the arts, humanities, and social sciences. There is more crossover in general.

Liberal arts students are also taking advantage of the opportunities to supplement their studies with courses in business and computer technology.

On campuses across America, curriculum reform is the order of the day. Much of the recent criticism of higher education has been leveled from within. The '60s concern for egalitarianism has been replaced today by a concern with quality and cohesion. The days of unlimited pass/fail courses, no requirements, and widespread independent study appear to be coming to a close.

Almost all institutions are in the midst of curriculum change. They are looking at ways to introduce students to the ideas and arts of non-Western cultures. They are developing new general education requirements and examining more closely the actual skills students are acquiring. They are concerned about competencies in writing and quantitative analysis. They are grappling with questions of assessment and discussing ways to measure their effectiveness with an eye toward using that information in planning for the future.

Edward Fiske, former Education Editor of the *New York Times,* thinks the roots of much of this academic self-analysis are political:

> The faculty is taking back the control that it gave away in the '60s, reinstituting requirements and establishing a core. This trend started at Harvard in the late '70s, which spurred lots of other schools to do the same. In the beginning it was a political rather than an academic event. The primary issue was control, not content.

More and more faculty and academic deans are expressing concern about academic overspecialization, the rise of preprofessionalism, and a lack of common goals, which are all too common on today's campuses. They are claiming that it is not enough merely to reinstate a hodgepodge of distribution requirements, but that it is essential to come to some cohesive view of what should constitute the core experience of education today.

Some schools, such as Princeton and Columbia, are quick to

point out that they never gave up their general education programs in the first place. Others, such as Skidmore, which went through major changes in the '60s and '70s, introduced a whole new core curriculum. Gustavas Adolphus reevaluated and essentially redid its catalog from scratch. The trend is definitely toward more control, toward establishment of a core academic experience for undergraduates. Just what should be included in this core curriculum is the subject of endless debate among deans and faculty, but there is no doubt that the content of college catalogs is changing again.

Life Outside the Classroom: The Changing Landscape

Gone are the amenities of genteel college living in the '50s and '60s. Few dormitory living rooms contain grand pianos and oriental rugs these days, and the ubiquitous color television in the lounge is likely to be bolted to the table. But college students of this generation are being well taken care of, from their culinary to their counseling needs.

"Retention" is a buzzword on all campuses, and some schools have even hired specialists in "enrollment management" to help them not only attract but also keep students. Consumer-minded students demand services that support their daily living, and colleges and universities have poured financial resources into out-of-the-classroom facilities—athletic complexes, student unions, and, in institutions such as the University of South Carolina and Northeastern University, complete shopping malls.

Elaborate sports complexes cater to the health- and fitness-conscious student population with weight rooms, Nautilus equipment, and saunas adjacent to Olympic-size swimming pools. Even small colleges provide students with more sophisticated and extensive facilities than the simple gymnasiums that were standard in the largest universities a generation ago. Translucent bubbles housing indoor tennis courts and skating rinks dot campuses all over the country. Some schools, such as the University of Miami, have built multimillion-dollar wellness centers to provide a full array of integrated offerings. With a 10,000-square-foot weight room, Miami's center provides nutritional assessment, physical therapy—even massages. Students congregate at the juice bar and indoor and outdoor conversation pits. The Evergreen State College in Washington includes a rock-climbing practice wall in its wellness complex.

Lavish student centers attest to the fact that today's students and their parents have high expectations of campus leisure facilities as well as of classrooms and laboratories. The University of Texas Union houses 575 student-run activities. Wilson Commons of the University of Rochester boasts a striking glass design by I. M. Pei. The Aztec Center at San Diego State sits on Mission Bay, a captivating waterfront wonder. George Mason University's 320,000-square-foot George W. Johnson Center is an innovative experiment, integrating students' academic and social lives. A hub for both students and faculty, this streamlined facility houses an academic library, professors' offices, and classrooms, along with a 310-seat movie theater, dance studios, bistros, and much more.

An entire community exists under one roof in many of these upscale centers—a bookstore, a bank, a travel agency, theaters and cabarets, video game rooms, art galleries, cappuccino bars, and food courts catering to an assortment of palates. Signs of the technological explosion are everywhere, from the reception desk, which may have a touch-screen computer that displays a campus calendar, to ATM machines, fax machines, computer terminals, and laser printers conveniently available for student use.

Wheelchair ramps and parking spaces for the disabled are welcome campus additions and are evidence of the increased access to college for all potential students. There are more cars on campus and more parking lots than there used to be. But complaints about parking from students, faculty, and staff are louder than ever.

MAKING CONNECTIONS: CAMPUS GROUPS

Activities fairs, a fall ritual on most campuses, provide a festival-like atmosphere with colorful banners, posters, and students distributing leaflets and invitations to join the campus radio station, newspaper, literary magazines, a capella singing groups and theater troupes, community service organizations and intramural sports teams, Young Republicans and Young Democrats. These kinds of organizations have been an important part of campus life for many generations.

The diversity of the current crop of college students is reflected in a mélange of a whole new set of campus organizations, which might not look so familiar to visiting parents. There are more groups than ever before, representing a broad range of backgrounds and beliefs. These include the Society of Women Engineers; the Hispanic Business Students Association; the Islamic Society; the Cultural Diversity Players; the Organization of United African-American Peoples; the Gay, Lesbian, and Bisexual Alliance; the American Indian Students Commission; and the Korean Students Association.

Most students thrive on the sense of connection that comes from affiliation with a small group united by a common bond, and these informal organizations are a vital part of colleges today. As students choose among this incredible range of campus groups, they are making a statement about who they are and who they want to be.

Students of Color: Ethnic and Cultural Groups

The racial and cultural mix on today's campuses brings new richness and intellectual energy as well as new tensions to the entire college experience. It influences the nature of the curriculum, the organization of the living units, and the scope of the social life. Students, faculty, and administrators engage in ongoing dialogue about what multiculturalism and diversity mean to the university and the daily lives of students.

Students of color on predominantly white campuses confront daily episodes of prejudice that take their toll. African-American and Latino students at the University of California at Irvine report that when they go to a local shopping center they are followed by security guards. Asian students from Maine to California complain that everyone assumes they are either premed or engineering majors, and they feel the thinly veiled hostility of their classmates who are worried about their raising the curve. Students from the Middle East sense the fear and mistrust of their peers whenever there is a widely

publicized incident in their part of the world. Chicano students
describe the humiliation of arriving at a fraternity party where the
Mexican theme includes Anglos affecting Spanish accents.

Minority student groups, both organized and informal, serve a
crucial need as a haven—a safe space where students of color can be
themselves, where they don't have to represent all people of their
race or culture, but can speak their own minds.

In *The Agony of Education: Black Students at White Colleges and
Universities*, Joe R. Feagin, Hernán Vera, and Nikitah Imani write of
their findings from interviews with parents and students:

> In contrast to certain critics of higher education like
> D'Souza and Bloom, many black parents see black stu-
> dents' sticking together in traditionally white places as
> necessary for their personal and academic survival, not as
> some type of organized anti-white activity. These peer
> group settings give many first-year college students a place
> to be themselves, and to find supportive friends, without
> the intrusion of racial barriers.[4]

The following student comments echo these sentiments:

> When you're a minority on a big campus, even if you have
> friends from other groups, it's nice to know that there are
> other people like you. Walking into the black student
> lounge is so comforting just because it's like my place. It's
> just your area, your own private study room, and if other
> people are there, they look like you. It's really neat.
> There's a huge picture of Martin Luther King and art from
> black students on the walls—it's ours.

■

> At Oberlin, the black student house provides a social life. If
> you have all this comfort and support and have all the things
> on a college campus that white students get to enjoy just
> anyway because they're the majority—the idea is that you'll

perform better, and you'll reach out because you'll be so happy with where you are and what you're doing—it will be natural for you to reach out. I really believe that's the case.

◼

It's important to me to be true to yourself. Joining ABS [Association of Black Students] was something I really wanted to do. Everybody fits into something. People look at you and decide where they are going to place you. Being light-skinned and of mixed heritage—that causes more problems for you 'cause it's less clear for people where they're going to stack you in their own minds in classifying you. Joining ABS was my way of establishing myself and telling people where I was. It's meant a lot to look at a group and say this is what I've invested myself in.

Many institutions have responded to today's diverse population of students by providing ethnic and multicultural centers. The Swarthmore Black Cultural Center, a large stone house adjacent to campus, is guided by a director and a committee of black faculty, administrators, and students and provides comfortable places to study or just hang out. It also contains a library, art gallery, and facilities for a wide range of social, cultural, and educational programs for black students and others interested in black culture. The Cross-Cultural Center at the University of California at Irvine houses student organizations for African-Americans, Native Americans, Asian-Americans, Chicanos, and Latinos. These are just a few samples of an increasing number of gathering places for students of color on campuses across the country.

Some campuses, such as Berkeley, where there is no distinct majority, foreshadow the American pluralistic society of the not-too-distant future. But many students at Berkeley report feelings of isolation in the midst of diversity. They use words such as *balkanization* and *tribalism* to describe the breakup of the student body into distinctly separate ethnic and racial groups at the expense of a common campus identity.

Other Berkeley students report that there is more mixing than meets the eye of the casual observer. Though students find support and social comfort by coming together with others of similar backgrounds, many also form bonds across racial and cultural boundaries as they struggle together with difficult chem labs, enervating athletic practice, or challenging community service projects. And as they celebrate their own culture, they often enrich the lives of their fellow students.

The conventional wisdom from a white student overheard giving a campus tour to a prospective freshman:

> The Asian Students Association has the hottest parties on this campus, especially on the Chinese New Year. Everybody goes. They always have great decorations, good music, and definitely the best food. They even have fireworks.

> ■

> Black Anthology is the most awesome student production on campus. There's singing, poetry, dance, even a fashion show put on by the art students. You have to come early or you don't get a seat.

At Washington University, students from a variety of ethnic groups have come together to form a coalition called Many Voices: One Vision, recognizing a need both to preserve their own identities and to foster a sense of a larger community. Their mission is to learn more about each other, support each other's programs, and through joint efforts, celebrate their commonalities as well as each unique heritage.

African-American students on predominantly white campuses face serious dilemmas and major struggles above and beyond the daily stresses of their white counterparts. Many have chosen to attend a school in which African-Americans are likely to represent less than 5 percent of the student body, to "brave it" in an environment that is at best tolerant and at worst hostile. There are subtle reminders daily that they are not welcomed by many of their classmates and professors—who don't recognize them or confuse them with other black students, fail to respect or acknowledge their insistence on celebrating the life and death of Martin Luther King, Jr., suggest that they accept a mediocre performance rather than reach for higher academic goals, imply that they have been admitted as a result of preferential treatment.

African-Americans, both on campus and off, live with a dual consciousness, with an ability to switch from their black world—a shared language, heritage, and music—to the world of the white majority and its cultural norms. This split is particularly exhausting and confusing at a time when a young adult is sorting out a sense of his or her own identity. Many feel forced to make a choice. A freshman at a prestigious college addresses a dilemma common to many minority students:

> If I join a black sorority or hang out with my friends from BSA [the Black Student Association], the white kids say I'm segregating myself. If I go out with some of the white kids on the floor or a couple of them I knew from high school, then my black friends give me a hard time and say I'm turning my back on my own. I almost went to Howard, and I still think I might transfer. It seems like such a hassle a lot of the time.

Recent studies show that students attending the top black colleges, such as Morehouse, Spelman, and Howard, statistically outperform black students who attend predominantly white colleges. Jacqueline Fleming, a black psychologist who specializes in the field of motivation and is the author of *Blacks in College*, notes the strong influence of the varied supports that black students have on an all-black campus—greater access to friends, relationships with professors who believe in them and support their dreams, and exposure to role models. She challenges black and white faculty and administration at all institutions to take note and to become mentors to students.

■

For many students of mixed heritage, it's hard to find a niche on today's multicultural campus. One student who is of African-American and Korean descent spent his childhood and teen years in a small rural community where he was routinely ostracized. Even though he is now a student at a cosmopolitan university, he still feels on the fringe.

A young woman comments:

> Both of my parents are of mixed heritage. It's very important that I get to be a woman of color of multiethnic heritage—that people don't put me in one box or another.

On many campuses, students have formed groups to celebrate and explore their mixed heritage. A member of an organization called Shades describes her experience:

> It was interesting to hear other people's experience, and the interesting thing about Shades is—a lot of members are mixed Caucasian and black heritage, but then there are people who are black and Asian or Asian and Caucasian. So it's very much a multicultural group. Sometimes we talked about being a member of ABS, sometimes about the greater college community. We talked about what it meant to have one parent who was black and one who was white, and at the same time you were talking to people who are Indian, who had similar experiences. I think every group of color has issues of complexion. Our talks served a lot of personal needs, but it was also academic in that you were sort of broadening your horizons a lot on lots of different cultures.

For students of mixed heritage, organizations such as Shades can strengthen and support their sense of identity at this crucial time of their lives. One member, whose father is black and mother is white, reflects on this need for validation:

> I think because of who my parents were and the nature of their relationship—they cared about each other so much,

and I was like a product of that, I was sort of like an entity—they didn't really work to give me a defining culture. It was bits and pieces of each. They were sort of pioneers the way they raised me. I was very loved and a very strong person in a lot of respects, but there was still this gap, and I really wanted to have a strong identity.

Religion, Spirituality, and Cults

Many of today's students are looking for a sense of purpose and community in an environment that often seems fragmented; they are looking for answers, for rituals and traditions in an era of rapid change and rootlessness. Increasing numbers are turning to faith communities on campus.

The number of students affiliating with religious groups is rising; across the country, participation at the Newman Centers and Hillels, traditional gathering places for Catholic and Jewish students, has increased markedly. And alongside these, the numbers of different religious groups are mushrooming continually—the Chinese Christian Fellowship, the Bahai Campus Club, the Muslim Society.

Young men and women attend traditional services, join Bible study groups, and some even live in small enclaves that carry on rituals or traditions of their faith. Students who join a group with a religious focus often find companionship as well as spirituality. Many of these organizations sponsor parties, cultural programs, or other social events. For some students, the identification with their own ethnic group is more important than the spiritual experience or religious ritual. Membership provides them with a longed-for niche on campus. For others, membership provides an oasis of calm in a stressful landscape.

This search for community even extends to the nonbeliever. A new group, the Campus Freethought Alliance, is a small but significant minority of atheists and humanists who have banded together to unite against what they see as the public religiosity of the 1990s.

Administrators on many campuses are concerned about students' susceptibility to destructive religious cults. Seymour Lachman, Dean for Community Development at the City University of New York and a Professor in the School of Public Affairs at Baruch College, explains that such groups usually have a "self-appointed messianic leader claiming divine selection who focuses followers' attentions exclusively on him and exercises autocratic control of them." Cults manipulate, control, and isolate their members. They demand unquestioning loyalty and obedience.

College campuses are prime targets for cult recruiters. Using coercive and deceptive techniques, cult recruiters have been known to position themselves outside the counseling service or in the student center, looking for students who appear depressed or lonely. Cult leaders know that students who are on their own for the first time, though pleased with their freedom, are anxious about taking responsibility for their own lives. Young people are searching for answers, for an identity, for some stability in their lives; they are vulnerable to the offer of instant community, a set of clear expectations, and ready answers to complex questions. International students, lonely and eager to learn about American culture, have a particularly difficult time distinguishing between genuine overtures of friendship from religious congregations and organized recruitment by cults.

For parents who are concerned about their own child, this is not the kind of problem to be tackled alone. This is a time to call the dean, the advisor, or another appropriate university administrator. Parents may also turn to their own clergy or to one of the organizations around the country that monitor the activities of cults. The American Family Foundation (AFF) does research, educates, and provides assistance to victims and their loved ones. The International Cult Education Program (ICEP), an arm of AFF, helps professionals in colleges and other institutions educate themselves and their students about cults.[5] Two books that parents might find helpful are ICEP's book, edited by Marcia Rudin, *Cults on Campus: Continuing Challenge*, and *Cults: What Parents Should Know*, by Joan Ross and Michael D. Langone.

Gay and Lesbian Support Groups

Reflecting the growing acknowledgment and acceptance of the homosexual community nationally, university-sanctioned student organizations commonly include gay, lesbian, and bisexual groups. Most of these support groups offer social and educational programs, and some serve as political action groups as well. They confront overtly discriminatory policies and incidents, and also attempt to sensitize the university community to the more subtle forms of harassment they experience.

The University of Pennsylvania employs an administrator and a fully staffed center, one of only a handful in the country, to support lesbian, gay, and bisexual students, staff, and faculty. In addition to programs, support, and advocacy, the center maintains a 24-hour telephone listing of events of interest to their constituency. The center's library of books and periodicals written for and about sexual minorities is a valuable resource for both students and faculty. The Penn's LBGA (Lesbian, Bisexual, Gay Alliance) home page provides links to other helpful campus resources, such as The Virtual Closet, featuring coming out stories, and The Youtharts Project, highlighting art and writings by lesbian, gay, and bisexual youth.

Campus recognition has changed the lives of many gay men and women, offering them a place to share their concerns with their peers—a far cry from the isolated, guilt-ridden secret lives of those in earlier times. While welcoming the safe haven of their own community, most are involved in all aspects of campus life. In spite of the improved climate, however, blatant antigay incidents still mar the lives of many gay, lesbian, and bisexual students.

Greek Life Today

Although some colleges such as Colby and Amherst have disbanded their Greek system, fraternities and sororities are definitely back in vogue on many campuses. With 400,000 members at 800 campuses, fraternities have more than doubled their membership since the low point in 1971. New chapters arrive yearly on campuses that spurned them a decade ago. They provide students with a family of "brothers" and "sisters" and an instant identity advertised by the pins, jackets, and sweatshirts they proudly wear. Many also provide affordable and communal housing.

Present-day Greek life is a study in contradictions. Fraternities are notorious for their wild parties, excessive alcohol consumption, and drug use. They now spend up to a third of their budgets to pay liability costs. Alcohol has played a major role in most of the claims. Many of the incidents have resulted in sexual assaults, serious accidents, and some even in death. As a result, some nationals are adopting alcohol-free houses, and most are altering their policies. Hazing, and its sometimes tragic consequences, has come under scrutiny, and the majority of states have passed antihazing laws.

On the other hand, an increasing number of fraternities and sororities have taken the lead in campus activities and community service. The black Greek system is noted for its commitment to lifelong community service and for the ongoing connections that it provides for its members.

The Greek system has opened its ranks along with the rest of the university. Most nationals no longer tolerate restricting membership based on race or religion. Though more diverse than they used to be, however, they still cater mainly to the affluent, and the students who are excluded still suffer the pain of rejection. Today's students see "networking" as a plus in the stampede for professional success, and these coteries provide the first stop on the "old boy" express and its "old girl" equivalent. Those who are excluded from membership often feel that they have been exiled permanently from the mainstream.

■

Today's colleges and universities have officially acknowledged the value of students' extracurricular involvements, whether through Greek life or social, religious, or political groups. Under the aegis of the dean of students, a cadre of student development professionals advises student groups and provides training in leadership skills. They coach and teach and act as confidants and mentors. Their mission is to help students gain confidence and competence in the world outside the classroom.

In their concern about their child's ability to meet academic demands and maintain a high GPA, many parents view student involvement in nonacademic activities as a frivolous pastime. Yet research by Alexander Astin highlights its positive influence on the way students grow and develop. Students who are active campus leaders bring that confidence into the classroom and tend to be active participants there as well. Charles Schroeder, Vice Chancellor at the University of Missouri, urges parents not to discount the impact that the extracurricular experience can have on their child:

> We try to encourage broad-based student involvement in a variety of settings. The intent is to promote character development and values, leadership skills, and the ability to communicate well. Much of this comes from involvement outside the classroom. Students spend approximately twelve to fifteen hours a week in class. Just think about how many hours kids spend together talking, drinking, playing sports, working together in a host of student activities. The intensity of their relationships is powerful. Part of what we do in Student Development is help students make meaning out of the collegiate experience.

BEYOND THE IVY-COVERED WALLS: CHANGING NEEDS AND SERVICES

Beyond the venerable old edifices and dazzling new facilities that pervade the campus, there are a legion of services for students that didn't exist thirty years ago: career centers, psychological counseling centers, study skills and writing centers, multicultural centers, and women's centers. Lively and energetic residence-hall staff join psychologists and specialists in reading skills, student programming, and alcohol and drug abuse in the daily pursuit of helping students to develop as well as to cope with the stresses and strains of college life. These are the adults who are on the front line and are likely to have the most interaction with students, particularly freshmen and sophomores.

In previous generations, house parents or proctors who lived in dormitories enforced codes of discipline and provided a haven for "tea and sympathy" as needed. There were clear-cut rules and expectations, and the concept of *in loco parentis*, a Latin phrase meaning "in the place of the parent," was a court-ordered fact of college life. The landmark decision in the 1911 *Gott v. Berea College* case stated that college authorities would stand in place of parents to watch out for the welfare of their children while they were under the college's care. Colleges and universities operated according to these guidelines until the late '60s, when *in loco parentis* disappeared altogether on most campuses, along with curfews, stringent rules, and young people's trust in adults over 30.

In the late '60s and early '70s, students assumed power in all areas of their lives. Along with civil rights and women's rights, students' rights became an issue in itself. In addition to their challenges to the national political status quo, students mobilized changes on campus, from the dissolution of parietal rules to a more open and varied curriculum. They became responsible for monitoring their own behavior in all facets of their lives.

Edward B. Fiske, former Education Editor of the *New York Times*, recounts the impact of these sweeping changes on large numbers of students and on the colleges and universities themselves:

> The faculty gave away control of the curriculum, and the administration decided it was going to get out of *in loco parentis*. All this freedom worked for some kids, but for lots of others, it didn't. Colleges and universities realized this and began to pick up the pieces with expanded health centers and counseling services and career centers. A whole set of professionals stepped in to serve kids who couldn't handle the freedom. As Ernest Boyer (of the Carnegie Foundation) put it in his book *College: The Undergraduate Experience in America*, we moved from *in loco parentis* to *in loco clinician*.

The services that emerged in response to the needs and demands of students in the '60s and '70s are now as much a part of college life as the library and the lecture hall. A whole body of research exists about the development of college students, providing theoretical grounding to the work carried out by the student affairs professionals on campus.

Students today are searching for more structure than students of twenty-five years ago. They actively seek out advice from adults and seem more willing to accept restraints. Almost all schools are reassessing the needs of their students and the role that the institution should play in their total development. Although there is virtually no interest in returning to *in loco parentis* as it existed in the '50s or early '60s, today's colleges and universities are designing programs to involve faculty as active advisors and mentors and to increase their presence in the lives of students outside of the classroom.

Residential Life

Although residence halls on many campuses have been mixing the sexes since the early '70s, first-time parents of college freshmen are often shocked by the sight of young men and women actually living side by side, brushing their teeth together, mingling in the halls in their bathrobes, casually sprawled on the beds in each other's rooms. The following tongue-in-cheek comments from the mother of a brand-new freshman at the University of Pennsylvania speak for the anxieties of many parents:

> Initially, I was horrified by the fact that the small, squalid bathroom two doors away from Peggy's room was to be shared by students of both sexes. I had been prepared for the coed dorm and even for the coed floor, but the idea of sharing a bathroom with only a torn shower curtain between my naked Peggy and some unshaven lout was an ugly shock.

"Some parents are very naive about residential life in college," warns Karen Tidmarsh, Dean of the Undergraduate College at Bryn Mawr:

> Today's dorms are hard places for students to live. The
> rules and regulations that we used to have gave students
> something to bump up against. When I went to college,
> we signed out to where we were going. I felt safe because
> someone knew where I was.

If Dean Tidmarsh were a student today, chances are that no one
would know where she was at any given time. She could spend a day
or a week away from school and not be required to check in with
anyone. Parents are often horrified by this fact, but as one director
of residence halls at a large university remarked during a parents'
orientation meeting. "We haven't lost a student yet!"

Curfews, visitation restrictions, and sign-outs belong to another
era. On most campuses today, the rules are minimal. The good news
is that residence halls are laboratories for self-development; students
have to learn to say no when the university doesn't do it for them.
The bad news is that without the boundaries of a stringent code of
conduct, the residence halls can be chaotic. Blaring music and spontaneous beer parties make studying in one's room an exercise in frustration. And fines for vandalism are routine additions to some parents' housing bills.

Residence halls range from the small, decrepit, and charming to
the high-rise, impersonal, and air-conditioned—from the convenient fall-out-of-bed-into-class variety to those located a bike ride
or bus ride from the center of campus. It is not uncommon for residence halls to provide fitness studios and exercise rooms for their
residents. Many have computer laboratories that are staffed all day
and into much of the night; an increasing number have dorm rooms
that are directly wired into the campus computer network. At the
University of Pennsylvania, students' rooms are furnished with four
jacks, allowing a student to watch an instructional cable-television
show, chat with a classmate on the phone, and surf the Net for supplementary information all at the same time. Some dorms are single-sex; others are coed and separate the sexes by wing, floor, or
room. Many offer choices of quiet floors, no-smoking wings, or
suites of students with common majors or interests.

As we enter a new century, substance-free dorms or floors have become a popular alternative for many students. Recently, at the University of Maryland, 1000 of the 8000 students in campus housing chose this option. Some want to stay free of temptation, but most want a quieter and more civilized living environment. Indiana University offers nonvisitation units or limited visitation units for students who want the privacy of their own living space without worrying about running into a stranger in the hallway late at night.

Increasing numbers of colleges and universities provide living environments that encourage a sense of pride and commitment to a community. At Stanford, ethnic theme houses such as Ujamaa and Casa Zapata provide support and a home away from home, as well as cultural programming and resources. The Program Houses at Cornell provide a haven for students of similar backgrounds but have sparked controversy about the impact of self-selected separation by race or ethnicity.

The time-honored "houses" and "colleges" at Harvard and Yale have remained constant during periods of residential upheaval. With faculty-in-residence, they have their own libraries and dining facilities and support an active intellectual and cultural life.

A growing number of colleges are attempting to make the academic experience an integral part of residential life. For example, as part of the University of Pennsylvania's Academic Programs in Residence, faculty members live in the residence halls, advising and interacting with students daily as members of the same community. At Duke University, as part of a major shift in their residential plan, East Campus has become an all-freshman enclave that integrates residential living with academic and social programs. Duke's Faculty Associates Program links professors with living units throughout the campus, hoping to bring the intellectual energy of the formal classroom into the informal settings of the dining halls and lounges. The Living-Learning Center at the University of Vermont is a home for students who study subjects around a common theme of their choice. The University of Michigan, the University of the Pacific, Princeton, Bucknell, and Colby are among schools that have innovative housing systems that bring the living and learning experience into closer harmony.

Without rules and regulations, who keeps the typical residence hall from deteriorating into total anarchy? In many schools, the heroes and heroines in the trenches are graduate or upperclass students, often called resident advisors or assistants. The RAs, who frequently receive compensation such as room and board, act as the on-site supervisors and counselors responsible for the daily functioning of residence hall floors. On 24-hour call, an RA may be found rescuing a student who is locked out of a room, encouraging a stressed student to get a calculus tutor, admonishing a noisy resident, or counseling someone who is severely depressed.

RA training is often intense and extensive. The best is usually year-long, with supervision by graduate student residence directors and student services staff. RAs participate in workshops on everything from suicide prevention to time management; they discuss and learn about such issues as test anxiety, racism, homosexuality, and eating disorders. At the very minimum, RA training includes information and communication skills to help them be alert and reach out to students in need, listen attentively, and refer students to resources and professional help.

Career Centers

Career centers are among the busiest offices on campus these days, and their habitués aren't just second-semester seniors dressed in their interview suits. On most campuses, the placement offices of yesteryear have expanded into multifaceted high-tech centers. They help students with career development throughout their four years and assist them with their job hunt when they graduate. On many campuses, part-time and summer job listings are available at the career center as well.

Students have a chance to meet with career counselors as early as their freshman year to begin the search for knowledge about themselves and the world of work. Through individualized counseling, workshops, computer guidance programs, and career resource libraries, students learn the process of career development—a process that will prove invaluable since most of them will have many jobs and several career changes after they land their first position.

Contrary to what many students believe, there is no test that can tell them what their perfect career is or what they *should* be. But counseling and career interest testing can help students begin to focus, become aware of their interests, skills, and values, and decide what fields they want to explore. Fortunately, most of today's colleges provide students with a lot of opportunity for exploration. In addition to the written materials housed in career libraries and information garnered from electronic databases, career panels of local graduates, networks of alumni career advisors, and mentoring programs all serve to bring students together with role models and information sources.

Innovative internship and cooperative education programs give students valuable work experience while still in school, helping to solve the age-old dilemma that most recent graduates face—"only the experienced need apply." More and more career centers have reached out into the community to arrange on-the-job apprenticeships and internships. Many of today's upperclassmen, especially those who might have been tempted to desert the humanities, supplement their intellectual nourishment with these pragmatic stepping stones to the work world.

Career centers help with the nuts and bolts of job hunting too. Students learn how to write résumés, target job leads, collect references, and hone their interviewing skills. The best equipped of today's high-tech centers offer a sophisticated array of resources. Students can use a computer program to generate a résumé. They can do practice interviews and critique themselves on video. They can search local and global databases for job leads, fax their résumés, and interview with a potential employer thousands of miles away via video-conferencing. Most centers serve alumni as well as students, reflecting the contemporary view that career development is ongoing and career change is a common occurrence.

Counseling Services

Counseling centers that were embryonic or nonexistent thirty years ago are now standard fare. Staffed by psychologists, social workers, and counselors, their primary mission is to help students grow and help them surmount the normal developmental hurdles that are so common to late adolescence.

A member of the counseling staff of a private southern university elaborates:

> My role is so varied depending on the student. With some I'm probably not very different from the housemother I had living in my dorm thirty years ago—reassuring, letting a kid know that what he is going through is normal and to be expected. With others I'm an educator, a teacher of a variety of coping skills to deal with the incredible academic and social stresses that are part of their daily lives. And I am, of course, a psychologist, helping students to correct distorted perceptions that cause them to stumble.

"To stumble" often means to suffer from anxiety or depression, the most common problems students bring to counseling services. These can be brought on by anything from a disappointing grade to a broken romance or problems at home—the kinds of concerns that have always plagued college students. But the complications of contemporary family life, financial pressures, and the bewildering array of choices facing today's students have brought them in increasing numbers to university counseling centers. A lot more students seem to be willing to ask for help, and it is not unusual for them to recommend counselors to each other. Most students' needs can be met by these centers, but because colleges often place a limit on the number of visits a student can make, it is common for college counselors to give referrals to professionals in the community for more extended counseling.

Through the World Wide Web, students have access to instant information on a variety of psychological and developmental issues. For example, the University of Minnesota at Duluth offers information on issues ranging from procrastination to depression and sexual assault. At the University of Chicago, the Student Counseling Virtual Pamphlet Collection links students to counseling information Web pages at colleges all over the country, sharing their collective wisdom. For some students, this factual information may be enough; for others, this is a first step toward calling and making an appointment to talk directly to a counselor.

As trainers and consultants to RA staffs, campus leaders, and peer counselors, counselors are often well known to numbers of students on an informal basis. Although much of their work addresses the normal developmental tasks of college students, counselors also present educational outreach programs to deal with some of the critical concerns of contemporary college students, such as date rape, eating disorders, drugs and alcohol, and safe sex.

CAMPUS PROBLEMS

Crime

Crime is at the top of most parents' "worry list." In this era of crime consciousness, colleges have appropriated large sums of money for security measures to protect students. Gone are the days when bikes were left unlocked in campus bike racks and dormitories were left open until midnight. Today, computerized card systems replace locks on many campuses; special lighting and emergency phones have been installed on pathways to and from residence halls; escort services provide nighttime transportation to libraries, labs, and studios. On a lot of campuses, newly arrived freshmen find an orientation packet that includes information on security, rape prevention tips, and crisis hot line numbers. On city campuses, this comes as no surprise, but students who arrive at a halcyon collegiate setting outside of city limits are often skeptical about the message that they too are vulnerable.

Date Rape

From Stanford to Swarthmore, from Cornell to San Diego State, counselors and public safety officers actively address rape prevention with workshops and self-defense programs. But far more prevalent on college campuses, and more insidious than rape by a stranger, is the crime of date rape, sometimes known as acquaintance rape.

According to a three-year study of 7000 college students, under the direction of Kent State University psychologist Mary P. Koss, one out of every eight college women indicated that she had been forced to have sexual intercourse against her will through use or threat of force (the minimum legal definition of rape). Almost 90 percent of them knew their assailants. These shocking statistics are not an anomaly. In studies at Auburn University and the University of South Dakota, one in five college women reported having had sexual intercourse against their will. Because they are unlikely to use the term *rape* to describe what happened to them, and they often feel guilty and ashamed, most women who are forced to have sex with an acquaintance do not report the incident officially. But the aftermath can be as devastating for them as the consequences of rape by a stranger.

Colleges and universities are focusing attention on this widespread problem. Many campus organizations, such as Stanford's Rape Education Project and Princeton's SHARE (Sexual Harassment/Assault Advising Resources and Education), provide students with emergency phone numbers and offer films, discussion groups, and workshops on prevention and protection. Brown University's SAPE (Sexual Assault Peer Education) program offers interactive theatrical pieces such as "When a Kiss Is Not Just a Kiss" and "Love's Not Supposed to Hurt," which stimulate lively and thoughtful small group discussions.

Programs often focus on the miscommunications and misconceptions that lead to sexual violence. They challenge the beliefs of many young men, rooted in existing sexual myths—"She provoked it," "Women say no, but mean yes," "I just lost control; you know how men are." Counselors and peer educators instruct students about sexual rights and responsibilities and teach women how to say no. They also emphasize that it is essential for both men and women to make active, responsible choices, and point out the role that alcohol plays in increasing the risk of miscommunication and poor judgment.

Since recent research indicates that freshmen are the group most at risk for date rape, many schools now include videotapes or student skits and peer-led discussions on the topic during orientation. And it's not unusual for fraternities, sororities, and residence hall staffs to follow up with related programs as the year progresses.

Increased awareness about the prevalence of date rape has also produced student demands for more sophisticated campus support services, such as a specifically designated women's counselor, survivors' support groups, more accessible campus reporting mechanisms, and more responsive judicial procedures that take into consideration the special psychological dimensions of sexual assault cases.

Students can find information on date rape and sexual assault on university home pages as well as the Sexual Assault Information Page on the Internet. If a student has been assaulted or raped, the computer is no substitute for personal counseling by a chaplain, psychologist, or counselor. The World Wide Web can be helpful in providing resources and reassuring advice, however, for friends and family who want to give support.

Eating Disorders

A mixture of psychological, sociological, and environmental stresses make today's college women particularly vulnerable to eating disorders. Though some students have a history of anorexia or bulimia in high school, others turn early in their college career to the starvation diets that characterize anorexia, or the binge eating and purging through vomiting, laxatives, diet pills, or fasting of bulimia. The combination of leaving home, coping with the stresses of college life, and the societal obsession with thinness cause some women to engage in these destructive, sometimes deadly, behaviors. College counselors address these issues daily in individual and group counseling. But they also reach out to educate both students and staff about the pitfalls of excessive dieting and the physical and psychological implications of eating disorders. Web sites abound on subjects relating to diet, nutrition, compulsive overeating, and other eating disorders.

In addition to individual counseling, resources on college campuses range from one-session workshops on body image to multidimensional approaches. For example, George Washington University has strengthened links among university departments to intervene actively on a variety of fronts. Residence hall advisors receive training during their orientation; the athletic department provides a support group for women in sports, a population at high risk for eating disorders, to help them develop alternative strategies for managing stress; the student health service coordinates treatment with the counseling center to assure attention to students' physical well-being along with their psychological needs.

The University of Georgia has developed a comprehensive, ongoing plan to address the problem of eating disorders on the campus: distributing relevant literature; presenting films and discussions as well as educational programs that emphasize responsible nutrition and dieting; offering consultation to faculty and staff, friends, and roommates about how to deal with students struggling with this potentially dangerous problem.

Drugs and Alcohol: Use, Abuse, and Policies

Bathtub gin in the '20s, rum and cola in the '50s—alcohol is certainly not new to the college scene. But the extent of alcohol abuse is. College presidents today rank alcohol as the number one student problem on campus.

A 1993 Harvard School of Public Health study of over 17,000 college students on 140 campuses revealed that binge drinking (defined as five or more drinks in a row for men, four or more for women) is widespread and alarming. Half of the college student binge drinkers had already begun this behavior in high school. The rate of binge drinking varies from a low of 1 percent of students at denominational institutions to a high of 70 percent at north-central and eastern colleges with high student involvement in fraternities, sororities, and athletics. Those least likely to binge drink are African-Americans, students attending college on the West Coast, and women who attend women's colleges.

Although there are more students who don't drink at all than in years past, the problems of binge drinking have remained intractable and the consequences can be lethal. When students drink excessively or experiment with drugs, inhibitions fade, and young men and women have to come to terms with questions of unplanned sex and irresponsible aggression and vandalism. On Monday mornings, deans and residence hall directors routinely review incident reports of the weekend's personal and property damage. The incidents run the gamut from lacerations and chipped teeth to wrecked cars and falls from windows. More private consequences, such as having sex and regretting it later or humiliating oneself in front of friends, rarely show up in official documents, but may produce more permanent scars than the physical damage. Many of the reported cases of date rape involve substance abuse, and most university administrators agree that on a college campus, it is difficult to address the subjects of substance abuse and sex separately.

Reflecting the heightened national awareness of alcohol as a pervasive societal problem, colleges and universities are now providing educational and support services on a number of related issues. Adult Children of Alcoholics (ACOA) groups, Alcoholics Anonymous (AA) chapters, and alcohol education programs can be found on many campuses. Chapters of BACCHUS, an acronym for Boost Alcohol Consciousness Concerning the Health of University Students, are active on a number of campuses, led by students advocating responsible drinking. Many schools have full-time administrators to plan programs, educate, and counsel students about substance abuse. Information on drug use and addiction is part of most RA training sessions and has even become part of the curriculum at some schools. As already noted, many schools offer the option of substance-free dorms or halls. Fraternities and sororities on many campuses are turning to "dry rush."

The alcohol problem among undergraduates has become increasingly complicated since 21 became the legal drinking age throughout the country and the Drug-Free Schools and Communities Act was passed. This legislation requires every institution of higher education to certify that it has implemented a program to prevent the illicit use of drugs and the abuse of alcohol. Colleges and universities have had to come to grips with the fact that for most of their undergraduates it is illegal to drink; thus they have tightened their alcohol policies to protect themselves from legal assault. This poses a dilemma. If they can't drink at public parties, some students simply move the party to the fraternity house or other private quarters. University administrators want to be responsible but also realistic. Many are ambivalent; they are worried about liability, but don't want to institute policies they can't enforce. Consequently, the alcohol policies on a number of campuses are ambiguous and confusing to many students.

"I can drink at a party in a friend's room, and that's OK," said a freshman at a small liberal arts college. "I can get totally smashed upstairs and nobody cares. But if I walk downstairs to an official party in the lounge, it's no beer 'cause I'm underage. It doesn't make a hell of a lot of sense."

Though alcohol is the drug of choice for most students, a 1990 survey by the University of Michigan's Institute for Social Research indicates that during the prior year, 33 percent of the students surveyed had used some illicit drug. Approximately 29 percent had used marijuana and 5.6 percent had used cocaine. Students' use of illicit drugs has declined over the past twenty years, but temptations and opportunities still abound. On most campuses, hallucinogens and designer drugs, such as Ecstasy, are readily available.

Students don't have to search very far to find what they are looking for. They don't even have to be looking at all. The odor of marijuana wafts down the hall, and vodka bottles and beer cans decorate the windowsills of dorm rooms. Alcohol and other drugs are part of the college scene that invades students' lives whether they wish to take part in it or not.

Sex: Private Issues and Public Problems

The wide range of behavior that is acceptable to today's college students stands in contrast to the unwritten codes of earlier generations. Perhaps nowhere is this more dramatic than in the area of sex.

The sexual standards on college campuses before the late '60s were for the most part clear-cut. The double standard operated: nice boys did, nice girls didn't. Women were supposed to ignore sexual longings. For them, the underlying message was, "Sex is dirty; save it for the one you love." There were accepted stages of courtship and dating, and although many deviated from the norm, the public stance of most college students was to follow the rules. And many rules there were.

Women's dorms above the first floor were off limits to the opposite sex. "Man on the floor" meant a father carrying a heavy suitcase to his daughter's room. In men's dorms, women might be allowed to visit, but there were parietal hours and rules. The door to the room was to be left open no less than 6 inches. At midnight, droves of couples hid behind bushes in front of women's dormitories or dashed from parked cars as housemothers flashed porch lights to signal the midnight curfew. And there were notorious rules on many campuses, though hardly anyone can actually remember seeing them written down, that when men and women were together alone in a room, each of them had to keep at least one foot firmly on the floor at all times.

Women didn't have to depend solely on assertiveness skills to say no. There were rules and boundaries of time and space that helped them fend off the advances of dismal blind dates and that protected them from their own and their boyfriends' sexual impulses. Codes of conduct, right and wrong, were spelled out, and if one chose to behave differently, the burden of guilt or the label of "fast" would suggest that one had chosen wrong over right.

The social upheaval of the late '60s and early '70s, along with the ready availability of birth control pills, brought about a sexual revolution, which exploded on college campuses. The changes were radical: new freedoms, new notions of right and wrong, and the disappearance of rules, both institutional and personal, that had guided the generations before. Experimentation, spontaneity, and openness became the buzzwords of this new era—the celebrated Age of Aquarius. In the '50s, "nice girls didn't." By the 70s, women who "didn't" felt the pressure to join the sexually active mainstream.

When asked to describe the sexual patterns of today's college students, one college administrator thought for a moment and then said:

> This may seem like a strange analogy, but it's like fashions and hemlines. There used to be a standard. Women in the '50s wouldn't think of wearing skirts above their knees, and by the end of the '60s, they wouldn't wear them below. But now almost anything goes. People experiment and choose what suits them best. It's the same with sexual attitudes. Kids have no strict guidelines, although they might have parental or religious values that they have internalized. Many experiment, however, until they find their own "right" style. Some are comfortable and have few problems with their sexuality. But for most there is a lot of confusion along the way. And now, of course, the cloud of AIDS is hanging over them.

And a young woman, a junior at Boston University, comments, "I don't think you can say anything is rare or anything is the norm. I haven't seen anything I can say is the norm."

Today premarital sex is more the rule than the exception, but clearly there is no *one* standard of sexual conduct. Although some students engage in casual sex, a great many are more likely to have a series of relationships that include sex.

According to health service personnel on many campuses, students know less about sex and birth control than most adults think they do. In spite of generally available sex education courses, students remain surprisingly ignorant about the relative safety and risks of various birth control methods. One dean remarked that on her campus, April and May are known as the abortion months. "That's after the spring formals," she explained. At another university, an RA in an all-freshmen dorm called a member of the counseling staff the second week of school requesting a workshop on sexuality immediately; her residents were "bed-hopping" with what seemed to be little regard for the consequences of their behavior.

Most campuses provide workshops and seminars on sexuality. When peer educators run workshops for their fellow students, frank discussions usually follow—discussions that would not take place in the presence of an administrator or faculty member.

Parents might be surprised to see posters and banners promoting Sex Week, a health education series that's become popular at many schools. On one midwestern campus, a laminated banner hanging between two giant oak trees announced "SEX WEEK: IT'S ORGASMIC." Bulletin boards around campus were covered with flyers highlighting the events for the week: "Sex Bowl" on Monday, "Condom Olympics" on Tuesday, "Sexuality in the Jewish Tradition" on Wednesday, "Bisexuality Discussion Group" on Thursday, and "Sexually Speaking," a lecture by the famous Dr. Ruth, on Friday. Right after Sex Week, one young woman called to warn her parents, who were coming to visit, "Don't freak when you come to my room. My roommate was handing out condoms during Sex Week. She used the leftovers to spell out SAFE SEX on our wall. It's just a decoration!"

The whole subject of sexual practices among young people is changing as the threat of AIDS has reached the ivory tower. College administrators and students debate the format of educational campaigns—Should we dispense condoms? Should we educate about "safe sex" or should we address abstention as the only responsible solution to this frightening problem? Ethical, moral, and legal questions relating to university policy have brought into the public domain questions usually reserved for private and intimate relationships. And students respond with varying degrees of anxiety. Some toss AIDS off as a problem for gay students, wearing a cloak of invincibility typical of this age and denying the reality of the threat to the heterosexual community. Others have made significant changes in their sexual behavior and are reevaluating this whole arena of their lives.

As a result of the widespread media coverage of AIDS, students have become increasingly aware of the dangers of other sexually transmitted diseases, such as chlamydia, herpes, and genital warts, and these STDs are treated with regularity in college and university health services. Many students and parents are unaware that Hepatitis B is a serious STD that can be prevented by a vaccination. The vaccination requires a three-shot series that should be given over a 6-month period.

Although it is difficult to assess how much influence these developments have had on the intimate relationships and bedroom behavior of college students, there have been some recent developments that suggest major changes may be on the way. As students grapple with what this phenomenon means to them, "safe sex" no longer alludes simply to protection from pregnancy, but to protection from disease and even death. And *caution, abstention,* and *monogamy* are becoming part of the sexual idiom of growing numbers of college students.

■

It is clear that in spite of the timeless image they often project, the colleges and universities our children attend are not the same institutions they were twenty or thirty years ago. Reports and studies of today's students and campuses give us insight into the changes that have taken place. They confront the assumptions we tend to make based on our own experience and views, but they are by their very nature limited when it comes to understanding what our children are going through. College students have much to tell us about themselves and their generation. The challenge for parents is to listen to what they have to say; to encourage and advise; and without resorting to stereotyping and labels, to try to understand them within the context of today's college experience.

Part II

A PARENTS' GUIDE:
FROM START TO FINISH

4

GREAT EXPECTATIONS

"THANK GOD THE BEST YEARS OF MY LIFE ARE almost over!" a college senior yelled into the phone, leaving her parents stunned at the other end of the line. That all too common phrase "These are the best years of your life" had been uttered once too often and at just the wrong moment. She walked back to her room and slammed the door in frustration.

This phrase is familiar to most of us. We have probably heard it or said it, often with an added phrase, "so make the best of them" or "enjoy them while you can." As parents we transmit to our children countless images and expectations of college life. Whether or not we are explicit in our comments, we are likely to herald the college years as a golden time.

THE BIG BUILDUP

Although we are all well aware that no one is continually happy in any period of life, we and our children tend to develop great expectations about the next four years as we get caught in the big buildup that precedes entrance to college. The buildup culminates during the senior year of high school, but for many families, expectations about college begin when our children are infants, that wonderful time when they seem flawless and filled with infinite possibilities.

College admissions officers tell tales of parents of newborns calling for advice about preschools. Horror stories abound about Manhattan 3-year-olds being prepped for preschool interviews and parents hiring stretch limos so the family can arrive in impressive style. Parents of children as young as 10 buy *The Kids College Almanac—A First Look at College* to give their offspring a head start.

Applications to private primary and secondary schools are increasing each year. Prep schools throughout the country report that cheating is widespread and that many students seek counseling and medical care for stress-induced symptoms. One psychiatrist has coined the phrase "the valedictorian syndrome" to describe the condition of his steady stream of anxious, highly capable high school patients. It is not unusual for parents of college preparatory students to hire tutors when grades slip from A's to B's, as the jockeying takes place for top class ranks. Hoping to help their child stand out in the applicant pool, some parents hire consultants or plan exotic summer experiences, such as a community service project in a third world country or an internship on Capitol Hill.

Most parents of high school seniors, however, are already tightening their financial belts and are worried about the next four years of tuition bills. Though many families enter the admissions process in a low-key manner, they too may find themselves caught up in the whirlwind as classmates of their sons and daughters take prep courses for the SATs, go to private college counselors, and build their résumés with carefully chosen extracurricular activities. Are we letting our children down? we ask ourselves. Will they be left behind if we don't join the race, even if we find the race distasteful? And so we get caught up in the intensity of the pursuit, and in doing so promote the unspoken expectation that college is the be-all and end-all, the magical answer to all these years of preparation, as well as the ticket to continued success. We convey to our children that these will be four wonderful years, but that it's also important to keep the motor running, to keep up, to stay on track.

In high schools all over the country, there is more interest than

ever in the so-called hot colleges, a designation that shifts somewhat from year to year along with U.S. News and World Report's
rankings and with high-profile athletic championships. The number
of applications to selective colleges has increased dramatically in
the last two decades, and with the opening up of formerly white
male bastions to women and people of color, the whole admissions
scene is very different from what it was twenty-five years ago. Some
schools that were highly selective when parents were of college age
no longer are, and others have gone from regional obscurity to
national popularity.

The most selective schools claim that they could more than fill
their freshman class with straight-A applicants. The lower the percentage of applicants a college accepts, the more desirable it
appears, perpetuating the cycle of anxiety and rejection of highly
qualified applicants.

In spite of the increased competition for admission to a small
number of selective schools, competition among colleges for the
best and the brightest students is fierce. Many colleges compete for
academic superstars by offering attractive merit-based financial
packages. Some schools lure top applicants by promising research
stipends, guaranteed internships, or even employment upon graduation. Scouts and coaches pursue talented athletes with extravagant
treatment and lucrative offers.

A record-setting high school track star recalled the excitement
and pressure of the recruitment process:

> I felt a lot of pressure during the season. I knew people
> were looking at me. But most of the pressure came from
> myself. It was pretty exciting, though. The coaches called
> me at home and wrote me letters. They'd fly me out to
> Princeton, Penn. . . . They'd put me up with a campus
> athlete and show me a good time.

Although the number of college-bound students has declined
more than 13 percent in the last twenty years, the trend has recently
reversed and the numbers are on the way up again. Paradoxically,

most colleges have never been more focused on attracting the optimum freshman class, and students have never been more anxious about being admitted to the school of their choice. The atmosphere is highly charged on both sides.

College admissions staffs play their part in heightening expectations as they vie for position in the competitive scramble to keep their schools alive and well in financially shaky times. Twenty years ago a student inquiry to a college admissions office produced simply a catalog and an application form. Today, there are an ever-increasing number of slick view books, videotapes, and graphically sophisticated Web pages to attract prospective freshmen. Even the most selective schools employ large staffs who monitor their admissions techniques and formulate strategies to increase their yield of accepted students. College admissions departments do sophisticated marketing studies, and phrases such as "prospect lists" and "overlap schools" are part of the jargon spoken by admissions officers in every school in the country.

We are in collusion—parents and high schools and college admissions staffs—in setting up unrealistic images of the college experience. We are not doing this intentionally; we don't mean to be deceitful. Most of us believe that a good college experience is important—a once-in-a-lifetime opportunity. The unspoken message that often permeates the frantic years leading up to admission, however, is that college is also a haven of constant intellectual stimulation, wonderful friendships, camaraderie, and young love.

In actuality, the college experience can be rich with stimulation, wondrous new experiences, and relationships, a unique and special time that is never repeated in quite the same way. It is also a time of enormous stresses—a time of confusion, loneliness, and uncertainty; and this too has its own uniqueness, never to be experienced again from the vantage point of a young adult whose perspective is clouded by inexperience, insecurity, and the struggles of discovering a separate identity.

■

Where do parents get their idealized views of college? For some who have never been to college themselves, this may be a dream of what they never had, a fantasy of something special they missed. They form images from television and the movies, pictures of ivy-covered paradises, settings for romance, carefree romping among the stacks, wild fraternity antics, and intense discussions about esoteric topics. Or perhaps they remember idealistic young men and women of the '60s marching for civil rights and devoting themselves to causes that broke the boundaries of the Gothic quadrangles of their college lives. Rarely do the media images include the relentless everyday stresses of the classroom or residence hall living, and many of our frozen images are outdated.

Parents learn of college life from friends. Dinner party conversation is often sprinkled with happy news about successful offspring: "Alice is premed, getting straight A's, and immersed in her tutoring work in the inner city"; "Jack's an accounting major and already being sought after by companies at phenomenal starting salaries." Occasionally, we hear the war stories: "My daughter has spent the whole first semester miserable, trying to figure out how to get her roommate's boyfriend to move out. He's been living there since the semester began." But often when we hear about some of the more difficult times, they are mentioned with humor, after the fact, with the sleepless nights of parental worry omitted.

Many parents know about college because they went there. They often look back with rose-colored glasses and selective memories of the good times: the football games, first loves, an inspiring professor, immersion in fascinating studies. They tend to forget the all-nighters with No-Doz and countless cups of coffee, the periods of loneliness, the anxiety before midterms or dates, the boring lectures and tedious assignments, the times when first loves were no more. They also forget that today's college experience is very different from the experience of twenty-five or thirty years ago. Although parents know things have changed, they often don't really believe it—or they don't want to believe it. It is difficult to separate the fantasies, memories, and myths from the reality, and it takes a conscious effort for us and our children to develop realistic expectations about college, especially when we have become so caught up in the race for admission.

THE ADMISSIONS MARATHON

The admissions marathon usually begins in earnest during the spring of junior year in high school, with college visits and fairs and the inevitable onslaught of unsolicited view books. A veritable courtship between college and students has begun. SAT scores become a new identification tag, and the question "To coach or not to coach?" is the topic of discussion among parents and counselors alike. Today's students buy practice books or interactive CD-ROMs complete with music and colorful cartoons, hoping to raise their SAT or ACT scores. Students and parents surf the Web for college home pages and financial aid information. They browse through on-line course catalogs, take virtual tours of campuses, and check out the social life on campus calendars.

Most bookstores have a whole section devoted to college admissions. The shelves are lined, not only with SAT and ACT preparation books and college guides, but also with dozens of handbooks of the "how-to-get-in" genre. The diversity of today's campus is reflected in books targeted to a range of special populations, such as *The Multicultural Student's Guide to Colleges: What Every African-American, Asian-American, Hispanic and Native American Applicant Needs to Know about America's Top Schools*, or *The International Student's Guide to Going to College in America*. There are books specifically for women, athletes, gays and lesbians, and for students who are Jewish, disabled, first generation to go to college, or searching for a school that emphasizes community service. Though helpful, all this information can boggle the clearest of minds. Beyond the comprehensive directories filled with statistics, most students and parents also turn to a few of the college guides written by students or educators that offer a more colorful and subjective view.

Many parents and high school juniors start the college exploration process with a sense of excitement. It is a time of possibilities and dreams and an incredible number of options. Parents may enjoy looking at the college view books and videotapes more than the students do. They often find themselves reminiscing about their own college years, or simply about the days when they were 18. Although students are quick to acknowledge their desire to get out of high school, many of them seem overwhelmed by the choices now facing them. After showing initial enthusiasm about college materials, they may start to withdraw from the whole process. Conflict about deadlines, plans for college visits, and filling out applications seems to be de rigueur between seniors in high school and their parents. Most tend to look back on the year with a sense of relief after it is over.

Tension about whose decision this really is lies behind much of the conflict. Many parents believe that they know what's best for their children and that it's their responsibility to select the schools to which their child will apply. One mother described emphatically how she had picked schools for each of her five children because she thought she knew her children better than anyone else. Other parents bend over backward not to interfere and to stay totally uninvolved. Most parents try for a middle course, sometimes rushing erratically from one extreme to the other.

Parents can often be helpful by providing some structure in this emotionally laden and complex process. They can help students decide what's important to them and develop a list of priorities that might include location, level of competition, curriculum, social climate, availability of financial aid, diversity of student body, support for special needs and interests. One parent describes the approach she took to get her daughter started:

> Tiffany's very social and easily distracted. She got excited with each new school, but soon the novelty wore off and what was left was a pile of papers and view books on her bedroom floor. One night, we sat down with her and talked about size, location, and what her academic criteria were. We got rid of the extraneous stuff and helped her set up a filing system in a big box. She made fun of us, but after that she began to get things more in hand.

In helping his son to narrow down his choices, an African-American father stressed:

We spent a lot of time researching how welcoming and supportive the school was to people of color, both in the classroom and out. We spoke to students and their families; we looked at programs and visited campuses. We asked a lot of questions.

At some time during the course of the year, almost all families find themselves talking about college admissions more than any of them find palatable. A student at the University of Michigan reminisced:

I was scared to death my junior year in high school. I didn't want to think about college. I felt my parents pushed me too much. I needed them to push me, but not right away. I went to look at colleges the summer after junior year, but it was too much. At the dinner table, it seemed to be the only topic of conversation.

And a freshman in high school complained:

We spent this whole year talking about college because my brother was applying. I got so sick of it I felt like screaming almost every night. I don't think my brother liked it any more than I did, but my parents never seemed to want to talk about anything else. No one seemed bothered by my problems. I guess they seemed unimportant by comparison. It really bugged me.

A New England woman explained how her studied attempt not to repeat her parents' mistakes backfired. Thirty years ago she had gone to Smith because her father wanted her to. At that time she vowed that she would never do the same thing to her children:

When my oldest was trying to decide between Boston College and Springfield, I wanted him to choose BC, but I stayed out of it. He chose Springfield because he thought he would feel more at home there. Now he's finished with school, but he never lets me forget that he thinks I should have told him to go to BC. You just can't win.

Most college-bound students are inundated with college literature. National Merit Semi-Finalists may get as many as three or four hundred pieces of mail. Minority students with high SATs, musicians, and athletes often receive even more. Students often misconstrue these marketing efforts as a signal that the school wants them and has picked them out of the crowd.

The mother of a St. Louis high school senior wrote this description of her family's response to a typical marketing blitz:

The summer after Michael's junior year, the deluge began. Every day the mailbox was stuffed with view books and brochures—all slick and glossy, with pictures of beautiful young students strolling under trees laden with yellow and orange leaves. It always seemed to be fall in the view books. And in the few shots of winter, more beautiful students cavorted in snow under azure skies. Even in Minnesota and Maine, it didn't really look cold.

Michael showed only minor interest in the growing pile of information in his room. He was amused by the brochure with a half-page picture of a girl in a bikini stretched out in a tanning booth. Neither he nor we ever figured out any remote connection between that blatant attention-getter and the midwestern state university that sent it. Then there was the poster-sized picture of a moose in the middle of a field of wildflowers from a New England school. He hung that one in his bathroom.

We encouraged Michael to read the materials so he could set some preliminary criteria and begin to think in terms of types of schools that interested him. We thought we were being very reasonable, that we were providing gentle guidance, and that we would teach him something about decision making along the way. Well, he managed to ignore our increasingly direct suggestions about how to proceed, and he

went off to a job at a summer camp, leaving the unread literature in a heap in the middle of his bedroom floor. I think
he found the whole thing overwhelming.

Overwhelming is a word used repeatedly by parents and students
when they describe the college admissions process. There is, first of
all, the sheer quantity of the choices. And there is the intensity of
the rhetoric. After a while, one of the few things that most students
and parents agree on is that all of the view books sound as though
they were written by the same person. "Have you ever found a
school that doesn't claim to have an outstanding and accessible faculty, a diverse student body, and a commitment to excellence?"
asked a bemused high school senior.

Choosing a college is the biggest decision the majority of 17- and
18-year-old applicants have ever had to make. And because most of
them still think in terms of absolutes, they are likely to feel very
anxious about making the right choice. A lot of students respond to
this anxiety by procrastinating every step of the way. They may wait
until the last minute before they narrow down their list to a man-
ageable number of schools. Their overriding fear is that the school
they cross off may be "the perfect one." They wait as long as possible
before writing their essays, believing somehow that the right essay
may be just the key that will make the difference between admission
and rejection. It is not unusual for these students to carry their procrastination right down to the wire, exemplified by the enormous
number of applications that arrive at admissions offices all over the
country on deadline day via Federal Express.

It is important for parents to realize that young people have
diverse ways of dealing with their ambivalence about college applications. They also have different styles of making decisions. Some
students want as much help as possible from their parents and actually would prefer it if their parents assumed all the responsibility for
them. Others want no help whatsoever; for them it may seem too
threatening to take any kind of advice from someone they still see as
an authority figure without feeling as though they have to follow
what they have been told. Students need their parents to respect

their individual styles, and to help them stretch as they assume increasing responsibility for their own decisions. This is a delicate balance that is rarely achieved without turmoil on both sides, as parents and their children negotiate this aspect of separation.

Many students have a clear sense of what kind of college they want to attend. They make an informed choice, apply early decision, and if they are accepted, there is a familial sigh of relief. "I knew I wanted to go to Kenyon after I spent a weekend there last fall," said a freshman. "I sat in on three classes and slept in the dorm. I think I got a good feel for the place in three days. I was sure it was for me, and I still am."

Other students make their choices early, based on little knowledge about themselves or the college. They avoid information about other schools and refuse to consider alternative choices. If they visit the school, they look only for confirmation of the decision they have already made. The negative aspects of the school are avoided or unnoticed. They, too, apply early decision in an attempt to put the whole issue out of their minds. This method of coping probably causes less tension in the family than the more common one of procrastination, but it can lead to a disastrous match. Both responses may be methods of coping with the anxiety inherent in the belief that there is a perfect answer rather than a number of options for each student.

In recent years, many colleges have been accepting a higher percentage of their class early decision, provoking uneasy questions from anxious applicants: If almost half the class has already been accepted early decision, will it be impossible for me to get in later? Am I more likely to get in if I apply early? Will applying early decision affect my chances for a good financial aid package?

It's not easy to answer these questions, but almost any college admissions officer would say that students have a slight advantage if they apply early except at a handful of the most selective colleges. Even if they are deferred, their interest is noted, and this may tip the balance in their favor when decisions are made in the spring. Admissions counselors caution, however, that only students who are certain about their choice should use this option. Once they are accepted, they have made a binding commitment, unless the limited financial aid package makes it impossible for them to attend.

When it comes to financial aid, the implications of applying early decision vary from institution to institution. At some places, students who apply early are at a disadvantage, because the college may withhold more funds at this stage of the admissions cycle; other schools are known to award more favorable packages to early decision candidates. Conversations with high school counselors and financial aid officers may help parents get a sense of the established pattern at a particular school.

The college admissions process forces students to assess themselves, to face their limitations and define their values. As they go through the ordeal of writing essays and preparing for interviews, they come face to face with basic questions about their emerging identity. And for many, competition with classmates, even with dear friends, becomes a reality to be reckoned with.

A high school senior wrote the following as part of her application for admission to Dartmouth:

> When my older brother was applying to college, he became totally overwhelmed with the system of exams, applications, and interviews. In fact, it came to the point where he wouldn't request further information from any schools. His attitude amazed me. I mean, this was his future he was talking about, and he refused to take it seriously. I knew that when my turn came, there would be no problem. I would take it all coolly, setting up deadlines and schedules, while behaving in a mature and sophisticated manner!
>
> My perspective changed, however, once I was no longer the amused bystander, but the prospective candidate. When it came time for the PSAT, it was a scary feeling to sit down with my two freshly sharpened pencils and take the first of many exams that would supposedly affect the rest of my life. To think that filling in all those little circles could possibly help determine who I would become and what would become of me!

Senior year has definitely been a time of self-reflection and appraisal. When I went to my first interview, I was petrified. I could think of no reason why anyone would care to talk for a half-hour about me and my interests. I am basically a shy person, opposed to being phony or fake, so I was shocked to find myself talking to a stranger about such a variety of topics. I became flushed and animated. It was almost as if I were in a play, only I wasn't acting and there was no script. The whole time I had this terrible feeling that I was there to be judged, and heaven help me if I was not adequate. I think this is what has worried most of my classmates this year. We have had to look at ourselves and think, "Am I good enough? Am I an acceptable candidate?" That fear has changed some of us. People who have always been self-assured and poised refused to reveal their SAT scores, and blushed at the memory of their results. Everyone has become excessively competitive, and our school, though an excellent one, does not promote cutthroat competition. When preliminary class ranks came out, they were the topic of conversation for days. I criticized a friend who was complaining because she was number seven and not in the top five. However, I then found myself plotting murder to raise my class rank from number eleven to ten. I realized I was even gossiping over who deserved their class rank, and who didn't. This from a person who had always worked for her own satisfaction and pride, not to outdo anyone else!

The feeling of inadequacy and competition came to a head when I actually began to write my application. Academically, I have never felt inferior to anyone. Yet, when I looked at the questions and tried to answer them so they would reveal an appealing picture of me to the reader, they were not appealing, they were appalling! First I was afraid of being conceited; then I worried I was not being revealing enough; then I was too sappy; then, affected. On paper, I could not truly show who I was.

As students struggle with who they are, a conflict may arise between their parents' hopes and dreams for them and their own emerging sense of themselves. Many parents notice that their children withdraw during the months when college decisions are being considered. Closed doors, blaring stereos, and silent shrugs are familiar teenage strategies for shutting parents out. Communicative young people who formerly have been very close to their parents may retreat for a while. Conversations turn into parental interrogations or nagging sessions, equally unpleasant to parent and offspring alike.

A Philadelphia woman whose daughter recently completed her freshman year at Northwestern recalled:

> My daughter spent her senior year separating and rebelling. It was as though she had to make things really miserable here, so she could eventually leave. We fought a lot, and there were a lot of frozen silences. It escalated as the year went on. Nicole was always the kind of kid who spoke her mind, but this was a whole new ball game. She refused to go to family functions. She spent more and more time in her room with the door closed. She even withdrew somewhat from her high school friends, and talked on the phone a lot to friends from out of town whom she had met at a college summer school. Since I was in graduate school in social work at the time, I was very tuned in to the dynamics of what was happening. I made the mistake of telling her I accepted what she was doing, that I understood that she was separating from us and her friends. As I look back on it, that was not a helpful thing to say. It helped me to understand what was happening, but it didn't help her for me to try to explain it!
>
> The other thing I was aware of is how similar her behavior was to the symptoms of a substance abuser. You know— the typical clues about drugs to parents are a youngster who stays in his or her room for a long period of time, who is negative and secretive, who doesn't want to talk. I think this is also pretty typical behavior of a lot of high school seniors,

and it's easy to misinterpret it. I think parents should maintain a healthy skepticism. You can't be naive about drugs. By
the time you see what is going on, there probably is more
than you think. But you can't jump to conclusions either.
One thing that helped me to figure out what was going on
with Nicole was that there were still times, usually at 12:30
A.M., when she was ready to talk. And when that happens
you have to be ready to drop everything and talk. Those precious conversations can help to distinguish the kid who is in
trouble from the one who isn't.

The college admissions process can be particularly difficult for
students who are not academically successful, but are surrounded by
friends who are. And even the most supportive of parents are likely
to have unsettling feelings of their own, as this mother of a high
school senior describes:

> The other night I ran into one of those friends you make
> when your children are young and in nursery school
> together, when SAT and ACT scores are distant concerns. I
> asked her how her daughter, Becky, was doing. It was a friv-
> olous question, one made to be social. She said Becky was in
> the midst of applications to Stanford, Princeton, and
> schools of that ilk. I knew the answer to my question before
> I asked it. While it was fairly clear that her child would be
> able to get into her college of choice, we were holding our
> breath to see if Elisa would just get out of high school.
>
> Five years earlier, we sat in a position similar to Becky's
> parents. Our son, though perhaps not the number one stu-
> dent in the class, certainly had many choices for college.
> Parents, myself included, talked with one another about
> where our children were applying, which colleges met their
> long-range professional goals, and on and on. It was, in
> hindsight, a bit clubby. We absolutely weren't worrying
> about whether our kids wouldn't graduate or would be able
> to take care of themselves academically once in college.

So as my friend asked where Elisa was applying, I could hear the concern in her voice . . . or at least I imagine I heard concern when I mentioned a school that few have heard of. I felt a degree of embarrassment, a bit of bitterness, and a drop of jealousy . . . hard to admit . . . but true. I longed for that leisured relaxation of not worrying about your kid, which my friend had and which I had with my son. We are still holding our breath with Elisa.

Many college students remember their senior year in high school as a time of tremendous ambivalence. They want to be told what to do—to be given clear-cut advice about the choices facing them— and they also desperately want to break away, to be independent. They are worried about letting down the people who believe in them. And through it all they are struggling with who they are and how they will manage to separate from home and friends. A sophomore at Johns Hopkins recalls the pain of her senior year in high school. Even now a return to her parents' house brings back many of the feelings associated with that last year at home:

The application process was a real self-analysis for me. Who is Lauren Gibbons? What are her interests? Why is she applying here and not there? Why is she getting in here and rejected there? And on and on. What are your strengths? What are your weaknesses? What word best describes you? It was an unpleasant process for me. Home is still tied up with that process. There are a lot of memories of senior year that are truly miserable. And when I go back, they still surround me. I look on my bookshelf and find one more college book I forgot to throw out. And even though I'm happy here, when I go home it all comes back; there's that feeling of—I remember what that felt like. Every time I go home it gets a little better, but it's incredible to think how powerful those feelings are.

From October to March of my senior year, we were all consumed with the college application process. There was lots of pressure. I had lots of self-pity. I remember thinking, I don't do *this* well; I don't do *that* well. I disappoint my parents in *this* respect; my friends in *that* respect; myself in *another* respect. It was a time of very low self-esteem. I was very insecure about academics and SATs and all that.

The worst part was those few months when everyone in the world was asking: where are you going to college next year? I remember thinking over and over, what if I just said I'm not going to college? Then I would think, what would I do if I didn't go to college? What could I do? What would I be good at doing? Nothing. What do I want to do? Nothing, nothing, nothing! I felt really lost. I had no idea what I would study in college. I had no idea what I would really do in college. I began to worry, what would I do when I started missing Mom and Dad? What happens when my dog dies? What's going to happen to my friends from high school? Wait a minute, do I have any friends from high school? I started a total evaluation process of the people I'd been hanging out with for the past twelve years. Through the whole thing, I didn't talk to anybody about what I was going through. I just couldn't. I guess it must have been hard on my parents too.

Parental ambivalence about sending a child off to college, particularly a first-born, is common. The sense that family life will never be the same again, a sense of loss, even jealousy—all are likely to be mixed with the anticipated satisfaction of launching one's offspring. For many parents, in the midst of all the hustle and bustle of daily life, this is a period of reflection—of poignant memories about times past. For many there is a coming to terms with one's own limitations, while exploring the ever-expanding horizons of the next generation. A father wrote the following description of his recent tour of colleges with his 17-year-old son:

As we worked our way through several campuses in New England, the visits started to fall into a routine. Always

starting with registration at the subdued admissions office,
we gathered up a multitude of materials, took the student-
guided tour of the campus, and attempted to observe and
catalog our thoughts. Ever mindful of the role of overbear-
ing parent, I tried valiantly to hold back on questions,
deferring to Andrew, but each time finding it impossible
not to keep probing, attempting to unlock the subtle differences among the schools.

What was Andrew thinking about the people and
places we were seeing? Despite my urging him beforehand
to actively probe his hosts, he was virtually silent on the
student-led tours. However, he reassured me, "Don't
worry, Dad, I'm taking it all in." And I'm sure he was, just
as he always had. Rehashing at the end of each day, we
seemed to be very much in sync in our views of what we
had observed. While I sat happily conversing with this
suddenly grown person in the same Cambridge restaurant
and Maine lobster shack where I had carried him in my
arms fifteen years earlier, my mind shuttled back and forth
across time.

As the week wore on, it was clear that my excited
anticipation of the trip was being realized. The sheer freedom of moving about a favorite part of the country, the
energy of college campuses, and the increasingly precious
time alone with my 17-year-old son exhilarated me. How
idyllic it all looked, too, even in the bareness of late winter, with the feel of old brick, patterns of walkways criss-
crossing the campus, venerable old buildings with venerable names, and overburdened bulletin boards.

For a middle-aged adult, time spent on a college campus
also brought some pangs of jealousy. In a period of life
when career, family, and financial demands sometimes
seem overwhelming, the prospect of spending four years in
a peaceful environment, with almost total devotion to
matters of intellect and one's own development, seems to
be an incredible luxury.

The mother of a Williams student explained that she too felt jealous when she took her daughter to the campus for the first time. She found that she couldn't help making comparisons between her daughter's opportunities and her own:

> My sense of envy surprised me. There is a certain irony to children budding into beautiful young women, when most of us are becoming more aware of aging. I've spent the last twelve years juggling career and family, and it's just beginning to get easier. When I took Carla to Williams for her interview, I kept thinking how wonderful it would be to be in that kind environment with so much support and only oneself to take care of. I also started to anticipate the loss of Carla. I knew I was going to miss her, and I kept mulling over the question—where has the time gone?

In this era of single parenthood and blended families, separation and family dynamics have become increasingly complicated. For single parents, the anticipated departure of a child may be particularly difficult, especially when that child is a treasured companion. Students from single-parent families often worry about leaving their mother or father alone. Children of divorced parents have had to deal with separation at an earlier age, and this leave-taking may echo the painful feelings of earlier loss.

The financial pressure of supporting a child through college is an issue for almost all families. Parents often find themselves sending a double message to their children. On the one hand, they are saying that education is invaluable, and they'll pay a premium for the best. On the other, they may imply that it is costing them a fortune, and the child had better take advantage of it. Taking advantage of it means different things to different families. For some, the message is clear: get good grades and go premed. For others, the implication is simply that it is OK to pay all that money for a so-called name school, but not for a lesser known private institution with a high tuition rate.

Robert Hedrick, Director of Admission at Sewanee, the University of the South, emphasizes that today's parents are concerned about cost. They see themselves as consumers. They are asking as they look at schools, Am I going to get my money's worth?

> If families are from a state that has a strong public system, such as Virginia, Michigan, or California, they are going to look very carefully at private college price tags. Parents not only want to know about the quality of the university, they want to know how strong a specific program is. They ask questions about rankings and about the success of graduates.
>
> More students today have parents who have been to college themselves. They have a lot of hopes and dreams for their children. They are hoping the student will be happy, the roommate will be compatible, the courses will be stimulating, and the grades will be good. If at the end of the semester the student's grades come home and they are barely a 2-point, and the tuition bill arrives the next week, those parental hopes and dreams may turn into expectations—which will in turn feel like demands to the student. It is not unusual for money to be a source of conflict between parents and their children during the admissions process and throughout the college years.

The popularity of resources such as *The Best Buys in College Education* and *Money* magazine's *Money Guide: Best College Buys* is a telling indicator of the role that money plays in college selection. Though the financial aid literature is confusing, filled as it is with its own arcane language and acronyms, it is well worth taking the time to become informed about it. Some parents narrow their child's options unnecessarily by eliminating all high-priced institutions from the outset. It is important to remember that it's not so much the college price tag as how much the parents will have to pay. There is a wide range of financial aid options, including combinations of grants, scholarships, loans, and work-study positions. Though there are no guarantees that aid will be forthcoming, many colleges offer attractive financial packages that make attendance possible for highly qualified students who otherwise would be unable to afford it.

Every college has a financial aid office that can help parents and students navigate this overload of information. The financial aid information pages at some college Web sites are a useful resource. For example, Haverford College's user-friendly financial aid information page has links to dozens of general scholarship databases. FastWEB (Financial Aid Search Through the WEB) provides a free searchable database of more than 180,000 scholarships, fellowships, grants, and loans. In addition, parents and students turn to books, to the federal government's financial aid hot line, and to financial planners to find the best possible package. College counselors warn parents to avoid organizations that offer scholarship information for a fee; this information is usually readily available through any of the above resources.

Discussion of college finances and financial aid packages often provides the first occasion for parents to share such adult family matters with their children. Honest conversations about what the family can afford, and what the plans and expectations are, can prevent tension and resentment on both sides later. Parents need to be clear about their guidelines. They should tell a child from the outset the extent of the financial aid package they will need in order for him or her to attend a particular school.

"Most parents find the financial aid forms intimidating," says Linda Jacobs, the Director of College Counseling at The Northwest School and an independent college counselor in Seattle. "I often suggest parents start out by meeting with their accountant. This is a time to be honest, not a time for great pride. Filling out the financial aid forms is the one place where the responsibility belongs to the parents, not the student."

Finances are often a factor in determining how far away students will go or whether they will go away at all. In addition, family tradition and unfamiliarity with other parts of the country, as well as the psychological impact of distance, all play a part in setting geographical boundaries. A sophomore at Harvard who grew up in the Bronx said laughingly, "My mother told me I could go as far as the West Coast to school—only to her, the West Coast meant Philadelphia."

And a senior at Carleton stated that her parents, both college professors, were emphatic about the locale they thought was appropriate for her:

> My mother wanted me in the Midwest. She wouldn't let
> me apply to Stanford. She talked as though California was
> going to fall off the continent and slip into the ocean. Her
> objections had nothing to do with distance, but according
> to my mother, there are weirdos in California, and she
> didn't want me there in my formative years. I think she
> was afraid I'd wander off into a cult.

The headmistress of a private school in New Orleans explained that parents of her students feel very tied to the place where they live. For the most part, they want their children to be within a day's drive of home:

> This has a lot to do with Southern tradition and a sense of
> place. It's also about identity and the comfort that comes
> from being a family everybody knows. Decisions about
> college are very much influenced by these family values.
> Sometimes the students' real needs get lost.

ACCEPTANCE AND REJECTION

After all the applications are finally in, there is usually a respite from the oppressively frequent discussions about college. But most students and their parents are still thinking about college admission even if they have stopped talking about it. As the notification dates approach, it is the rare family that isn't checking the mailbox at the first opportunity.

A woman who thought she had put the whole admissions game into its proper perspective, and prided herself on not being overly invested in her son's success, sheepishly admitted that she was a bit more connected and anxious than she had realized:

The kids and I were on vacation out of the country during the two weeks that Jim's college admissions letters were due to arrive. Jim seemed to have put the whole situation out of his mind, and I thought I had too. But the night before we flew home, I had a dream that the house sitter had thrown out all our mail, including Jim's college letters. I awakened in a panic.

When the acceptances and rejections start coming in, students and sometimes parents, too, rush home to see if the letter is fat or thin. When the acceptances to first-choice schools arrive, the dream seems to be in hand. All those years of preparation, the mountains of college literature, the essays and recommendations culminate—or so it may seem at the time—in one appropriately fat letter that starts with the word *Congratulations*. Surely this is a time to celebrate with our children. But in their enthusiasm, parents can unwittingly convey the message that acceptance to Yale is the essence of their child's value. In their relief and excitement, they may also perpetuate the expectation of four years of bliss and happiness in New Haven. We are not doing our children any favors if we convey the message that acceptance by a particular college means they've "got it made"—or that a letter of admission is a ticket to success.

Some parents have become so emotionally involved in the admissions process that they take credit for the acceptance themselves. Their public comments about how much money the family donated in order to help an offspring get in, or references to the importance of Dad's alumni connections, can deflate even the most competent student's self-confidence.

Inevitably, many students face rejection during the spring of their senior year. And for a lot of them, this is the first major rejection of their lives. The word slips through high school corridors instantaneously about who was accepted and rejected where. Unseen scores are tabulated, and friendships sometimes buckle under the strain. Parents may find themselves standing by, wishing they could comfort their inconsolable child. Sometimes, however, parents feel more devastated by the rejection than their children do.

Both parent and child may suffer a perceived loss of status and feel embarrassed to tell family and friends. Parents as well as students talk about feeling inadequate at this time. Admissions officers talk candidly about being deluged by phone calls from parents of rejected applicants, demanding an explanation or pleading for reconsideration. One admissions director recalls his first year in admissions work at Princeton. As rookie of the staff, he was assigned the task of signing 5000 rejection letters. After they were mailed, his phone rang constantly for three weeks:

> Congressmen called. Alumni called. Mothers, fathers, counselors called—crying, yelling, venting their anger on me. It was a horrible experience, especially since so many of the students we turned down were highly capable.

The way a student and his or her parents handle rejection is likely to have a major influence on the student's eventual college experience. Parents can play an important role at this time by empathizing with their child and then trying to be encouraging about the remaining options. If the parent has become overly invested in the first-choice college, this will not be an easy task. Too often students report that their parents were terribly disappointed about their rejection and sent them off begrudgingly to choice number two or three.

Unfortunately, this kind of parental disapproval and shortsightedness colors students' attitudes toward the school right from the beginning. They often seem depressed and unmotivated from the time they arrive on campus. It may take a lot of work on their part and assistance from deans and counselors to help them separate their personal desires and aspirations from those of their parents, or to relinquish their own lost dreams and embrace current reality. Only then are they likely to make a commitment to their college and their success within it. A parent who helps a child to enlarge his or her perspective and to understand that there is no such thing as a perfect college is bestowing a valuable graduation gift.

Edward B. Fiske, former Education Editor of the *New York Times* and author of *The Fiske Guide to Colleges*, urges parents and prospective students not to limit their horizons to the few dozen most competitive schools:

> The fact that you don't have a designer label on your diploma doesn't matter. There are hundreds of good schools. We have in this country a system of higher education that is the envy of the world. There aren't just ten places that are excellent. There are probably about three hundred. It's important to keep some perspective.

Once a student has been accepted by at least one college and is actively considering options, the pain of rejection often fades into the background. Some high school students have instituted a ritual of rejection parties, requiring that guests bring at least one rejection letter to gain entrance to the celebration. Paradoxically, of course, the rare student who received no rejections will finally be rejected—from the party. The students build a bonfire and burn the rejection letters along with their collection of college view books, a mock exorcism of the whole stressful year.

MAKING THE CHOICE

For many students, the stress continues throughout April, as they struggle with the decision about which of their acceptances to choose. This is a time of weighing definite offers against indefinite waiting list status. Is it worth waiting, or is it better just to get the whole thing over with? Questions about financial aid and comparative expenses add to the confusion. A Princeton admissions counselor suggests:

> At this point the best thing a parent can do is step back and help the child look at the pros and cons of each school. The key is to ask meaningful questions rather than give answers.

The father of a student who was trying to decide between the University of Pennsylvania and Dartmouth asked his son to make the proverbial list of the pros and cons for each school, then to make his decision and keep it to himself for two weeks. His son made the list and struggled with it for a long time. And after he finally made his decision, he didn't tell a soul. He lived with his choice for two weeks and then came into his father's study and announced that he had picked Penn. His sense of assurance surprised even his father, who had suggested the process in the first place. The young man explained that although he still saw lots of pros and cons for both schools, when it came right down to it, "Penn just felt right."

Part of the decision is based on what a particular school's image means to the prospective student. What will it mean if I become an Aggie? Will I be a different person if I go to a small rural college or a big city university? What kind of person do I want to become? Is it foolish to turn down a prestigious school for one that I think I'd feel more comfortable at? Is it worth taking out loans to go to Pomona when I can go to UCLA and graduate debt-free? Will I be able to get into the courses I need so I can graduate in four years?

One college freshman, who had straight A's in high school, recalled the challenge of making such a decision. He had dreamed of going to Stanford for as long as he could remember. He liked all the colleges he applied to, and since his widowed mother's income as an editorial associate was not nearly enough to pay for four years at a private college, he applied for financial aid and was nominated for a special full-tuition scholarship at Lewis and Clark College in Portland, Oregon. Although he was accepted to Lewis and Clark, he was awarded only a partial trustee scholarship.

When he received his letter of acceptance to Stanford, he was elated, in spite of the fact that the only aid was a small loan. Although he did make one unsuccessful attempt to negotiate for more funds, in his excitement he didn't pay much attention to the implications of the limited financial aid package. He began to spread the word to his friends that he was going to Stanford. "In retrospect," he reflected, "I could tell my mother was stressing out about it, but I was really into being a Stanford student."

Several weeks later, he received word that there had been a change at Lewis and Clark; they offered him the four-year full-tuition scholarship. And so he was faced with "the most difficult decision of my life." His mother said that it was his decision, but asked him to think about it seriously. After sleeping on it, his decision seemed clear:

> Suddenly the most difficult decision of my life became the easiest. While it was hard to give up the image of myself as a Stanford student, I thought of my mother and all the sacrifices she'd made. I had always really liked Lewis and Clark. And then I thought, When I graduate, which Jeremy would I like better after four years? And I knew that Lewis and Clark fit me better . . . its size and accessibility to faculty, the fact that I'd be able to run cross-country there. Stanford is a great school, but my joy in being accepted there was irrational. It was based on the name; it felt good to be accepted into this exclusive club. I love it at Lewis and Clark. I'm spending next semester in China and one semester of my junior year in South America, and this is all covered by my scholarship.

Not all students are this fortunate. For most, financing a college education includes some scholarship money, parental contributions, work-study, and student loans. The Northwest School's Linda Jacobs comments:

> Parents are sacrificing to the point that they can see through their towels, and their kid is talking about going to Costa Rica for the summer. I think it's not all bad for students to shoulder some of the responsibility, to take on a reasonable amount of loans.

Most financial aid offers are not set in stone, and students have nothing to lose by appealing what seems to be an inadequate offer. Parents and students may need to do this together. One university dean of admissions notes:

> We appreciate applicants who don't merely ask us to match the funds another school has offered. It helps if the parents explain their financial situation, while the students tell us

why they would prefer to come here. The most compelling cases are the ones in which students describe what they hope to do—what they want to study or be involved in— and demonstrate their enthusiasm for our school.

At a time when their personal identity is fluid and stereotypes about colleges abound, students often have a very difficult time making that final decision. The fear of closing off options can be paralyzing. Students may feel as though their whole future is at stake. It is not unusual for the decision to be made and remade several times before it is final, as this college freshman describes:

> When I first started thinking about college, I wanted to go to Carleton or Macalester. Later it became Bryn Mawr or Brown. After I was accepted at both, it was an arduous decision. It was really an awful time. I had lots of wonderful reasons I wanted to go to Bryn Mawr, and I had lots of wonderful reasons I wanted to go to Brown, but the reasons were the opposite. Brown has a lot of freedom and opportunities. I kept thinking Brown is like the real world that has both men and women. But Brown doesn't offer particular encouragement to women. Even if I wouldn't be as encouraged there, I told myself that's what it's like in real life. So it's good to be in a real world environment. But the other part of me wanted to be at Bryn Mawr where I could develop, where I thought there would be more support for me as a woman.
>
> One day I decided—I'm going to Bryn Mawr. I told everyone I saw all day—my teachers, people who wrote my recommendations, my friends. I think I did that so I could hear it out loud. I wrote it all over my notebook. It made it more real. But the next day I changed my mind, and I had to tell everyone I'd changed.
>
> For the first few months I was at Brown, I couldn't even talk about Bryn Mawr. All I could think of was all the good reasons to go there and I hadn't, and I wasn't very happy at Brown. But now I'm used to being at Brown, and

I see that it's not perfect. Now I like it. Part of it is I'm settled in and have gotten used to it and see its good parts.
Part of it is I've changed my expectations.

A springtime campus visit with time to sit in on classes, stay in the
residence hall, and talk to current students often tips the balance, and
the decision suddenly becomes clear. If students can't travel to the
school, they may be able to attend a college-sponsored gathering of
accepted students in their own city. Sometimes, a dialogue by e-mail
between accepted and current students provides the personal touch
that can't be found in traditional admissions literature. A call from a
coach, a faculty member, or an upperclass student can turn the tide.

This is a time for students with particular talents to ask questions
and compare the opportunities each school has to offer them: What
chance does a competent violinist who is not a music major have to
play in the college orchestra? How much competition is there to get a
beat on the campus paper? What is the athletic profile of the players
already on the football team, and what chance will I have to play?
What do I have to do to keep an athletic scholarship from year to year?

Rarely does the student make the college choice in a vacuum.
The pressure to go to a certain school comes from parents, peers,
and the secondary school itself. Students often buy the image of a
college and the lure of the success it will supposedly bestow on
them. Sometimes the most prestigious school or the toughest one to
get into isn't the best choice for a particular student.

Stephen Spahn, Headmaster of the Dwight School in New York
City, cites an example:

> One of my students who has been accepted at several Ivy
> League schools really wants a career in theater. I think
> she'd be best off at NYU, but it's hard to turn down the
> more prestigious offers.

Spahn sees the role of parents as path-clearers, who know their
children and can honestly assess their strengths and talents as well
as their weaknesses:

In choosing a college, parents should help their kids look at appropriate options, at paths that will use their assets. Then once the decision is made, they should give as much support and expression of confidence as they can muster.

And parents should put the college decision into proper perspective. Choosing a college is just one step in a process that begins when children are small. Parents start acting as path-clearers for their kids when they encourage them to play soccer, or take violin lessons, or volunteer in a hospital. Each choice is another step along a particular path, each commitment a limiting of alternative choices, so to speak.

For some students, the decision brings them face-to-face with the question of who they are separate from their parents. Family traditions and cultural values may seem to be on the line. Families that have always sent their children off to the University of Virginia may find it hard to understand when their child rejects the school they had always assumed was the best and chooses Vanderbilt instead.

A Washington University African-American sophomore rejected her parents' preference for her to attend an historically black college. Her father, an attorney and an alumnus of Morehouse, felt strongly that the black college experience would be an important phase of the education he wanted for his daughter. She found it difficult to make a choice that was in direct conflict with her father's firmly held belief:

> I went to a private school where we started talking about college in eighth grade. By the time I was a senior, I was sick of the topic. I applied to five schools. Only one of them was a black college, and the only reason I applied there was because my dad wanted me to. I was accepted by three of the five, including Spelman. My dad really pushed Spelman; it's the sister school to Morehouse. For a while I just couldn't talk to my dad at all. It was so confusing. If I decided to go to Spelman, I didn't know if I'd be going for him or for me. My dad and I are very close. We have that special father-daughter relationship; I'm his baby and all that. It was so hard for

me to decide what to do. I finally decided to come here, and now I'm glad I did. I know my dad was real disappointed, though. He still holds out hope for my sister and Spelman. I respect him and want him to respect me.

Respect for their choice was what students said they wanted more than anything else in our interviews with them. They want to be supported by their parents for the choice they have made, and though they don't always tell their parents directly, they desperately want to know that their parents are behind them. Even students who choose the college that was also their parents' first choice want to know that their parents see the choice as the student's own, not as an extension of the family or its traditions.

THE PRESSURE IS OFF

Just at the time when students, parents, teachers, and counselors are sure they cannot bear to hear another word about college, the race grinds to a halt. Students send in their reply cards to the colleges and then don't want to think or talk about it anymore. Thoughts turn to high school graduation and to fun and relaxation. Many parents stand by and watch their 17- and 18-year-old offspring regress to childlike behavior.

One mother described with incredulity the scene she found in the den of her house a few days after her son's last high school class:

I couldn't believe it when I walked in the door. There were my son and two of his friends lying on the floor playing with their old hot wheels cars! It was quite a sight. Three huge 18-year-old boys who are going off to Amherst and Grinnell and Macalester next fall, whizzing those cars around a yellow plastic track. They had Bob Dylan blaring from the stereo and a candle burning in the middle of the floor.

At last the pressure is off. Students brag about the crazy things they are doing and flaunt their irresponsibility. They watch TV more than they have for years, or go to the beach, or as they put it, "just veg out." There is a reprieve—some well-earned time before they turn their thoughts to the next phase. Many of them, even if they weren't particularly happy in high school, feel temporarily on top of the world.

Even as they are enjoying the freedom they haven't felt since the college marathon began, students and their parents are aware that their time together is going by fast. One young woman from New York said that from the time she decided to attend a midwestern college, she knew that she had made a decision that might permanently lead her away from her family, at least geographically. She knew that her mother realized it too:

> I was home alone with my mother for four years after my sisters were out of the house. After I graduated from high school, there were many times that my mother and I would be cooking dinner and my mother would say, "I can't believe you're not going to be here next year." And I'd say, "I can't believe it either." But we always said it lightheartedly, because we knew we were close and that I would come back for holidays and special times no matter what. We felt kind of solid about the connection. But once I had decided to go a thousand miles away to school, I knew that meant I might never go back to New York to live.

ANTICIPATION: EXCITEMENT AND ANXIETY

It is a long time from the fall of senior year in high school to the summer before the first year of college. Throughout that time, the anticipation mounts, a mixture of excitement and anxiety.

In interviews with prospective freshmen, we asked them to tell us what they were excited about and what their concerns were. Their answers to both questions were variations on the same theme. They told us they were excited about meeting new people from different backgrounds, but were concerned about getting to know different kinds of people, being lonely, and getting along with their roommates. They were excited about living in a more independent atmosphere and having freedom; at the same time, they were worried about handling responsibility, making decisions for themselves, and managing their time. They were excited about having fun and "wild times," and they were worried about handling parties, drugs, and alcohol. They were looking forward to intellectual challenges, and were anxious about doing well academically. And most of all they were excited *and* concerned about leaving home and family.

Just as students feel a combination of excitement and anxiety, so for the most part do parents. At the crux of this duality is the pull toward the new—toward risk taking and fresh starts—as opposed to the tug toward familiarity, safety, and family ties. And intertwined through all of this is the ambivalence about separation and letting go.

Parents and children express their enthusiasm about starting over. For many parents there is a reawakening of the feelings they had when their children were babies, feelings of the new possibilities that come with a clean slate. Perhaps John will finally get organized, or Carol will become more responsible or more social or more successful academically. There is always the hope that the so-called late bloomer will finally blossom.

Students, too, may look forward to shedding uncomfortable labels. Those who were unhappy or unsuccessful in high school may expect to create "a whole new me." And those who were high school superstars may have the equally strong expectation that they will repeat their high school experience in the broader arena of college. Either expectation can be a trap.

When freshmen leave for college, they take themselves along. They take their strengths, their weaknesses, and their capacity to grow and change. Even if college can't possibly live up to the idyllic scenes in the view books, or the idealized images in their parents' memories, it can provide students with special experiences that will help them to make the most of their natural capacity to grow and change as they discover who they are becoming. And that is the vital expectation with which we and our children can approach the college years.

5

READY, SET, GO

The Departure

MIDSUMMER, AND THE LIVIN' IS EASY—OR IS IT?
Sometime during the steamy days of late July or early August—after
the roommates have been assigned and the dorms designated—the
countdown begins.

TEN . . . A sudden catch in the throat as a parent realizes this
may be the last summer that this particular twosome, buddies
since kindergarten, still unself-consciously meander through
neighborhood streets with such carefree abandon.

NINE . . . Do I need name tapes or a laundry marker? Maybe I
don't need either.

EIGHT . . . A seemingly spontaneous—but carefully orchestrated—attempt to recapture frozen moments of family good
times with a nostalgic trip to a favorite ice cream parlor,
beach, bike path.

SEVEN . . . Will he stand still long enough to figure out what
clothes he needs to take to college so that I, he, or we can
get them?

SIX . . . Standing over her while she cleans out her room: Am I really so concerned about cleaning out seventeen years of debris, or is this a good excuse to reminisce together, assuring ourselves that our memories will retain what is being carted off in boxes? How does one weigh whether a note written in class, a program to a play, a beloved pair of jeans is worthy of the keep and store pile, the Goodwill pile, or the trash pile? How do we reduce the past to plastic bags neatly tied with wire twists?

FIVE . . . Lists of things to get: extension cords, masking tape, hangers.

FOUR . . . A flash of anger—or is it fear—at finding crumpled dollar bills falling out of jeans pockets in the washing machine, the front door left open once again, reappearances in the early morning after sleepless nights devoid of telephone calls, full of worry—how can this kid make it on his own?

THREE . . . Is it cheaper to ship via UPS or the college student trucking service?

TWO . . . Nightly rituals of good-byes as gangs of friends move from one house to another, taping each other's music, exchanging addresses, philosophical viewpoints, and emotions ranging from casual disinterest to sheer terror.

ONE . . . Blast off—the day of departure, the launch.

THE LAST FEW MONTHS

The prelude to the actual countdown starts with a familiar invasion of the mailbox—no longer overstuffed with shiny view books as it had been last year, but now carrying a steady stream of letters about housing options, campus organizations, and course selections, all with the same increasingly familiar college logo—a relentless reminder of the fall to come.

Parents often discover these letters unopened days or weeks after delivery, scattered all over the dining room buffet or discarded among the piles of dirty socks and magazines on the floor of their child's room. Noted writer Gail Sheehy describes an official-looking form stuck under her daughter's journal:

> "What's this?" A small alarm goes off. "It looks like the forms for your meal contract at college."
> "Mmm, yeah," She starts humming.
> "You haven't sent in your contract yet?"
> Here it comes. She knows it.
> "Where is your head, Maura? Why can't you ever follow through?"
> "Thank you," not allowing a nick to show in her expression. "Now would you mind leaving me alone?"[1]

Words like *ever* and *never* and *always* are pro forma in these exchanges between parents and children—exchanges that know no geographical boundaries but are familiar refrains repeated coast to coast. The underlying theme from the child's point of view: Leave me alone. Stop reminding me that I'm growing up and leaving. And from the parent's point of view: I'm not so sure you're ready to leave. I'm not so sure you can make it without me.

One mother from the Midwest describes her son's avoidance with an expression halfway between exasperation and amusement:

> The letter from Macalester sat on his dresser for weeks unopened. My curiosity turned to concern, and when I finally couldn't restrain myself another minute, I suggested that there might be something important in the letter with a deadline that needed to be met.

When her son grudgingly opened it, he found an announcement of a tempting array of freshman seminars—special offerings of the kind that had attracted him to Macalester in the first place. The announcement went on to say that if he was interested in participating, he was to choose one, and that each seminar was limited to twelve people and would be filled on a first-come, first-served basis. The young man barked at his mother, "Why didn't you tell me to open it?" She decided not to respond or attempt to discern the logic in this query from her tall, strapping, bright son who ordinarily bristled at intrusions into his life.

The summer between high school and college seems like a giant exhale—a release of tension, a respite from responsibility, perhaps perceived as a last gasp of childhood. To interrupt it with a series of new choices about meal plans, seminars, housing, and roommates seems an affront: *Somebody else attend to the nitty-gritty details for me. Let me be to wander with my friends, have a summer romance, do some mindless work that keeps my head free and my pockets full.*

A Harvard student recalls receiving a form to help with the selection of roommates—a form that seemed a "silly piece of bureaucracy"—a nuisance that he dashed off on the day it was due. When asked what kind of person he'd like to live with, he jotted down, "I don't care. I can live with anyone." He regretted it later when he found himself living with two extreme eccentrics. There were indeed people he couldn't live with, and he spent much of his first semester sleeping on the floor of a friend's room.

A member of the residence hall staff at Hollins College suggests that students fill out roommate questionnaires as thoroughly as possible, but adds that they should not expect all their preferences to be fulfilled. She explains:

> When the system works well, a student who asks for a quiet sunny room to help nourish her many plants will end up with a corner single with an abundance of light on a quiet floor. But obviously, it doesn't always work that way.

Almost all schools want to know students' preferences about quiet halls, smoking, coed or single-sex living, substance-free environments, and other basic conditions. Although residence hall staffs may not be able to provide ideal matches, students are more likely to find themselves in a compatible situation if they take the time to fill out the questionnaires thoughtfully and return them on time.

Parents may choose to offer advice about completing forms and meeting deadlines, but ultimately the responsibility lies with the student. Students who don't take the time to complete or send in forms learn to live with, and adapt to, the consequences. The young man from Harvard who found the roommate selection forms silly had a bit more discomfort his freshman year than he needed to have, but now he looks back with amusement and a new respect for and understanding of bureaucracy. The freshman who missed getting into the courses she wanted because she registered late often becomes the sophomore who plans ahead to make sure she doesn't make the same mistake twice.

Still, in their eagerness to see their child get off to a good start, parents may make a last attempt to take the reins. Even minor decisions can produce out-of-proportion hassles. A young woman from the Southwest describes her last summer at home:

> All through high school, my parents gave me a tremendous amount of freedom. I never had curfews. I had a car much of the time. I was treated as a pretty mature person. So for them to suddenly act very protective, and a lot more parental, was a shock. My mother was very nervous; she had always been so rational, and now she was absurd. We were supposed to send in a picture to be in the freshman face book. I didn't want to have my face in the face book. I knew that it wasn't important, and she just had a fit. She thought it was crucial that I do everything correctly. I lectured them and reminded them that I was 18 years old and could take care of myself and everything would work out and I wouldn't be rejected and I would have a social life despite the fact that my mother said that no one would ever call me if my picture wasn't in the face book!

Although it is helpful if parents back off as their children assume the responsibility for their own decisions, there are certain circumstances in which it is important for parents to be involved. If, for instance, a child has special problems or needs, parents should make sure that appropriate university professionals are informed. The health service should be told about chronic illnesses; the dean, or appropriate office, about learning disabilities; and the dean or residence hall director about family problems that may affect the student's adjustment—a recent death, an impending divorce, a severe illness in the family. Whenever a parent informs the college about special needs or problems, the child should know about it.

Alice Drum, Vice President and Dean of Educational Services at Franklin and Marshall, receives numerous phone calls from parents about everything from course selection to health and learning disabilities. She explains:

> I like to be informed, but whenever possible I prefer that the student make the call—or if this is particularly difficult, that the student and parent contact me together. This can be an important step in the student's assuming responsibility for dealing with his or her problems.

Some of the summer mail is addressed directly to parents, with information about parent orientation, tuition payment, and health insurance options. These call for careful assessment. In many schools, there are a variety of payment options that may be advantageous, and university health insurance may turn out to be a necessity even for students covered by their parents' policy. Some schools require health insurance and build it into the tuition charges.

One health service director at a midwestern university, where the university health insurance policy is not required, urges parents to seriously consider university health insurance programs in this era of managed care. She recounts an incident that, though seemingly extreme, is becoming more common. A student broke his hand during finals. His parents' East Coast HMO would not approve payment to the local hospital and insisted that he fly home to Boston to have it taken care of, making a difficult situation even more disruptive.

The residence hall and roommate assignments that arrive in the midsummer mail begin to make concrete what up to this point has been a rather distant, vague, and idealized image of college living. Often students convince themselves that they have to get into a particular dorm in order to be happy, or that all will be lost if their roommate isn't a potential best friend. They may agonize over which tapes they will bring with them or whether to take a bicycle. They may pore over course catalogs, trying to pick the perfect schedule, or spend hours trying to decide what color blankets to buy. Instead of facing their general anxiety about leaving home, they may focus on something that seems totally out of proportion to perplexed parents. Tension in the household begins to build again.

Finding oneself assigned to a triple or to the less popular off-campus housing brings disappointment and even tears to some, as if anything short of perfection is a harbinger of a ruined freshman year. Because many prospective freshmen still see the world in terms of polar opposites, right and wrong, they truly believe that if they don't make perfect course choices or get the perfect room assignment, the implications will be disastrous. Some parental reassurance may help students to see the subtleties and shades of gray. But logic and information and even the best intentions of parents are not sufficient to change the mind of an adamant 18-year-old. It usually just takes some time. Some of the things that loom so large during the summer fade into the background as freshmen settle into the day-to-day flow of college life.

One young woman's comments reflect her change in perception over the course of her freshman year at Haverford:

> I didn't dwell on it, but I was upset last summer when I was assigned to the apartments. When I had visited and stayed in a dorm, the woman I stayed with said "anything but the apartments." I had always imagined myself in the dorm when I thought of myself living there, and now I had to reorient myself. Actually, there are some real positive trade-offs living in the apartments. I guess I discovered that anything is the best or the worst depending on your vantage point.

How does one know if one's housing or roommate is "good"? There is no way to know ahead of time, of course; stereotypes are often all one has to hang one's hat on—so coed dorms are "good" and single-sex dorms are "bad." If your roommate's name is Brooke, "she's probably a snob"; if he's from Nebraska, "he's probably a hick." Atlases are dusted off and brought out to check on roommates' addresses. Is Edina a rural town in Minnesota? No, it's a suburb of Minneapolis. Is Essex Junction, Vermont, even on the map?

Parents can be helpful at these times by simply acknowledging their children's anxiety or disappointment, and by helping them put information in perspective, dispelling myths and sweeping generalities and encouraging them to get more information, if they can, from upperclassmen at their school.

Unfortunately, some parents are more intolerant and anxious than their children. Residence hall personnel rarely hear requests from students for roommate changes during the summer. It is the parents who are more likely to intervene because of a name or address that suggests a certain nationality, race, or social class, and parents' prejudices as well as their overprotective involvement take over.

One staff member at a midwestern university told of a mother calling him more than ten times during the summer wanting her son's room changed because his roommate was from Puerto Rico. It was clear from their conversations that she had all sorts of assumptions about this young man's background and social status—all of which turned out to be completely false. In most cases, residence hall staffs will not make changes unless it seems as though the situation will be truly problematic for all involved. Usually, the student is not the one who perceives the situation as a problem, and often he or she is embarrassed by a parent's intrusion. Indeed, parental intervention of this sort may impede a student's growth. The university's diverse student body is a rich resource. To understand, tolerate, and negotiate with people whose values, habits, and cultures are substantially different is a large part of the out-of-classroom learning that can take place in college.

Many students seem to take housing and roommate assignments in their stride and suspend judgment until school is underway. Some do write or call their roommates, though, to begin to make contact. Finding that a roommate listens to funk music, or likes to go to sleep at 1 A.M. may be a future freshman's first encounter with the inevitable compromises of dorm living. A woman from a middle-class family in Iowa recounted her shock when her future roommate from Virginia called and said she was bringing her horse to school with her. And a Chicana woman from New Mexico, on a full scholarship, recalled the awkwardness she felt when her roommate from the north shore of Chicago asked if she was bringing her stereo with her to Wellesley. The diversity of the college campus had expanded these students' limited horizons, reminding them in personal ways that life was going to be different from now on.

A young man from Pittsburgh, who was entering Colgate, was reassured after talking to his roommate:

> I called my roommate. We talked and found out some interests in common, who would bring what to school, and when we were going to arrive. As soon as I talked to him, I felt like I knew one person there. When I saw him at school, I just picked up from where we had left off. I asked him how his job at the pool that summer had gone. It really made a difference talking to him ahead of time.

Some students prefer to contact their future roommates by mail. Searching for words of introduction can be awkward, however. A vivacious young woman of many talents tried to think of ways to introduce herself to her future Berkeley roommate in a letter: "If I tell her I was a cheerleader, she'll think I'm just a boppy airhead. I can't describe myself in two paragraphs," she wailed. Music seems to provide a shorthand that helps youngsters to place themselves in a context. "He listens to Hootie and the Blowfish and the Dave Matthews band; he can't be half bad," one young man from Portland exclaimed after an introductory letter from his roommate-to-be at the University of Maine. "She's into the Grateful Dead; she wasn't too thrilled when I mentioned Vivaldi," was the essence of a quick conversation with a Tulane student's assigned roommate. An entering freshman at Brown reported the good news—"She likes jazz, does sports, and goes to bed early"—and the bad, "It all sounded good until I mentioned the word *feminist* in a sentence, and there was this silence. She just said, 'Oh.'"

Based on numerous interviews with college students, there seems to be little or no correlation between roommates' initial contacts and their ultimate compatibility. Too often, single letters or abbreviated phone calls encourage fantasies of becoming best friends and soul mates—only to discover later that a liking for yellow quilts and James Dean doesn't guarantee friendship or similar lifestyles.

■

For students entering large universities, the summer before freshman year often includes a visit to the campus for an early orientation program. Many large universities have tried to reduce the chaos and impersonal atmosphere of orientation and registration by scheduling summer orientations, staggering smaller group programs through the summer weekends. These visits often ease the transition process, but may also burst the bubble of idealized college life. The dorm rooms probably look small and bare, and the food isn't like home. Preregistration and the frustration of dealing with prerequisites and closed course sections introduce students to the realities of institutional bureaucracy.

This slice of college life may seem out of sync with the summer's steady pace—a frenzied few days of the new and unknown interrupting the security of familiar friends, family, and surroundings. Some students panic, usually just for a brief period of time, and wonder what they are getting into.

One midwesterner, despite the additional expenses of travel and time away from her summer job, flew to Burlington for the University of Vermont's summer orientation. The program included preregistration, and she was afraid she wouldn't get into the classes she wanted if she didn't attend. Although she had fallen in love with the school on an earlier trip by herself in the spring, she called home daily during the few days of summer orientation, teary and miserable. There were relatively few out-of-state students; most of the students who showed up drove with parents or friends from nearby cities and neighboring states. Many seemed to know each other from high school, and she felt lonely and worried that she might have made the wrong choice of schools. After several late-night phone calls, her parents prepared themselves for the fact that she might withdraw and go instead to Indiana University, closer to home. As she stepped off the plane wearing a University of Vermont sweatshirt and a beaming smile, they knew they had been premature in their assumptions.

THE LAST FEW WEEKS

By August, a flurry of activity breaks the relaxed cadence of long summer days. The students who are procrastinators continue to put off shopping or packing, but the tempo of their social lives may increase as time with friends begins to run out. Couples linger together, planning ways to stay connected during their next nine months in different locations. The seesaw of snapping tempers and unusually tender exchanges between youngsters and their parents are reminders of their ambivalence toward separation—and its proximity.

One woman gave a moving account of her family's celebration of this rite of passage. Several weeks before the beginning of school, she and her sister planned a ritual for the whole family to mark their children's impending departure.

> I have been reflecting for some time on the need for tradition and ritual in my life. I read about a "leaving home" ritual, and since my sister's daughter and my son were leaving for college at the same time, we decided to plan one together. We picked poems and music and decided to have the ceremony in my parents' garden. We invited each member of our extended family to write something to honor Sarah and David and to bring a gift that symbolized their sentiment about them.
>
> It was a powerful and moving experience for all of us, as we each summed up in our own unique ways what David and Sarah mean to us. I was so glad that the kids were able to witness the love and honoring of their individuality

from their parents, grandparents, and cousins—three generations of our family. It is something I hope they can carry with them to each new adventure and renew continuously.

Wanting these last weeks at home to be quality time, parents try to restrain themselves from commenting as their children sleep away mornings or party away nights. Time becomes the most precious of commodities—moments together to be begged, borrowed, or stolen. Some of this is spent on the practical aspects of the move, the question of getting to school; who's going, when, and how; the shopping, packing, and sending of clothes and equipment. Many colleges send suggestions, even lists, of what to bring. Most include specific information about computing facilities on campus and advice about purchasing personal computers. Hometown upperclassmen at the college, as well as their parents, can help prospective freshmen. Much, if not all, of this can be handled by the student alone, but more often than not, parents are actively involved.

Sometime during this period, the decision is usually made about how the student will actually get to school, whether alone or accompanied by a parent. In some families this isn't even discussed, especially when there are family traditions or norms:

> My older sisters flew to school by themselves. I'm not sure who decided to do it that way, but by the time it got to be my turn, I just assumed that I'd fly too.

In other families the child makes his or her wishes known directly, or economics and distance dictate a particular decision. But many families find themselves approaching this topic delicately. It seems laden with everyone's feelings about the impending physical separation and the simultaneous desire to establish independence.

Some students are very clear about their preference, wanting a family member to take them either for reasons of practicality—to stuff the car with the last-minute accumulation of belongings—or for emotional support. Washington University's Associate Dean of Freshmen, Delores Kennedy, explains:

Freshmen may not spend much time with parents once they finally arrive on campus, but they take comfort in looking over their shoulders and seeing that Mom and Dad are there. If students express an interest in having their parents accompany them, it's probably a good idea to try to do it. It may boost the student's confidence just at the time he or she needs it most.

Just the opposite is true for some students, who find making the trip on their own a great confidence booster. Those who want to go by themselves may feel more secure and better about themselves if they are allowed to do so.

But, as is true with so many of the decisions facing parents and students at this time, the impact one way or another isn't likely to be a major one. If parents don't accompany their child to school in the fall, they may find it even more satisfying to come later for Parents' Weekend when the turf truly belongs to their child. Those who do go, however, will have the chance to begin to put some names together with faces and places right from the beginning—laying a foundation for sharing experiences as the year wears on.

As they concentrate on organizing and checking items off on last-minute "to do" lists, parents and children often neglect attending to the central long-range issues that will involve their continuous interaction throughout the college years. Families might save themselves unnecessary friction and misunderstanding if they put aside some time, before college begins, to think and talk about four key areas of concern: communication, finances, academics, and social life.

Most parents approach their children's college years with expectations and assumptions about these four areas, although they may not express them explicitly. As a matter of fact, they may not even be conscious that they have assumptions at all. But all too often, college students and their parents find themselves locked in frustrating battles about money, grades, a live-in boyfriend, or a dearth of phone calls home, because they were each operating on a different set of assumptions. Just talking about these issues ahead of time obviously doesn't create a united front of common assumptions, but substantive conversations and attentive listening ensure that each will have a better understanding of the others' expectations and views.

How does a family come to this understanding? Lectures by pontificating parents are definitely not the way, in spite of the fact that it can be tempting for even the most well-meaning parents to take that last chance to express a disdain for hard drugs or expound on the financial sacrifices they are making and what they expect in return.

By the time a family has a child old enough to leave for college, their patterns of communication are well established. Some families actually sit down to talk weekly, with discussions as focused as they are at an office meeting. Others sit at the dinner table in a leisurely fashion night after night as the conversation glides effortlessly from topic to topic. Still others manage to squeeze in bits and pieces of their ideas and thoughts on the run at unpredictable times, whenever the spirit moves them. Periods of intimacy and long discussions are interspersed with weeks of hellos and good-byes and grunts and groans from teenagers who are always in motion.

As families prepare for their child's departure, the most effective means of talking with each other will probably be the one that is most familiar. This isn't the time to adopt a new style of family communication, no matter how well it works for someone else. If parents think through these issues, examine alternatives, and come up with a conscious set of assumptions and expectations, they can discuss them with their children in whatever way and to whatever extent feels most comfortable and natural. And in doing so, they will be setting the groundwork for the inevitable changes and challenges that they and their children will confront as time goes on.

COMMUNICATION: HOW WILL WE KEEP IN TOUCH?

It is helpful for families to come up with a tentative answer to this question before the miles separate them literally. Students may not actually tell their parents how important it is for them to hear from the family. They may not even realize it themselves, or admitting it may belie their independent stance and their attempts to separate. But students do count on parents to keep them informed about what is happening at home, in the family, in the neighborhood.

Some parents claim that they have nothing interesting to write about, especially those who also speak to their children regularly. But letters or e-mail notes communicate something more than the actual facts and events they describe. Hearing about the mundane daily comings and goings of brothers and sisters, neighbors, and friends lends a sense of permanence and familiarity to a tenuous time. It is no coincidence that we use a word that suggests a safe harbor, rootedness, and stability to describe the nightly television newscaster—anchor— steady and familiar. Parents, too, serve as anchors when they dispense the news from home as reliably as Peter Jennings or Tom Brokaw.

A freshman at the University of Tulsa spoke with affection of the regular mail she received from her mother:

> My mom would write about how the street looked in front of our house—or about our cats. She'd tell me that our neighbor painted his door red, or that my old school won its first football game all season. Football isn't really important to me, but home is, and she made it come alive for me in her letters.

In the midst of their busy lives, most students write home sporadically, if they write at all. But whether or not they do, mail from home is almost always appreciated. Reassuring letters from family members can be read and reread, giving a boost to a wounded ego and reminding students that they are not forgotten. Their identities feel shaky in their constantly changing external and internal worlds, and recognition and acceptance from home can restore a sense of continuity and self-worth. Some parents send clippings from the local paper; some just send the Sunday sports pages with a brief note attached. There are innumerable ways to stay in touch—to let your child know he or she is on your mind. Students rave about care packages and holiday cards and surprise gifts, no matter how small.

A Colorado College sophomore from Long Island spoke fondly of his mother's regular correspondence:

> I live so far from school that we don't talk on the phone too often, but my mother often sends me a quick note saying, "I'm at the office writing a report and was thinking of you." Or she'll send me a silly card. It's great just to be remembered and get something in my mailbox.

And a junior from Montana State reiterated, "Mail is important. Going to an empty mailbox is the worst. Parents should let their kids know they're out there."

Another woman, a senior from Manhattan, said, "My parents send me cards—you know—on birthdays and Halloween and Valentine's day. But my roommate's mom sends her real letters, and she gets cookies once a month. I get to eat the cookies, which is great, but I have to admit I'm kind of jealous."

Some parents are very casual about their expectations for written communication from their children. They don't expect to hear from them a lot, or they are comfortable with long periods of silence interspersed with spurts of cards and calls. Other parents have definite ideas about letter writing, and they make their expectations clear to their children. A Texas mother of three explained:

> The requests made of our children when they went away to school were few and simple: do your best and write real letters. We insisted on weekly correspondence. They followed through—most of the time. The early examples from each were pitiful, but month by month, we could see marked improvement. Their diplomas validate most of the knowledge and skills acquired in those four years, but fail to note that each had developed a personal, literate style of correspondence.

For more and more families, electronic mail has brought a whole new dimension to keeping in touch. Parents who had been com-

puter-phobic become e-mail aficionados as they discover the fun
and informality of this new mode of communicating. A mother of
two daughters notes how this computer connection changed the
way she kept in touch:

> During my oldest daughter's first year of college, we wrote
> weekly and spoke by telephone every Sunday. By her
> senior year, the letters dwindled to once a month. I saved
> them and gave them to her when she graduated. When
> my second daughter went to college, she had a computer
> with an e-mail account, and I have one at the office. We
> were slow to use it, relying on letters and phone calls. One
> day, I sent her a message, and before we knew it we were e-
> mailing each other twice a day. I printed all her messages,
> kept them in a large binder, and gave it to her when she
> graduated. Both girls have enjoyed reading their "college
> chronicles" and commented how grateful they were to
> have them.

As e-mail becomes more popular, a lot of parents hail its virtues:

> My husband is not a letter-writer, nor does he talk much
> on the phone before turning it over to me. However, he
> does e-mail our daughter when he wants to find out some-
> thing or make arrangements with her. I am no longer the
> "middle man" for them.

> My son seems to tell us so much more in e-mail than he
> ever does on the phone. It's on *his* time. He usually writes
> us at about 3 A.M.

> My daughter tells me she likes to e-mail her father because
> he doesn't interrupt her.

E-mail provides an avenue for quick bits of information or news in the middle of the day or long late-night musings. It can combine the best of letters and phone calls—the chance for revision of the written word, but with the quick access of the phone call. And for many young people who feel the pushes and pulls of being on their own, it is an avenue for connection with their parents in a casual and therefore perhaps less threatening way.

There can be some pitfalls, however, as this mother recollects:

> When I first got e-mail it was like a new toy. Every time I had a thought or a question for Jessie I went straight to the computer. It was irresistible. When I noticed that there were a lot more messages going out than coming back, I asked her if it bothered her. She said no, but I began to temper my urges a bit.

E-mail can be as intrusive as letters or phone calls when it's overdone or peppered with lectures and a barrage of questions: Did you study for your biology test? Did you get your grade back on the English test? Did you write your résumé for summer jobs? It's Aunt Sue's birthday; don't forget to send a card.

One father cautions:

> You have to be careful about your response because it's so quick. Kids are reaching out—they want encouragement from Mom and Dad—and sometimes they throw you a curve. You've got to stop and think before you respond, 'cause you can't retrieve something once you send it.

Many schools now provide voice mail automatically for all resident students. The parents of a Duke freshman acknowledged: "Sometimes I call Marc even when I know he won't be there and leave a message, 'Just thinking of you.' I'm sure it's as much for me as for him."

This same parent reflects on phone calls to her "quiet" son:

He's a self-contained person. We don't usually know what
he's feeling. But we knew when he left for school this year
that all his supports were gone, his girlfriend, his music, so
we worried. We called fairly often to touch base. He called
his girlfriend daily, but would only call us when he wanted
something—usually a care package—trail mix or
microwave popcorn or cookies.

When he came home for winter break, we sat down with
him and told him that we don't know what's going on with
him or if he's down or sick, but there's a big chasm for us. We
told him that it would be thoughtful for him to remember
that we need some contact and would like him to check in.

Many parents expect to keep in touch weekly by phone. Some
arrange to call their children once a week at a particular time, often
on weekends when the rates are reduced. For many families, the regular weekly phone call works well, with little need for modification
throughout the student's college career. For some students, however,
regular phone calls from home seem intrusive and controlling. They
would prefer to do the calling themselves, when they are sure to
have privacy and to be awake, alert, and undistracted. Their parents
may provide an inducement in the form of a Call-Home card, a
credit card good only for calls to the parents' home number.

Wanting family members to be there for them when *they* do the
calling rather than the other way around is not a sign of selfishness,
but another indication of the need for students to take charge of
their lives. For example:

I think it's important that I do the calling, because then I
don't resent them. If they call, and I'm grumpy, the whole
conversation goes downhill from there.

◼

My mother doesn't seem to get the message. She calls me
at eight in the morning and says, "I called because I knew
I'd get you in." Of course I'm in. I'm asleep.

◼

There is a problem with parents calling too often. My friend's mother called daily. Everyone on the hall knew about it. It upset her—it was embarrassing.

Many students mentioned how much they appreciated their parents' open-ended invitation to call home—or even to visit, if they live nearby. A Tufts freshman recalled her father's parting words:

He said, "You're only a plane ride away—a one-hour shuttle ride—if you ever want to come home for just the day." I never did, but knowing I could made a difference.

Anne Schroer-Lamont, Dean of Students at Washington and Lee, suggests:

Invite your child to call home when needed. Kids can't plan to limit their crises to Sunday evenings. Some parents tell their children, "We can only talk for ten minutes"—but you can't budget a child's problems. Often they need the first ten minutes to check out how everyone at home is—what's going on. They may be worried about their parents' relationship or other problems at home and need to deal with these before they are ready to let you know about theirs. So try to include phone calls, especially in the first semester, in your college expense budget.

Parents should remember, however, that reaching for the phone at "down" times is a freshman phenomenon, and that parents often receive a skewed view of their son's or daughter's psychological well-being. The "ups" are reserved for friends and the "downs" for them. Moreover, most family budgets cannot absorb the strain of frequent long-distance phone calls over an extended period of time, and even open-ended invitations to call may eventually evoke limits.

Whatever plan a family begins with is likely to undergo adjustments eventually, often after just the first few weeks of school. Students who share a phone will have different needs from those who have private phones. And adjustments will continue over the long haul, as students and their families weather the predictable and not so predictable crises of this time in their lives.

Paradoxically, the theme of separation permeates this practical discussion about communication and maintaining connections. The issues of control and independence, the need to touch base and yet establish autonomy, are at the heart of all the logistics.

Laurence Beede, Associate Dean of the Faculty of Hampshire College, urges parents and students to think about the importance of communication and its role in the evolution of their relationship:

> College is a time for communication between parents and students. Parents who call at regular intervals to find out how their son or daughter is doing without asking the student are not likely to be really helpful during this trying and exciting time. On the other hand, students who refuse to tell their parents anything could possibly be inviting confrontation when it comes time for the parents to pay the bill. We try to encourage direct communication back and forth on every possible occasion. In fact, good communication should foster the process of letting go.

FINANCES

Money may not be the root of all evil, but it can become the rope that binds children to their parents with stifling knots. A clear discussion of expectations can help to prevent this. In fact, sound financial planning can foster a student's growing independence. If parents can be straightforward with their children about financial realities, their children will often surprise them with their resourcefulness and willingness to assume responsibility.

Indeed, an increasing percentage of today's college students are taking financial responsibility for a portion of their education. It is not unusual for today's graduates to incur debts of $13,000 or more.

So money is very much on the mind of today's college students and their parents. As a senior at a private university put it:

> I've got $4000 in grants, $3500 for being an RA, $3000 from parents, $3000 in loans, and the rest from summer jobs. I try not to think about it too much.

Filling out college financial aid forms may have brought out into the open a subject that has typically been taboo in many families— How much money do we have? What is the accurate picture of our financial worth? For many families, however, this is still an off-limits subject, and some students leave for college with only a vague notion of their family's finances. Some simply know that they are comfortable and that their parents will support them financially and are not concerned about money. Others are confused by mixed messages:

> My parents never talk about money, but I can see them trying to cut corners all the time now. And I know it's 'cause of the big tuition bills.

> ■

> My parents say they are strung out by college expenses, but they just redecorated our house.

> ■

> My mother and father are divorced. My tuition is due and it's gone up substantially from last year. My mother says, "Ask your father." My father says he can't afford any more, but he just took his girlfriend on a cruise. Sometimes I feel guilty, and other times I'm just plain mad.

It is important for parents to be straightforward with their children about what their limits are, what they will be contributing to, and what the student's responsibility will be. Before a student leaves for college there may still be some unanswered questions regarding money. Parents and students can often find helpful information about estimated living expenses in the official college catalog or parents' handbook. It's also a good idea to talk to sophomores and juniors at the college to get an idea of how much money to set aside for extras, such as snacks and Sunday dinners, lab fees and art supplies, laundry, entertainment, and long-distance phone calls. But only time will tell exactly how much will actually be needed for expenses, or whether the student will be able to handle academics and a part-time job. Some basic guidelines and open discussion while the student is still at home can set the tone for later negotiations.

Some parents feel comfortable with sending a prescribed monthly allowance for expenses. Some make it clear that they can contribute to tuition, room, and board, but that the student will be responsible for any added expenses. Other parents agree to pay for travel home or for books but not for incidentals. One mother of a Yale sophomore took this approach:

> We said we'd pay for books; we didn't want him to pick his courses by the price of the books. But clothes and all other expenses came out of his summer savings.

The decision about who will pay for what is made on the basis of available resources, priorities, and values. Parents who are sensitive to the issue of developing autonomy will set up a system that allows their child room for financial choices and responsibility:

> My dad asked me to keep track of my daily expenses for two months. From that we arrived at an amount for a monthly allowance. It was a good exercise for me because it made me realize what I spend money on. I decided to get a job second semester, though, because I liked having a little extra in case I wanted to be extravagant or travel to see a friend.

■

> My parents used to send me money as I needed it my freshman year, but I really hated it. I always felt guilty

when I asked for more, or like I had to justify where I had spent the money. Now I get one lump sum at the beginning of the semester and that's it. I like it a lot better. I know what I have, and I can budget accordingly. If I want to blow it on a ski trip or a couple of six-packs, it's my business—and I'll scrimp for a while to make up for it.

■

My parents told me they would supplement my financial aid package and would take care of the remaining tuition and board. All the other expenses are up to me. I thought I had earned enough last summer, but I ran out by March. Luckily I picked up a part-time job to keep me solvent.

Most colleges and universities have banks and ATM machines on or adjacent to their campuses, making it convenient to have an account locally. Opening and maintaining a checking account helps a young person to feel more competent about handling his or her own affairs. For the student who has never done this before, it is one more step on the road to independence.

The mother of a William and Mary freshman describes her daughter's stumbling attempts to manage her money during freshman year:

It's been a learning experience. We're big on finding someone within the system to help you. Brenda found a "nice lady at the bank" who helps her. We told her we were not going to bail her out when she overdrew her account. Apparently she did from time to time, because once when she was home, an envelope came for her from the bank and before opening it she said, "Oh God, I've overdrawn." I asked her how she knew and she replied, "That's what the envelope for that looks like."

The same parent described how her oldest son, when he was a freshman at Williams, convinced the family that it would be a good idea for him to have a credit card:

> It would never have occurred to us to give him a credit
> card. We're not a credit card family. He came home second
> semester and presented us with a rational plan for why he
> wanted one. He wanted to establish credit for himself; it
> made it easier for him to cash checks, and it would be use-
> ful in a crisis situation. This made a lot of sense to us. After
> that, we gave all of our children cards and told them that
> the first month they couldn't pay their bill would be the
> last month that they would have the credit card. Our mid-
> dle child did miss a plane once and had only $18 with her.
> Nobody would cash a check, and with her card, she was
> able to spend the night at a hotel.

Credit card companies court college students. Some students get three or four cards and juggle the payments from month to month. This generation was brought up on credit cards, and the "spend now, worry later" mentality often leads to delinquent loan payments and ruined credit ratings when they enter the workforce. A number of schools have begun to include information about this problem in their literature and urge parents to warn their children about the difficulties that arise from the misuse of credit cards.

The introduction on many campuses of all-purpose identification cards, sometimes called "smart cards," is both a convenience and a potential hazard for freshmen who haven't learned to manage their money. For instance, at Columbia University, each student is issued a university photo ID that is used for many functions, including access to university buildings and dormitories, library privileges, and entrance to athletic events. It can also be used as a debit card at the university bookstore, dining facilities, and vending machines. At some universities, vendors in the local community also accept uni-versity smart cards, making it all too tempting for students to drain their balance on pizza and beer.

The major expense of college tuition may bring to the surface once again financial tugs of war between separated and divorced parents. Counseling services in colleges and universities regularly see students caught in the continuing crossfire of bitter ex-husbands and wives who seem to lose sight of the fact that their child is the loser in this battle. Obviously, it is in the child's best interest for the financial arrangements to be clearly spelled out and understood before he or she leaves for school, even if it takes, as one divorced woman put it, "mini-summit meetings" to do it.

The child also loses when parents use money to make an unspoken bargain, the "after-all-I've-done-for-you" syndrome. A pamphlet for parents of Wittenberg University students advises:

> Some students feel that their parents use what they have done for them to bribe the students to be "good" or to do what the parents wish. Such coercion often courts exaggerated rebellion. Money can be used in that way . . . as a bribe or threat to produce the kind of behavior a parent wants. Students are very sensitive about being used as "ready made products." They want to feel some of their own control over their lives.

As students move through their college years and struggle to become increasingly independent, money and financial ties to parents inevitably cause concern. For many students, the struggles for separation and independence are complicated by their prolonged years of financial dependence. Parents can help loosen the financial tie by encouraging their children to assume responsibility for the management of their financial affairs, by being honest with them about family finances, and by being clear about their expectations right from the beginning of their children's college career.

ACADEMIC EXPECTATIONS

"Just do the best you can." These are the standard parental words of advice to offspring when the conversation turns to the academic side of college. But if "the best they can" has meant A's and B's until now, most parents expect that to continue. Many students complain of the double messages they receive from parents. "I don't care about your grades as long as you try" may have as its hidden message, "I know if you try, you can get an A." Students are acutely tuned in to their parents' expectations regarding academics, and they feel enormous pressure to "pay them back for their financial sacrifice" with A's and B's.

A lot of students place pressure on themselves to get good grades. Actually, most of them want the same academic success for themselves that their parents want for them. They want to be excited about their courses, stimulated by their professors, and they want to do well. They would love to get all A's and B's; there are even some who would be truly satisfied only with A's. Many have glided or plugged their way through high school without a C or a D, and as they begin their college careers, they want, and perhaps expect, to keep up their stellar record.

Some of the superstars will find themselves in academic situations that are totally different from those in high school. In the most selective colleges, which fill their freshman classes with the upper 10 percent of high school students, 90 percent of the students will be in an unfamiliar position—no longer at the top of the academic heap. And half of them will be in the bottom half of their college class. Obvious as that may sound, it can come as a shock to students and their parents when they have become accustomed to the accolades that accompany acceptance to the most prestigious colleges and universities.

Parents of these very successful students may be particularly susceptible to heightened expectations about their children's academic performance. Some have even touted their children to family and friends as a "4-point" or a "3.8," as though those numbers describe a total person. One who understands this numerical shorthand might do well to ask, "What else can you tell me about him?" "Is she excited about what she is learning?"

Parents of high academic achievers probably haven't spent much time worrying about their child's academic performance. They may have come to take it for granted and focus their concern on other aspects of development. Some even hope their youngsters will relax more in college and take more time for friends and extracurricular activities. They may not realize that they have high expectations and assumptions about academic performance until their child hits an unexpected academic snag. One woman commented:

We finally accept the idea that our children won't be all-American or Arthur Rubenstein—but we still expect them to excel academically in all their courses. My son was a bacteriology major, took philosophy and got a D. We were shocked. We expected him to be good at all subjects. That may be as unrealistic as the mentality that says we should all weigh 110 pounds. If we can accept the fact that a kid who is 5'7" won't play college basketball, then we should be able to accept academic liability.

Parents whose children did not do well in high school may have thought a great deal about what they expect from them in college. Their expectations are often mixed with anxiety that the high school pattern will be repeated, and the eternal hope that the student will turn over a new leaf at last. These are the parents who are prone to giving late summer lectures to their children about study habits, discipline, and buckling down. The more they lecture, the more their children turn a deaf ear. But the temptation to "tell her one more time" is difficult to resist, in spite of the rational knowledge that it's out of their hands, and now it's up to her.

A Cincinnati woman whose son was about to leave for Oberlin said:

Ted didn't really work in high school. He managed to do OK, but not great, with very little effort. I don't think he was ever turned on to a course. He just didn't get much out of school at all. He'll have to work harder at Oberlin, and I expect him to make a reasonable effort to hit the books and stretch his mind. He doesn't have to get all A's and B's, but we're paying too much for him to just jerk around. I'm not concerned just about grades; what I really want is for him to open up intellectually. I want him to be interested in what he's doing. He's so narrow now; he's not curious or adventurous intellectually. I'm hoping Oberlin will be broadening for him. He's going to a place that fosters caring about the world and other people. I'd rather he become really excited about a European history course and get a C than take yet another math course that he hates and get an A. But it's hard to get away from the subject of grades. They are the inevitable barometer; they are some reflection of what is going on.

For most parents, even if grades aren't paramount, there is a grade threshold—some number below which a grade-point average becomes unacceptable. That number will vary not only from parent to parent but from one child to another in the same family, and for the same child at different periods of his or her career. Likewise, the messages that parents transmit may mean different things to different students. Telling some students not to worry about grades may be a license not to go to class. To a young person who has always been a plugger, the message "Do the best you can" may simply increase self-imposed pressure and the tendency to be a workaholic. The same message to a more easygoing sibling may not be clear enough; she'll be likely to benefit from more specific guidelines— perhaps even a mutually agreed upon grade-point average to aim for during the freshman year.

There are some parents who not only expect a certain grade-point average from their children but also assume that they'll select a certain major—usually one leading to a high-status career. It is not uncommon for parents to introduce their children who are barely out of high school as "Jane's our premed; Jim's our prelaw." Some parents even threaten to withdraw financial support unless their child follows a prescribed course of study. Students who are embarking on their college years are just beginning to explore their own interests and capacities. Parental expectations and assumptions about what they should study act as barriers to the student's development. The underlying communication to the student is "I know what's good for you better than you do."

Every college counseling staff in the country can tell war stories about students who have been pressured to study business or biology or engineering against their will. And though consciously trying to appease their parents, these students may also be fighting for their own identity. Some finally come to a turning point during their later years of school and choose the course of study that they really want, but only after having paid a painful price.

James E. McLeod, Washington University's Vice Chancellor for Students and Dean of the College of Arts and Sciences, advises:

> This need for freshmen to have a certain future, to know what they will be in 2010 or 2020, runs counter to their growth and development. It leads to low or no risk whatsoever. They need to pursue interests—to reach and stretch. They *do* need to know the implications of their choices. They need to have conversations with faculty and advisors, people who know about the institution and about life. But a certain future is not the thing to seek in their freshman year.

Eventually, if they are to separate and become independent, students must take responsibility for their own academic goals and the consequences of their performance. They have to decide whether they are willing to work hard enough to get the grades it takes to be accepted to medical school, to keep a scholarship, or to graduate with honors. They have to discover what they are capable of and what sacrifices they are willing to make. Many students feel more secure when they know what their parents expect from them at the outset. And perhaps parents feel more secure too, when they know they have made themselves clear. But as time goes on it will be up to the student to decide to what extent parental goals really fit with his or her own aspirations. And the challenge to parents will be to remain supportive and to be flexible and open to change.

Dean McLeod believes that it's important for parents to acknowledge this shift in the relationship:

> I'd like parents to let their child know, "I am an interested party. I remain engaged in who you are and who you are becoming." But the baton needs to be passed to the child. The student needs to have license to take the baton—to take charge of his or her own life. Parents and students are in the race together, but it's the student's chance to carry the baton.

SOCIAL LIFE: CHOICES AND RESPONSIBILITIES

I drank a lot those first few weeks. I found myself in situations that were really hard for me to handle, and I didn't handle them the way I would have sober. I finally woke up well into the first semester and realized I didn't have to be a "party girl" to have friends and a social life, but it was hard to get people to take me seriously.

■

I smoked a lot of pot in high school. When I got here I decided to hang out with a different kind of crowd. They're into drinking, and sometimes it gets out of hand.

■

One night I took a girl out and after the movie I invited her back to my apartment. Before I knew what was happening, she went into the bathroom and came back out without any clothes on. I panicked!

It is the rare high school graduate who hasn't had to grapple with personal decisions about alcohol, drugs, and sex: Should I or shouldn't I? How much? What kind? Where?

By the time students arrive on campus, they are well on the way to formulating their own value system, usually based on many years of observing and listening to parents and peers. Their actual degree of experimentation varies widely, but almost all of them will find that college life brings them face-to-face with more choices than they have ever had before. More choices, more pressures—and now perhaps for the first time, no familiar parental boundaries to keep them in line.

Throughout their teenage years, young people have been used to a certain amount of structure and limit setting by their parents. "I have to be home by midnight." "My parents wouldn't let me walk out of the house wearing that." "I better not have another drink 'cause I have to check in with my mom when I get home." "We always go to eleven o'clock Mass as a family Sunday morning." Phrases like these have saved many teenagers from having to take a stand—making it easier to say no when under intense pressure from peers, or to refuse to try out a new behavior before feeling ready. Students may find parental rules arbitrary and aggravating, but often they depend on those rules to keep their behavior within safe limits.

Sometimes college students don't realize that this parental backing is missing until they are in the midst of a problematic situation. No one in college will be checking to see when they come home, or even *if* they come home. Roommates and friends won't be checking for red eyes or alcohol breath. Students have to put themselves on the line; they are responsible for setting their own limits.

The Dean of the College and the Dean of Student Life at Brown University send an annual letter to parents and guardians of freshmen, asking them to do their share in preparing students to live in a campus community:

> The freedom of our atmosphere has on occasion, unfortunately, led some to lose sight of their corresponding responsibilities to themselves and to the community. We therefore ask your help in reminding your children that boundaries do exist at Brown and that serious penalties are imposed on those found guilty of overstepping them.

The letter expresses concern about the misuse of alcohol and other drugs, and makes a particular plea to parents to join the university as partners in dealing with this problem.

> It is our hope that parents will take time to review issues of chemical use with their children, including their expectations for behavior at Brown. In a country where rules and customs vary so greatly from region to region, students can easily be confused as they make choices of their own. Parental direction can be of great value to children and provide enormous service to those at Brown who wrestle with this vast national problem.

When Andrew Edmiston was Director of the Counseling Service at Lehigh University, he wrote a sensitive and comprehensive pamphlet, "Life at Lehigh: A Conversation with Parents." He challenged parents to formulate and discuss their values and to communicate directly with their children. On the topic of drugs he advised:

> Every student and every parent is faced with the task of formulating his own personal position with regard to the use of various drugs.
>
> There is never a guarantee that you and the student will see eye to eye on these matters, but mutual respect is a sound beginning. Furthermore, learning about drug types, drug usage, and possible effects helps to create a foundation upon which intelligent opinions can be built. Young adults respect those who are well informed and willing to discuss objectively the complex issues involved. Parents who recognize that the problems associated with drug use and abuse are complex can better avoid the pitfalls that occur from misunderstanding and misinformation.
>
> There is an important difference between communication and confrontation. If you have concerns about these matters, share them. Do so in a manner that conveys your earnest desire to understand your student's world and the challenges he faces. Whatever else you may feel or do with regard to these matters, keep in mind that lectures, threats, and ultimatums may lead to doubt and sometimes result in everyone involved retreating into defiant and defensive positions.

Edmiston also tackled the issue of sexual conduct:

> Your student may find, as many do, that his attitudes relating to sex will be challenged many times. He may be forced to do some hard thinking about his own attitudes, particularly so in a climate that encourages him to be his own person and to make up his own mind.

The foundations he brings to the University, upon which he builds or against which he protests, are those that have their origins within the family.

Parents are confronted with an infinite number of "teachable moments," and the challenge, of course, is to recognize some of them when they occur. The father of a Bucknell freshman described how he almost blew his chance to talk to his son in a meaningful way about marijuana use:

Two weeks before Tim left for school, I was driving home from work and reached into the glove compartment to get out a map. A packet of cigarette rolling paper fell out with the map. I could feel my blood start to boil. "Now he's smoking pot in the car!" was all I could think.

I barged into the house and was about to start in on a tirade, but something inside me stopped me, and I calmed down and just presented him with the packet and said, "Come on in and talk. I'm worried about this."

At first Tim just looked at me sheepishly, and then he said angrily, "What do you want me to do? Tell you every time I smoke a joint?"

I said, "No, of course not. But you're leaving the evidence that you're smoking, and I'm concerned about how much, and what it will do to you when you're off on your own." He kind of relaxed and started talking—reassuring me, giving me space to ask more questions. I probed a bit, but mainly listened. He told me about a lot of stuff he'd been exposed to in high school and let me know he'd done lots of thinking about his own limits and how to deal with pressure from other kids. One thing led to another, and before I knew it almost an hour had gone by and our conversation had run the gamut from cocaine and a messed up friend who was in jail for dealing, to spirituality in nature and organized religion. What was best was, he did most of the talking. And I was able to tell him something I've been wanting to say for a long time—that if he's ever in a jam, no matter what it is, I want him to feel as though he can come to me for help.

A Kansas mother of three gave each of her daughters—at Smith, Trinity, and the University of Kansas—the same advice at the beginning of their college years:

> I will never relinquish my right to give advice, but at this point you are no longer obliged to take it. I have done what I can to give you the equipment to make your own decisions. Never let anyone else tell you what to do. Never make a decision and say, "She made me do it." If you choose drugs, sleeping around, whatever, it will be your choice. Don't close any doors behind you. Don't not do something because it's expedient.

Students fortunate enough to have older siblings who will counsel them often turn to them rather than parents for advice. A freshman at James Madison University recounted a precollege conversation with his older brother: "He basically told me to wait until I was sure of what I was doing—to use my best judgment and not to do anything for someone else."

Another experienced upperclassman advised his younger sister, "Just make sure you always leave yourself a safety net. If you're going to drink a lot, don't go back to a guy's room with him. If you're going to go to his room, don't drink."

Counselors often see the casualties from the first month or two of college—students who have jumped into new lifestyles too quickly without taking into account the consequences or their personal values. One counselor regularly advises freshmen not to make any major lifestyle changes during the first month of school: "It's better not to jump into dramatic experimentation—whether the experimentation is with sex, alcohol, or a new religious commitment." Many students regret starting off by creating an image that doesn't reflect their real sense of themselves, and find backtracking an awkward and stressful process.

Parents may feel that being honest and direct about their values and concerns seems fruitless at times, when confronted with "Yeah, yeah, Dad," or eyes that roll back in disgust, or tolerant amusement when talking about such provocative topics. But, though loathe to admit it, students do care about what their parents think, and often these discussions at home can serve as a grounding to refer back to when the students are faced with difficult choices at school.

THE LAST FEW DAYS

There does come a time finally when the suitcases are brought down from the attic or the trunk up from the basement. The very act of packing may be another reflection of the way a student handles leaving home.

Parents speak of their children's underpacking:

> The night before she left, she threw some things into a backpack and some duffels. I was horrified, but she kept reminding me that they sold tissue and toothpaste in Ann Arbor, so not to worry.

And overpacking:

> She seemed to be moving her entire room to Penn—her bulletin board, high school yearbooks, stuffed animals, wall hanging. We packed five or six large boxes to send UPS the week before, plus a trunk and the suitcases she took on the plane. I tried to explain that she would have trouble fitting all that into a small room with another person and her things, but it seemed so important to her, I guess. At the time I thought I was being too indulgent, but it really seemed to help. She kind of "nested" when she got there and seemed to relax when she replicated a corner of her room at home in her new surroundings.

In these last hours of packing, the most ordinary actions can take on a special magnitude. Cleaning out a closet becomes a night-before-departure ritual, and the gesture of taping the last box is done with emphatic finality. All the while, nostalgia permeates the scene.

In a letter to the editor of the *New York Times*, Deborah Frankel Reese, a New Jersey mother of two, writes wistfully of her own departure for Skidmore a generation ago, as the images from that time mingle with the present reality of her daughter's leave-taking:

> I believe that part of the mixed pain and joy I felt as we packed the college-bound boxes and bags were the memories of my departure for college more than twenty-five years ago. My own remembered clothes—Bermuda shorts, McMullen blouses, madras, and circle pins—kept getting tangled up in my daughter's very different clothes as we filled the suitcases.
>
> Just as she, opening the doors to her new life, believes everything is possible, so did I. Her small cartons of books reminded me of the Emerson, Byron, and Camus I took with me, certain in the knowledge that I, too, would one day write a book. I smiled at the favorite stuffed animals my usually pragmatic, practical daughter gentled into her trunk, particularly the small, green kangaroo—given to me so long ago by the boy I was so certain I would one day marry.

Each leave-taking is unique and has the stamp of that child's own personality printed on its style and pace. A mother of two college-aged children recognized the characteristic patterns of their approaches to new adventures. Her sensitivity to their individuality helped her to support them in different and appropriate ways:

> When our daughter was young, she always rushed into things and then got scared. She would race to the top of the slide and then get scared at the top, and I would come and help her down. Our son, on the other hand, would

stand next to me and watch for a long time until he'd figured it out and then he would attempt it without looking
back. They left for college the same way. Steven went
first to the University of Michigan. He researched it and
spent time during the summer talking about it and planning. We talked over details endlessly. He was miserable
for the first twenty-four hours, but never after. Stephanie
didn't seem to want to talk about it or think ahead at all.
She went to Michigan also, packed the night before and
went off fearlessly, or so it seemed, but then she got scared
and had a hard time. We did a lot of long-distance hand
holding.

And so the journey begins . . .

6

ORIENTATION AND
DISORIENTATION

IMAGINE YOURSELF STANDING AT YOUR FRONT
door with your bags packed, ready to leave on a long-awaited journey. This is a special trip, different from the family vacations or business travels you are accustomed to.

■ You are leaving behind everyone you know and moving
to a new place where you have made a commitment to
spend the next four years of your life.

■ When you arrive in this strange place, you look around
and see a landscape of unfamiliar faces. A lot of these
people talk differently from you; they have strange
accents and use expressions you've never heard before.
Some of them wear clothes that are different too. They
all look smart, confident, and outgoing.

■ No one here knows anything about the status you had
in your previous position—or about any of your past
accomplishments.

- ■ You have left behind your family, friends, colleagues—all the people who are important in your life.

- ■ You're not too sure where anything is or who might be able to help you.

- ■ You have to share a small room with a perfect stranger. There are no set guidelines about bedtime, use of the phone, stereo, radio, or entertaining guests. You have to negotiate everything.

- ■ You have more work to do than ever before, but you're not too sure how you will be evaluated or what people will want from you. You may not get your first evaluations for many weeks.

- ■ You have a lot of unscheduled time and there are plenty of distractions: sports centers, concerts, movies, parties, clubs—and lots of attractive potential partners.

- ■ You need to keep track of a little plastic "smart card" so you can unlock your door, check out library books, buy your meals, or get into the gym. And you have to handle financial and housekeeping matters that used to be done for you or, at least, shared.

- ■ You're not too sure where your work and new relationships are heading, and you don't know where or how you will ever fit into this new place. But everyone has told you that your whole future depends on your doing well during these four years—preferably better than those other bright, confident-looking people who live here with you.

This is the freshman's journey. The student who arrives at college is confronted with a totally new world, as alien as a foreign land.

And when seen from this perspective, we may wonder how anyone survives freshman year. Of course, most will survive—even thrive. Yet in many families, college has been a topic of family conversation for so long, especially during the senior year of high school, that parents may lose sight of the magnitude of the transition that freshmen encounter.

ORIENTATION

Most colleges and universities plan carefully orchestrated orientation programs to help freshmen get their bearings. Though larger schools often get an early start during the summer, in many colleges, orientation is a three- or four-day affair that kicks off the fall semester. More schools than ever before begin with an intense small-group experience, from Colby's COOT (Colby Outdoor Orientation Trip), exploring the surrounding hills and coastline of Maine, to Columbia's Urban Plunge—a full day of community service in nearby New York City neighborhoods. Students who participate in these programs usually rave about them and feel that they have a head start.

The official orientation period, no matter how it begins and when it takes place, is designed to take advantage of new students' eager attentiveness, imparting vast amounts of information and immersing them in social activities that encourage friendship and keep homesickness at bay. Seminars and speeches, parties, tours and excursions, a seemingly endless series of meetings and greetings fill the first days. And, through it all, upperclassmen, administrators, and faculty attempt to introduce freshmen to the resources, philosophy, rituals, and culture of their new home. In retrospect, students are often both grateful for and disparaging of the bombardment of back-to-back programming. But most of them emerge with tentative feelings of belonging to a new culture and new place, using campus acronyms and nicknames as though they had always known them, talking about "my friends" or "my advisor" with a possessiveness that bespeaks a long-standing acquaintance.

Parents who come to campus with their children are kept busy too. Many attend the brief orientation programs that are offered especially for them in an increasing number of schools, introducing them to the resources of the college, telling them what to expect, and encouraging the process of letting go. Most of the programming is planned so that parents and students are separated from each other for a significant portion of the day. Parents have an opportunity to ask questions without fear of embarrassing their children, and to gain a firsthand exposure to their child's new world.

Parent orientation is, to some extent, an exercise in reassurance and letting go. All parents want to know, of course, that they are leaving their children in good hands. Knowing what the campus security system is, or how the advising system works, or what the Learning Center and Counseling Service offer, is not only reassuring, it is also information that may help parents to foster their child's independence. Later on, when a child calls home with a problem, a parent who knows what kind of assistance is available is more likely to suggest using the appropriate service on campus rather than trying to take over the problem and solve it. Parents who understand something about the rigor of the academic program will find it easier to give much-needed support to a discouraged and tired freshman rather than offer unsolicited advice about studying harder. College orientation directors and other administrators urge parents to take advantage of the sessions planned for them and learn how they can help their children find help for themselves.

Whether or not parents actually attend the orientation sessions on campus, they all have access to information about campus services and academic programs through bulletins and brochures, which can be tucked away in a readily accessible place. These might come in handy when least expected. Even if they are never used, most parents feel more secure just knowing where to turn if help is needed.

■

On the day fall orientation begins, the campus starts to bustle early in the morning with a steady stream of new arrivals. Some students arrive in airport vans with only a backpack and small duffel; others, in their parents' cars, loaded with suitcases and trunks and racks of clothes. Though some have traveled across the world, and others have commuted from across town, the air is thick with anxiety, tension, and excitement for all. Parents and their children can be heard snapping at each other in spite of the fact that they all want this to be a perfect day. The new students walk uneasily, often with heads down, looking up as they pass each other and exchanging awkward glances. Many wear T-shirts with advertisements for the status they used to have—Silver Lake Tennis, Ypsilanti Basketball—or where they spent the summer—Yellowstone, Paris, Oak Bluffs. Others sport the names of their high schools or favorite rock groups, all in an attempt to hold on to and present to others who they are.

During those first hours on campus, it is easy to distinguish the freshmen from the upperclassmen who serve as resident advisors and orientation assistants. The RAs and OAs, as they are called at many schools, typically move with the grace and ease of those who are at home in their environment. They greet each other enthusiastically, share breathless tales of summer adventures and unself-conscious hugs. They all seem to look fit and happy and relaxed. It is not unusual for a freshman to look at them and wonder, "Will I ever be like that? Will this place ever feel like home?"

The very first moments of collegiate life are filled with the ubiquitous pastime of waiting in line. There are lines of cars in front of the residence halls, waiting for their turn to unload. There are lines to pick up orientation packets and keys, lines for luggage carts and elevators—all before the students even get into their rooms. Then there are lines at the bookstore and drugstore and bank and telephone service. And more lines to see advisors and financial aid officers. The larger the school, the more numerous and longer the lines. After all the preparation and anticipation and emotions of departure, college begins with a series of tedious waits.

Parents, too, feel the disorientation of arrival on someone else's turf, where customs and logistics are unfamiliar. Suddenly their child is just one of many, and the family unit joins the ranks of outsiders. The son or daughter who had been eager for their presence may now walk self-consciously five or six feet ahead of them—

already placing distance between them, reminding them that the time to part is near. One mother, when asked how the first day was going for her, answered bemusedly:

> As well as can be expected, considering I drove 500 miles yesterday and now my son is telling me I can sit in his suite but should stay out of his room—that it's OK if I talk to other parents, but not to students. He literally jogs ahead of me. He's keeping his distance. And he and his "friends"— he met them this morning—are going out for pizza tonight.

Many parents are surprised by the subtle and sometimes not so subtle cues from their son or daughter that their presence is a mixed blessing. As one faculty member said to an assembled group of parents at the opening orientation session of a small liberal arts college: "This person you brought with you, who was clinging to you two hours ago, won't even know who you are three hours from now."

An exaggeration to be sure. The pull toward separation and the desire to make the break are coupled with the wish for parental reassurance—or just a bit of help with the mundane tasks of moving in and getting settled.

A freshman at Colorado College, who had asked his parents to drive him to school, described with a wry smile:

> Having my parents at school with me when I got here was nice. I cannot say that we had anything to do, but it was nice not having to walk in completely alone. Once they had taken me to get Wal-mart stuff, I was ready for them to leave. I felt like it was time for me to deal with making friends and they could do nothing to help me. So, I wanted them to leave a little earlier than they did. After they left, I called them every day for a month.

A student who emphatically tells his parents he wants to be alone and unpack by himself urges them a moment later to be back in time to meet him for lunch. Another, who had handled the packing and departure from home with utmost bravado, tells her mother she wants to spend the first night with her in her hotel. This desire to surge forward and then to check back with parents is a familiar echo of the separation behavior of the 2-year-old, who careens off into new worlds, only to run back anxiously to make sure that Mother is still there. The beginning college student is also plunging into new worlds, and the lure of adventure and separation from parents, as well as the need for security, may produce behavior during these opening days that is as inconsistent as it was those long years ago when he or she was a toddler.

Parents who bring their children to college with preconceived expectations of sharing the orientation experience in a particular way may miss the very rich experience that is actually available to them. Dreams of a last family dinner together at the best restaurant in town are often dashed by a student's scheduled orientation event or spontaneous first meal with a new friend or floormate. Images of an idyllic shopping spree to buy plants and prints together may never materialize. Not only that, but the weather may not cooperate. Instead of the anticipated crisp, cool fall day, students and parents often find themselves moving in on the hottest day of Indian summer or in the midst of a downpour.

Expectations of gracious living are relinquished to the reality of lounges filled with worn furniture and long, dimly lit hallways. Even the glass and steel high-rises that dot many campuses usually reveal interiors that include modern amenities but lack imagination. Parents are sometimes angered by the physical limitations of the residence halls, especially when at an expensive school. "But," explains a dean at Barnard College, "I'd like parents to understand that our focus is on quality education. Poshness is not one of the important offerings."

Parents may feel like awkward bystanders in a world that is quickly enveloping their child. Relishing the opportunity to provide tangible assistance one more time, they assume the roles of porters, gofers, and personal shoppers. The mother and father of a University of Minnesota student laugh as they describe a frenetic thirty minutes at a Minneapolis discount store while their son was getting settled in his room:

We madly ran from aisle to aisle filling our cart with essentials and nonessentials, everything from double-stick tape to plastic drinking cups; from a popcorn maker complete with a jar of popcorn to a big, shiny red wastebasket. We even threw in a tie. We must have looked like those prizewinners in a supermarket contest: "Fill your basket with all you can in thirty minutes!" The truth of the matter is we did it as much for us as we did for Ted. We knew he wanted to stay in the dorm and unpack by himself, and we had all this nervous energy and this was something concrete we could do. When we brought the stuff back to the dorm, it was clear that it was a hit. The popcorn maker was our best bet. We got a kick out of seeing Ted and his roommate leave for their first floor meeting, carrying the wastebasket filled with freshly made popcorn.

It isn't always easy to refrain from last-minute hints about study habits and course selection and discipline and making friends. It may even be difficult to stand back and leave the bed unmade and the suitcases half full. A Bowdoin senior recounts:

My mother hadn't set foot in my room since I was 13. When we arrived at college, she wouldn't leave until she had made my bed; it freaked me out. She got upset because I brought my favorite bedspread, which had holes in it. She was acting as if my college career was doomed because I had three holes in my bedspread.

It is not uncommon to hear students and parents fighting in the campus store about mundane decisions, such as what color sweatshirt to buy, or which type of desk lamp is best. Some parents even try to have dorm rooms switched, or show up at meetings for students and advisors, or make special requests to the RAs to look out for their children. All of these actions, no matter how well intentioned, make it more difficult for the new freshmen to separate and assert their independence.

Though many schools invite parents to accompany their children to school, they also gently encourage them to leave campus after the parent programs are over. Phrases such as "now that parents have departed" and "dinner with your classmates while your parents enjoy the restaurants in town" appear in most orientation schedules, pointed hints that it is time for parents to go. It is apparent to college faculty and administrators that even the most self-confident freshmen feel uneasy when their families linger on beyond the activities intended for them.

As the moment of parting draws near, many students seem anxious to say good-bye to their parents; others have last-minute jitters and become tearful and panicky. The long imagined final good-bye may be, in fact, a self-conscious and hurried affair in the student-filled lobby. One father said wistfully of the last minutes at Kenyon with his son:

> Like most symbolic moments, we have a picture in mind of what it will be like, but it's not finished off like a Kodak commercial. I can't even remember the actual moment of parting, because he was surrounded by his RAs and friends.

The orientation experience isn't picture perfect for students or their parents. But parents who approach this experience with open minds, who are flexible and willing to take their cues from their children rather than attempt to direct them, are likely to feel the deep satisfaction of having shared an important passage even as they are parting.

DISORIENTATION: THE FIRST FEW DAYS ON CAMPUS

"A whirlwind," "a blur," "a fog"—these are the words students use in retrospect to describe their earliest days on campus. Overwhelmed by new places and people and rituals, they have a sense of unreality and a world turned topsy-turvy. The first glimpse inside an ivy-covered brick dorm is often a shock. And the dormitory room itself, bare and colorless, shows little promise of the home it will eventually become. A University of Oregon student recalls:

When I got to my room, my roommates' stuff was there, but they weren't. I started putting sheets on the bed, and I broke down. It didn't look good. Anything that unfamiliar that I know I'm committed to for the next ten months couldn't possibly have looked good—to sleep at night with total strangers—and wake up the next morning in this strange place.

And a Vassar student remembers:

I had a single and I was really glad about that. But when I saw it, I just couldn't imagine how I could ever think of it as my place. The first thing I did was set up my stereo, so at least the sounds would help me mellow out.

For a University of Vermont freshman, the first problem was finding her room. It certainly didn't seem funny at the time, but now she chuckles as she tells the story:

I asked my dad to drop me off at the dorm, and made plans to meet him later. I knew I didn't want him to be there as I met my roommate. I grabbed two of my suitcases and took the elevator to my floor. When I got to the room, there were two girls already in there. It was then that I found out I was in the wrong dorm. I was too embarrassed to go back down in the elevator. I was afraid someone would see me and know what happened, so I took the stairs. Later that day I was supposed to go to a freshman barbecue, and I couldn't find it. Everything seemed to be going wrong. I was really in a daze. It was sort of like floating around in a sea of people. I felt very vulnerable.

Indeed, many college students talk about how vulnerable they felt during their first days on campus; they acknowledge with hindsight that the road to becoming a suave sophomore is paved with a series of minor embarrassments. They remember desperately wanting to make a good first impression while trying to decipher the codes of their fellow students' behavior. As they meet their roommates and floormates, with whom they will spend the next year, they are confronted with people whose lives thus far inevitably have been different from their own. Dean Alice Drum of Franklin and Marshall observes:

> When students come to college, they bring a whole series of cultures with them: their individual family, their high school, their town, their part of the country. An only child may find herself rooming with someone from a family of ten. Even if the two students are from similar racial, religious, and class cultures, their personal family cultures are foreign to each other in many ways. One has most likely never shared a room with anyone; the other has never had a room alone. One student may be appalled by the other's casual borrowing of clothes and other possessions; the other may think that the roommate is selfish.

And in this era of diversity on college campuses, a lot of students will also find themselves living with classmates who *do* come from different religious, racial, and class backgrounds. They may use different slang, or even speak a foreign language. Soon after their arrival, students are confronted with a mélange of styles, values, and attitudes—a coming together of many worlds:

> My roommate went to boarding school. That wasn't part of my world. She had her friends from St. Paul's.

> ■

> My roommate was from Puerto Rico and spoke practically no English whatsoever. When my parents left I thought, Oh no, I'm being left here and I don't know anyone and my roommate doesn't even speak English. I was jealous of the girl down the hall who had a Puerto Rican roommate who did speak English.

> ■

I wasn't prepared for the racism I encountered here. It's sometimes subtle and sometimes not so subtle—like if I play my music at the same decibel level as a white student, I'm the one the RA tells to lower the volume.

■

I was very conscious of the eighteenth-generation Harvard people because my father was so into the fact that his daughter, the daughter of an immigrant, was going to Harvard, the quintessentially American university.

■

I'd never met anyone who was Jewish or black before. Half my floor was from Long Island and didn't even know where Minnesota was, much less my small town. Everyone started calling me Blondie, and I thought, Wait a minute, my hair is almost brown. It was overwhelming.

■

I came here—to this Ivy League bastion—with a chip on my shoulder about prep schools because I went to a big public, urban high school where half the class dropped out by senior year, and most of my friends don't have much and a lot of them went to community colleges. I was surprised by how much people mix here.

Although many students find the discovery of this diversity exciting, parents sometimes intrude in an attempt to ensure that their child won't stray far from the fold. A young woman from Cleveland recalls a series of phone calls from her parents the first week of school:

My parents had talked to other parents when they dropped me off here. There happened to be a few other people whose last names ended in *ski* in the dorm, and Mom and Dad asked them if they were Polish Catholics.

They wanted me to meet all the people on the floor who were Catholics. It happened that my roommate was the youngest of seven from a big Catholic family, and they thought that was really neat. They kept calling and asking about these people. They were really concerned that now that I had left, I was going to leave my religion too, and they wanted to make sure that I hit the Newman Center as much as possible.

Overanxious parents, even those whose values include an appreciation of the richness of different cultures, may find themselves seeking out potential friends for their children. A freshman from suburban Atlanta exclaims mockingly:

I can't believe my mother. She keeps asking me if I've gotten to know that nice Jewish girl from Bethesda who lives across the hall. My parents have never even noticed if my friends were Jewish before!

In response to the plethora of new people, some students themselves initially cling to anyone who is remotely familiar—a long-lost buddy from fifth grade, a fellow Bostonian, a former cabin mate from summer camp. International students and students of color find it particularly comforting to make connections with others from their own backgrounds; indeed, they can be a lifeline to one another, and many schools plan special programs to help them meet. Some students respond with enthusiasm to the opportunity to meet so many new people and join the party crowd immediately. But even the most outgoing feel disoriented as well as excited by the fast pace and their new surroundings.

The hallways and walkways reverberate with fleeting conversations as strangers make their introductions—"What's your name?" "Where are you from?" "What's your major?" The questions and answers are an endless echo.

In spite of efforts to concentrate, it is impossible to keep names and faces straight. Two students may engage in an impromptu half-hour conversation at the soft drink machine and walk away without knowing who the other is. Time seems distorted, the way it does to travelers in a distant country who are bombarded with countless new experiences in the course of a day. Nothing is connected to the routines and rhythms of life at home. It is exhilarating and exhausting.

There are a lot of choices to be made, and students are often concerned about making the right ones. Is it important to go to the orientation session on note taking, or should I skip it and play softball in the quad? Should I wear a Polo or tie-dye? Would it be better to go to the freshman ice cream social or out for a pizza with the kids down the hall? Should I go to a French film with my roommate or party at the frats? What courses should I sign up for? What activities should I get involved in? How much should I drink at the party? Should I or shouldn't I try out for the choir? Do I want to be called Peggy or Margaret or use my middle name instead?

Parents may receive frantic phone calls from confused and over-stimulated sons or daughters who just days before brushed off attempts at last-minute advice, now wanting immediate right answers. The father who is a pragmatic business executive may be strongly tempted to respond from his own perspective to the question "Do you think I should take cultural anthropology or economics?" If he can take a deep breath and then ask some probing questions, he will be teaching his child something about decision making and helping him move toward independence. Questions such as "What do you see as the advantages and disadvantages of each?" and "How do the faculty compare?" are more effective than a directive answer. The mother who in her own college days was fiercely anti-Greek and receives a bubbling phone call from her daughter announcing, "I've gotten a bid from Pi Phi. Do you think I should join?" is challenged to pause and open a discussion that will help her daughter discover her own best answer.

This North Carolina mother reflects a year later on her handling of the sorority situation:

> I made the mistake of putting down sorority life when our daughter called. She did join anyway, but I never responded positively when she talked about it. It went

against so many of my own values. But as time went on, I realized that it provided her with a structure for her social life that she needed—and also gave her better housing opportunities than she would have had on such a big campus. The bottom line was she had investigated all of this and had more information than we did to know what was best for her. I just regret that I wasn't more supportive at the time, and I've learned to trust her judgment more.

It is easy to succumb to the lure of simple right and wrong answers that these dilemmas seem to evoke. But these moments are a perfect opportunity for parents to promote and encourage independent decision making with an expression of support for whatever is decided.

At stake in the aggregate of these decisions is the freshman's sense of who he or she is going to be in this new place where the labels of high school and family and community no longer stick. What affiliations will he make? What groups will he become part of? What image of herself does she want to present? What commitments will she make? What is important? In the company of strangers, a clean slate opens up the possibility of developing a clearer identity—a more solid sense of self that is not merely a reflection of, or reaction to, parents and family expectations. It is exciting to think about the option of change, as well as frightening to think about the possibility of losing oneself. It is almost always disorienting, as exemplified by the comments of this Mills College sophomore:

> When I was first at school I felt like I was floating. I kept having to remind myself who I was—what my name was, where I was from. I felt like I always had to explain this is my name, what I do, who I am. I needed to assert this all the time. With all these strangers it was so discouraging; I had to start all over again. Everything I had in Memphis didn't matter. It took me several weeks to realize that who I was hadn't really changed. If I just went on living normally, people would discover who I am. I didn't have to keep putting it out like it was my résumé.

A University of Rochester student from Omaha recalls:

> In high school I was quiet and mild mannered. People saw
> me as an athlete and a scholar. My good friends saw the
> outgoing side of me, the clown, but that was reserved for
> them. It was fun coming to Rochester. A whole new
> beginning. Nobody knew Liza from Omaha and so I could
> start out any way I wanted. I could be the clown or stay in
> my shell. I thought, If I want to make college something
> I'll remember, I want to meet as many people as possible
> and especially in the first week. It was a fresh start. I could
> have my own identity here. No stereotypes were attached
> and everyone was in the same boat. We were all academic
> type people, and there had to be someone to break the ice
> and provide comic relief, which I did.

And a freshman from Haverford explains:

> When I got to school, I decided to use my real name,
> Amelia. It's a name most people don't have, and it's more
> sophisticated than Amy. Amy had served me well when I
> wanted to blend into the woodwork. I thought I would be
> happy if I could bring Amy, but call her Amelia.

The issue of identity is predominant as freshmen find ways to present themselves to each other. Having left family and long-standing
friends behind, they are anxious to make connections that will
begin to fill the void. Some immediately create their own Web
pages, colorful and imaginative representations of their persona on-
line.

They also communicate who they are by how they dress and what
they do, by the music they play and the way they decorate their
rooms. Most students plug in their radios or stereos before they even
unpack. The music they select blares into the hall, a communiqué to
passersby. It is an introduction, a way to break the ice, an excuse to
wander in—a common language, drawing together like-minded

admirers. It also fills this alien space with familiar sounds that entertained and soothed them back home.

Throughout their rooms, students scatter bits and pieces of home,
a reminder to themselves and a message to others. Pictures of family
and friends and pets, beloved stuffed animals, posters, and yearbooks
take their places of honor. Even those who were miserable in high
school or whose home life is precarious tend to bring some tangible
part of their past for display.

Roommates stack up their beds double-decker style or take them
apart and put mattresses on the floor. They build lofts and hang
kites from the ceiling. Some strive for a white wicker and green
plant look; others for '60s retro with Indian spreads and incense.
One way or another, they create an ambience and put their personal
stamp on rooms formerly devoid of character.

Roommates who do this together face their first challenge: two
strangers making the kinds of decisions usually reserved for intimate
friends or couples. As they make plans about space and supplies and
decor, they may have their first disagreements. These initial difficulties are a chance for them to begin to learn about accommodating
each other's needs, about standing up for themselves and engaging
in the art of compromise. Through dealing with each other they
begin to develop skills that they will use in many other situations.
And as the transformation of the room takes place, they also begin
to build the bond between them; they feel more competent and
independent. Parents who intervene and take charge of setting up
the room before they leave unwittingly deprive their children of an
important opportunity, more important by far than the perfect rug
and matching bedspreads.

Whether the formal orientation period lasts a day or a week, most
upperclassmen look back on that time and smile at how naive,
scared, and hyper they were. Emotions tend to be at a peak and
change from moment to moment.

There are countless triumphs and defeats as students navigate the
first few days of college life. They feel pulled in different directions.
They suffer bouts of loneliness and homesickness, doubting that all
these new people will ever measure up to their dearest friends at

home. Everyone else looks happy and secure; it will take time to develop friendships and to find out that others share their feelings. Freshmen may enjoy the camaraderie and sociability of constant activities and impromptu get-togethers, but worry about how they will ever have privacy and time alone in such close quarters. Many liken it to summer camp. Others remark incredulously that their fellow classmates "act like high school kids."

Students find themselves suddenly responsible for "grown-up" tasks: arranging for a telephone, opening a bank account, interviewing for work-study jobs. As one young woman put it, "All of a sudden I feel like I have to be independent. I feel like my parents. I feel old. The child is gone in a second."

Even the hallowed collegiate rituals are confusing to a freshman who as yet has no context in which to place them. A freshman walks out of the convocation ceremony, where the provost has spoken, turns to his roommate, and asks, "What's a provost?" His roommate shrugs his shoulders. Another watches with disbelief as a procession of faculty dressed in academic regalia streams into the somber chapel; she whispers to the student next to her, "Do you think these people are our teachers?" Later another student quips, "I wonder what we should call them. Professor? Doctor? Your Majesty? Hey you?" And a student at Brown recalls:

> We have these gates at Brown. They're only opened twice, once at convocation and once at graduation. At convocation, the first day of classes, we all file through these gates in rows. I did it barefoot; I couldn't resist. There we are, all the freshmen with no idea what is going on. Some administrator I don't know is telling me what to do. It seemed impersonal and strange. There were all these people giving talks we had to listen to and we're the ones who don't know them. It was all done as if they were doing it for our own good, but it had no meaning to us.

Some students become so absorbed in the euphoria and intensity of their new lives that promises to call or write home are temporarily forgotten. They lose track of time, and when they do think about calling it's 2 A.M. or their roommate is on the phone. As one college dean told a group of parents, "If your children don't call home for a week or so, it probably means that they are busy, healthy, and haven't run out of money yet." Some students, though, call a lot in the beginning—perhaps even daily. They may want to talk about everything that is happening, or they may simply want to hear a parent's voice yet offer little information or insight in return. Occasionally, they tell just enough to set parents on edge. A Trinity student called home breathlessly a few hours after her arrival in San Antonio to report, "I'm in love with the guy who gave me a ride from the airport!"

DISORIENTATION: PARENTS' FIRST FEW WEEKS AT HOME

Of course, the world at home hasn't remained completely stable. A child's departure always has an impact on the parents who are left behind. Some feel the jolt at the moment of parting. Others find themselves reacting after the fact, their feelings taking them by surprise.

During the weeks before his son's departure, the father of a Lawrence University freshman had been trying to console his wife, who was having a difficult time. He repeatedly told her that she should focus on the positive aspect of the upcoming event, that they had been preparing their son for this day for eighteen years and now it was time for him to leave. He urged her to think of this as a time for celebration, for after all, they had a terrific son who was going off to a fine school. It was all very logical. But after they dropped their son off at Lawrence and were heading back home on the interstate, his wife looked over at him and noticed his tear-streaked face. He describes that unexpected moment:

> I guess it didn't really hit me till then. I did feel really good about Kurt and about the experience I think he's going to have at Lawrence. But there was no way around it. We had just been through a passage, and I started thinking about the stage of life I'm in—that I just turned

50 and my mother is an old woman who can no longer share in this joy and that an important part of my life is coming to an end. My wife and I spent the next three hours driving through the cornfields, reminiscing about Kurt—both of us alternately laughing and crying.

A mother of three found that each child's leaving was different. She remembers most vividly the departure of her third:

The last was the most difficult. In some ways it surprised me. I have a ritual—after they leave, I change the sheets and clean up their room. Jossie, the youngest, left a long, sentimental note and I found it under her pillow. I wept.

There are many factors that affect parents' reactions—their own marital status, the size of the family, the birth order of the child, how pleasant he or she was to have around. Most parents feel mixed emotions after they have sent a child off to college. It is a bittersweet time of excitement and nostalgia, of weighing and evaluating gains and losses. Waves of feeling tend to emerge and recede at unpredictable times, when walking past a daughter's uncharacteristically neat bedroom or glancing at her baby picture on the wall, after a son's telephone calls or long-awaited letters describing his new friends. One father whose son and last child had gone to the University of Denver told of leaving a pair of his son's old track shoes in the front hall for weeks to ease the hollowness he felt whenever he came home from work.

In a newsletter to parents of high school seniors, Barbara Kohm, a school principal in Clayton, Missouri, writes her impressions after her last child left for college:

I love the freedom my husband and I enjoy, and I love the quiet orderliness of a clean house. I love having my car to myself, and I love having the radio permanently set on the classical music station.

At the same time, I miss the exciting confusion that the children and their friends provided. I miss the dinner

table discussions about parties, poetry, politics, and
English assignments and the silly songs we sang as we did
the dishes. I even miss helping them solve problems
although my memory may be a little fuzzy here. I'm ready
to go out to dinner more and to cook less, but I'm not sure
I'm ready to have my primary parenting years behind me.

What hurts the most is that for twenty-five years I've
thought of motherhood as my main job. Now that job is
reduced to a weekly phone call and an occasional piece of
advice—although even that isn't needed very often. I
have a hunch that this bittersweet rush of mixed emotions
will never entirely go away, that it will linger for the rest
of my life, not as an irritant, but as a reminder of the real
depth and meaning of life.

Many women, including those who have long-standing, demanding careers, share this feeling that being a mother has been their primary role, and the bonds that they have formed with their children
often make the separation process more difficult for them than they
had anticipated. When her own daughter left for college, Pulitzer
prize-winning columnist Ellen Goodman wrote:

A long time ago, I thought that mothers who also had
work that engaged their time and energy might avoid the
cliché of an empty-nest syndrome. A child's departure
once meant a mother's forced retirement from her only
job. Many of us assumed that work would help protect us
from that void. Now I doubt it.

Those of us who have worked two shifts, lived two
roles, have no less investment in our identity as parents,
no less connection to our children. No less love. No less
sense of loss.

Tomorrow, for the first time in 18 years, the part of my
brain that is always calculating time—school time, work
time, dinner time—can let go of its stopwatch. The part of
me that is as attuned to a child's schedule and needs as it is

to a baby's cry in the night will no longer be operative. I don't know how easy it will be to unplug.[1]

For single parents, a child's leaving may be particularly poignant. A divorced woman who holds a high-level position in a major corporation describes the change in her home life:

> Eliot and his sister have been the focus of my family life for more than ten years. Eliot's father took him to college, so I missed out on all of that. I tried to get my former husband to describe everything to me, but that didn't work. His values and perceptions are so different from mine (that's what split us up in the first place) that when I'd say things like "How's the dorm room?" he'd say, "It's messy!" That's not what I wanted to know. Anyhow, the weekend after Eliot left, I cleaned out the garage. I kept imagining Eliot's voice. I kept expecting to turn around and hear him say, "Hey, Mom, it's looking good," in that characteristic way of his.

Just as the freshmen are orienting themselves to the college world they have entered, their families back home are changing old patterns and finding ways to adjust to the new configuration their own world has suddenly taken. Siblings' relationships change; the threesome that was always a study in shifting alliances becomes a united duo. A father suddenly finds himself the only male in a family of women; he'd never thought about his daughter's common bond with his wife before. A divorced mother finds herself living alone for the first time in her life; she alternately revels in her freedom and weeps at the solitude. A couple look at each other across the dinner table night after night, wondering what is left of their marriage or cherishing the opportunity to talk at last without interruption. The only child still at home challenges her parents not to be boring—to pay more attention to her now that a favorite brother is no longer there to joke and commiserate with her.

While parents are struggling with a sense of loss, a younger sibling may rejoice at the possibility of her new position in the family. A Los Angeles woman smiles as she recalls what happened the day after her first daughter left for the University of California at Santa Barbara:

> The next morning I got up very early and was engrossed in typing a long letter to Molly, trying to tell her all the things I'd forgotten to say, without letting on how much I missed her. I felt very emotional, crying as I was writing. Suddenly, the bedroom door opened and in bounced Beth, my youngest, dressed totally in Molly's clothes!

In many households, as soon as the departing child walks out the door, the rest of the family scrambles for the space that's suddenly available. Brothers and sisters who have shared rooms grab the chance to have one of their own. Empty nests are replaced with newly redecorated studies or exercise rooms filled with the latest equipment. Parents may later be surprised when their children are hurt or angry at finding their rooms redone or taken over; their reaction seems out of sync with their self-proclaimed independence. But when everything else is changing in their lives, their room and all their childhood memorabilia represent grounding and continuity. Clearly, cordoning off an underutilized room in an overcrowded apartment or house is impractical. But it is the wise parent who discusses these changes with sensitivity *before* they are carried out.

The period of launching children typically coincides with the normal developmental issues of middle age. Parents of college-age children are often concerned about elderly parents; they may be caught in the middle, assuming financial responsibility for parents at the same time that they are taking on the burden of college tuition. There is anxiety about finances, both present and future. Women are approaching or going though menopause. No longer taking their health for granted, men or women become more concerned about staying fit and taking care of themselves. Stimulated in part by the excitement and possiblity of their child's new adventure, they may be reevaluating their own careers, thinking about switching gears, about increasing or decreasing work or community commitments. Or they may be coming face-to-face with their own limitations and letting go of long-held dreams. The changes implicit in a child's leaving for college may heighten parents' awareness of other changes in their lives, and although still in home territory, they often feel a sense of disorientation themselves.

And so at a time when children may be checking back for the reassurance of the routine and familiar, family members may be feeling shaky and off balance as they shift to accommodate the loss of one member. On the home front, senses are heightened and emotions more raw, swinging between elation and deep sadness as the reality of the loss becomes evident in the routines of an ordinary day—unconsciously setting the table for four when only three sit down for dinner, hearing the silence of an evening without the abrasive interruptions of the phone ringing, suddenly aware of the freed-up Saturdays that had been spent watching high school football games.

Young men and women ask for little more at this time than a steady and rooted home base to return to, just as they had many years ago when they hurried back from their adventures across the playground to find Mom and Dad sitting on the park bench where they left them. To provide this sanctuary and still stay out of the way is an artful balancing act. It requires sensitivity to the often confusing dynamics of separation and to the long journey the freshman has begun.

7

THE FRESHMAN YEAR

Academic Life and the College Scene

THE ACADEMIC YEAR ON COLLEGE AND UNIVERSITY campuses has its own predictable rhythm, but that rhythm—the markers and intervals—may be quite different from the one parents and children have grown used to at home. As parents pull sweaters out of mothballs, feeling renewed and invigorated by the clarity of cool autumn weather, their freshman sons and daughters may be approaching midterms, feeling especially jittery and vulnerable as they prepare for the first tangible measure of their college work. Campus traditions and rituals become part of the fabric of students' lives: fraternity and sorority rush, fall break, homecoming, winter carnival, registration for the next term, housing selection, reading period, and finals.

The particular markers and their exact timing vary from school to school, and the reactions to these events vary from student to student. But within all this variation there is a common flow, common rituals and patterns that pervade college campuses at particular times of the year. And since the campus environment is different from home, with different priorities and different cycles, it is no wonder that parents and children sometimes feel out of sync when they talk to each other across the miles from their separate worlds.

TO EVERY SEASON: THE RHYTHM OF THE FRESHMAN YEAR

During the first few weeks of school, the frenetic pace set during orientation continues. Classes begin, teachers are sized up, and students approach the freshly printed syllabus for each course with good intentions and high expectations for success. They may shop for courses, sitting in on numerous classes before they actually finalize their schedules. Trying to integrate their own impressions with the collected wisdom of their advisor and the upperclassmen they talk to, freshmen often drop and add courses until a cutoff date forces them to make their first academic commitments. They tend to want certainty, perhaps believing that if they search long enough, they will find the perfect courses and the perfect schedule. "It was so confusing that first semester," recalls a current junior:

> When I came to school, my advisor told me to look at the catalog and just pick my courses. She told me I could drop and add later. I was already having enough trouble just having all these choices in that huge catalog. I just wanted somebody to tell me what to do. Telling me that I could change my mind made it even worse. I was holding onto an old high school idea that you can't change your mind, that if you start something you have to finish it. And if I changed, I'd be responsible for that change, and what if I didn't make the right choice?

Beyond the classroom, freshmen are faced with an explosion of activity: parties and sporting events, concerts and plays, and a tempting array of extracurricular organizations all trying to lure freshmen recruits—not to mention a seemingly endless series of impromptu get-togethers as students wander from room to room in the residence halls, listening to music together and talking and wondering how they will ever get any work done.

Everything is new—exciting or frightening, overwhelming or stimulating. Some students thrive on the onslaught of activity and choices, hyper but happy with the overstimulation. Others seem bewildered and overwhelmed and retreat into bouts of homesickness and self-doubt. Students' reactions to school tend to be intense during these early weeks: they either love it or hate it or alternate between the two extremes, sometimes during the same day, sometimes even during the same phone call home. Almost unanimously, they complain about the institutional food, announcing that they can't find anything edible except salad and pizza.

Three or four weeks into the semester, freshmen tend to settle down a bit, to come to the realization that this is not just, as one student put it, "summer camp with homework," and that they have made a long-term commitment. It is often a sobering time:

> I suddenly realized that I was staying—that this wasn't like camp or a vacation from home, that this was real life, and I got a funny sort of feeling. I had been swept along by the excitement of it, and I hadn't really let it sink in that this was now my home.

This realization may evoke homesickness from students who were euphoric during the first few weeks. Many reach out to high school friends at other schools, and they wonder whether they will ever find comparable friends at college. E-mail, phone calls, and even visits from campus to campus are common attempts to establish continuity in an ever-changing period of transition.

One student from Seattle at a small Pennsylania college decorated his home page on the World Wide Web with photos of the San Juan Islands and his beloved dog, a visual introduction to his list of:

Things I Miss

- My family
- My friends from back home
- My dog, Wolf
- Gourmet food
- Gourmet coffee, including lattés, mochas, and the like
- The words *phat*, *hella*, *filthy*, *fresh*, and *bomb*

- Water
- I really miss coffee . . .

Things I Don't Miss

- Having to drive places
- Living near none of my friends
- Crappy classrooms
- Unfriendly people
- The drug dealers across the street from my house
- The Seahawks

Students who were overwhelmed and homesick at first may find comfort in the familiarity they are beginning to feel with people and places and the day-to-day rhythms of life in college. They have taken the first of many steps in the year-long freshman task of finding a niche.

As classwork progresses, idealized expectations of intense intellectual discussions in the local coffee house give way to solitary sessions in the library or bouts of boredom in the classroom. Freshmen discover that long stretches of daytime with no classes and no assignments due the next day make it easy to succumb to the temptation to sleep late and watch *All My Children* on the lounge TV or sit in front of their computer playing Tetris. For some, serious studying is limited to the middle of the night, the only time when, along with the brightness of daylight, the distractions temporarily disappear. Others find themselves filling every available hour studying, often inefficiently plowing through what appears to be an endless amount of reading, unable to decide when they are allowed to take time out to play.

During this second month of school, social life may also start to be tempered a bit as the pace slows down. First impressions begin to fade, and students who were wary at first learn that they can live together in spite of different backgrounds, values, or tastes in music and wall posters. Students who formed instant friendships during the first few weeks of school may find that the novelty and comfort of those relationships are starting to wear thin. The roommate who had been a constant companion during mealtimes and sojourns to the library may now seem more like a leech who never seems to be out of the room and whose obsessive neatness is nerve-racking. No longer treating each other with the tolerance accorded strangers, roommates often have their first major disagreements at this time of the year, and complaints to residential life staff about roommate problems inevitably increase. Students gravitate toward loosely formed groups in their search for companionship and a sense of community. Most are still wondering just where they will fit in.

As the semester approaches its halfway point, first major papers are due and midterms are scheduled, and an air of tension envelops most campuses. Students move across diagonal pathways to and from libraries, labs, studios, and computer centers, heads down, faces serious—even somber, carrying the weight of several academic texts in the ubiquitous backpack. Many freshmen pull their first all-nighter during this time, a rite of passage—a time of desperately seeking to reclaim the many hours that seem to have disappeared during the previous weeks. They spend an inordinate amount of time studying and worrying about studying. Not surprisingly, the campus health service treats a constant stream of exhausted students complaining of sore throats, colds, and the flu. And the counseling service readies itself for the onslaught of students who are trying to cope with the psychological stresses that predictably emerge during this pressured time.

The aftermath of the first set of midterms often evokes a period of intense self-doubt. Students who sailed along effortlessly in high school may be shocked to realize that the success they had come to take for granted is no longer necessarily going to be theirs. The first failing grade, or even a C in a course, can be an affront to the confidence of many students, especially when their identity has been tied to their academic prowess. They may even start worrying that the admissions office made a mistake in accepting them and begin to think, This is the wrong school for me. Premeds who encounter a disappointing grade in biology or chemistry may panic and question their whole future.

Some students breathe a sigh of relief when they see the results of midterms. Intimidated by war stories from parents and high school teachers suggesting that they will no longer be able to get A's and B's when they reach college, those who continue to do well feel the satisfaction of getting past the first academic hurdle of their college career. Whether or not their initial academic ventures have been successful, once they have moved beyond the midsemester point, most students begin to see the differences between the demands of high school work and the more sophisticated academic challenges of college. And at this point some of them begin to make the adjustments necessary for their academic success.

By late October, students start to talk eagerly about their Thanksgiving holiday plans. Some feel homesick for the first time. In numerous parts of the country, November brings signs of gloomy wintry weather, adding to the anticipation of the upcoming holiday and a break from campus life. For children of divorced families, the question of where to go for Thanksgiving often resurrects painful family conflicts and questions of allegiance. Some students who don't go home for the vacation struggle with an outbreak of homesickness, missing the familiar traditions of this family-oriented holiday. Others delight in the opportunity to be independent and try something different, whether it is a visit to a roommate's home, a trip to a nearby city, or cooking turkey with friends for the very first time.

Although many students can't wait to get home, once they arrive and check to see that the refrigerator is stocked and the old place looks pretty much the same, they are out the door for an extended round of visits to high school friends. Trying to explain their new worlds to each other, students begin to realize how much has happened to them in the few months since they left home. With the excitement of reunions and rounds of parties, it is often a confusing and disorienting time.

In spite of the brevity of their time at home, some students take this opportunity to let their parents know that college is changing them. As they try on different identities, students may surprise their parents with new hairstyles, modes of dress, accents, or food preferences. One bemused mother recounts:

> Three months ago, all Tim would eat was spaghetti, ham-
> burgers, and fries. When he came home for Thanksgiving
> I fixed all his favorite foods only to find out that all he
> wanted was tofu and brown rice.

Most students return to campus from Thanksgiving break to face several weeks of intense work, culminating in their first set of final exams. "It's hit-the-wall time," explained one student. "It can feel pretty grim in spite of all the campus preholiday traditions and hoopla. We all show up at these Christmas get-togethers tired as hell. But of course we manage to squeeze in our share of partying too."

As the days before winter break come closer, students plow through long hours of studying and writing final papers, trying to hold themselves together until the long-awaited holiday. Freshmen have a foot in both worlds, immersed in their studies and new college friends while fantasizing about going home, being taken care of, and reconnecting with old friends from high school.

Most students want nothing more than some time out when they arrive home for winter break. Parents are often dismayed by their first glimpse of their exam-weary son or daughter, with dark circles under red-rimmed eyes and ten pounds heavier—or lighter—than usual. The typically energetic freshman is likely to want to sleep or "veg out" in front of the TV for a few days and consume as much food as possible. Parents, meanwhile, energized by the hustle and bustle of the holiday season, may want their son or daughter to get moving, to participate actively in long-established family traditions. They may even feel angry at this apparent inertia and cynically question why they are spending so much money on education if these are the results. For a while, at this particular juncture, the rhythms of the calendar and academic years seem markedly mismatched.

Winter break is a much-needed refueling time for students. It is also a time that stirs up for parents and their temporarily returned off-spring new struggles over separation and letting go. Students often make emphatic attempts to assert their independence and establish their emerging identity. Coming home night after night at 4 A.M., sporting multiple earrings and multicolored hair are some of the more visible manifestations. There are, of course, deeper and more subtle pushes and pulls, as students test values and limits and new ideas in the context of old, familiar ground. Students struggle too with questions of intimacy, wondering if their new college friendships are truly meaningful and at the same time questioning if they will be able to, or want to, maintain their old friendships at home.

When the winter break is over and students return to school, the residence halls are filled with the excitement of coming together again. Animated meetings and greetings, warm reunions among friends and roommates, and eager attempts to catch up with each others' worlds are in telling contrast to the hesitant, self-conscious arrival on campus of this same group of freshmen the previous fall. For many students, this is the moment of recognition that they actually belong to a community, that this place has become a focal point in their lives. For some, it feels like coming home. They have finally begun to believe that the place is theirs.

■

As they settle into the rhythm of the second semester, many students thrive on the comfort of knowing the ropes, of knowing where things are and who does what. They are often beginning to see their college friends as their close friends; many are giving up the illusion of the perfect high school group. They approach their course work with a newfound confidence. Although still wavering in their attempts to manage time, they have learned something about pacing themselves and setting priorities. The sense of urgency and anxiety they felt first semester is replaced with the satisfaction of having more control over their lives, and as one student put it, "knowing what I have to do and what I can get away with."

Some students, however, feel let down and homesick when second semester begins. They may find it hard to readjust after being at home, comfortable and secure, with few responsibilities. The long list of academic demands looms ahead of them, and still feeling burned out from first semester, they wonder if they can survive the same cycle of papers and tests all over again. Those who did not do well first semester often feel a combination of self-doubt and determination to do better. Many students rethink their initial plans. Premeds often question their choice as they plunge into the second round of courses in a rigorous curriculum. During this period, freshman deans hear from a lot of students who are thinking about transferring. Feeling lonely or perhaps uncommitted to anything at the school, students worry that they have made the wrong college choice. Some send away for catalogs and applications to other schools. Others make their first commitment to an activity outside the classroom, taking another step toward creating a niche for themselves.

In many parts of the country, the first two or three months of the semester coincide with dreary winter weather. Not surprisingly, students' moods often plunge with the temperature. This is the time of year in most schools when students have to make sophomore housing plans; they decide who they are going to live with and where they want to be. As they scramble to pair up or form groups of four or six for suites and apartments, inevitably some students end up feeling left out and unwanted. Midterms, which usually come at a particularly bleak time of the year, only exacerbate the situation. Most schools in cold climates plan special events and festivals to counter the frigid weather. And many students head south for a respite and the time-honored tradition of fun in the sun during spring break. Others use this vacation time to explore summer job opportunities and set up interviews in their hometowns.

When spring finally arrives on campus, the social pace picks up in earnest. Students revel in their access to the outdoors, and impromptu Frisbee games, concerts, and parties pop up all over campus. This can be a wonderful time for students who are comfortable in their friendships or who have found romance. But for some, spring can trigger feelings of intense loneliness. As couples pair off, those who are unattached see a tableau of their classmates walking hand in hand amidst inviting greenery. It looks as though everyone is in love and carefree, making it all the more difficult for the many students who are neither.

Most freshmen agree that the second semester goes by more quickly than the first, and before they know it the end is in sight. They have a pile of papers to write, exams to study for, and a host of decisions to make: Do I store my things here or ship them home?

How am I going to get home? And then there are the concerns about how to finance next year's college expenses and what to do during the summer. Students flock to the financial aid office in search of the latest information on available money and to the placement office in search of summer jobs.

For most, the academic year ends with rushed good-byes and promises to friends to keep in touch over the summer. As soon as they have finished their last exam, tired and bedraggled students throw their belongings into suitcases and storage boxes. They depart a few at a time over the course of several days, in a very different fashion from their simultaneous and emotion-filled arrival the previous August or September. The last to go find themselves wandering through quiet hallways and lifeless rooms, perhaps realizing more than most how much their feelings about college are intertwined with their fellow students.

For many, the decision to go home for the summer raises familiar issues about separation, as well as independence, identity, and intimacy. Is it possible to go home and maintain a newfound, but still shaky, sense of independence? Is it feasible to hold on to a separate emerging identity and not fall back into the role of family peacemaker or jester or superstar? What will it be like to separate and leave behind intimate college friends, or a lover who is a constant companion?

Some students decide that they don't want to spend the summer at home. They may get jobs near the campus, surrounded by friends who have made a similar choice, all hoping to enjoy the college environment without the pressure of academic demands. Or they may choose to work abroad or at a resort far from home. Parents who had been looking forward to their child's return are often disturbed by such decisions, and it may be hard for them to accept that their child wants and needs this opportunity. Once again parents are challenged to let go.

By the time summer vacation rolls around, college freshmen have been away at school for approximately nine months. Their sense of time is likely to be very different from that of their parents. As one freshman put it, "Every day goes by so fast, but it feels like I've been here forever." They have met a whole new set of people; they have struggled with new ideas and knowledge and values. There have been countless firsts in all arenas of their lives. "My world has exploded," said a 19-year-old from Minneapolis. "There are so many new elements—I find it hard to figure out where my parents fit back into that."

In the context of parents' lifetimes, nine months have been but a moment, and in comparison to the universe of their college student offspring, their's has remained relatively stable. Fitting back in is a given; parents expect their child to have matured, to be more reasonable, more considerate, and to tell Mom and Dad where he or she is going each night and for how long. Their child's idea of independence is that he or she be trusted, left alone, and not accountable. The freshman year has ended, and the family has come together again, if only for a while. So much has changed; so much has stayed the same.

◼

To follow the sequence of the freshman year from fall to summer in a linear fashion captures the peaks and valleys of the year, but misses the complexity of any given time. Simultaneously trying to adapt to academic demands, new social relationships, and the freedom and responsibility of the campus scene, college freshmen are deluged throughout the year with challenging experiences in all domains of their lives. The combined effect is more than the sum of the parts. Students don't have the luxury of compartmentalizing the challenges they face, or handling them sequentially. It is not possible to wait until homesickness is conquered, the roommate problem is resolved, and the noise and excessive drinking in the hall settle down before tackling the first big chemistry exam. Students have to try to handle everything all at once, and through the course of the year most of them do.

Yet, for parents to understand more about what the freshman is going through, it helps to examine separately each of the central elements of the freshman experience: academic life, friendship and social life, and today's campus scene.

ACADEMIC LIFE: THE FRESHMAN PERSPECTIVE

Paradoxically, the area of a college freshman's life that parents are the most interested in is the one students may speak of least. To transmit in writing or a phone call the excitement of new learning or the heady feeling after a provocative seminar with a talented professor is difficult at best. Moreover, for many students the academic side of life has been too closely associated with grades and expectations. A parent's question, "How is your English class?" may be heard as "How are you doing in your English class?" or "Are you keeping up with the work in your English class?" As a result, a student may cut off the conversation with an abrupt "Fine" and move on to less threatening subjects.

Some students are turned on by their courses and long to share their excitement with their parents. Parents who give them the opportunity speak of discovering in their children a new and previously untapped curiosity about art or politics, philosophy or physics. Some students call home and spill forth their delight in a particularly brilliant lecture by a favorite professor or their first glimpse of the connections between renaissance art and literature.

When a parent responds seriously or in jest by saying "What can you do with art history to put bread on the table?" or a student even senses that a parent's thoughts may be moving in that direction, the conversation turns flat and the wind is knocked out of the student's sails. But parents who set a tone of openness and interest, who reflect the enthusiasm they hear and ask for more details, may be rewarded by hearing about the best that college has to offer.

Questions such as "What's your favorite class? Tell me about it," "What are you reading? What's the professor like?" convey the message "I'm genuinely interested. I want to know what your new world is like, what you are learning, how you are maturing, and I appreciate you discovering your own interests, opinions, and strengths. I value your intellectual development and growing independence."

Parents can participate in a student's experience in other ways that show they care. One student who discovered women writers during her freshman year recalled:

I read *The Awakening* and just loved it, and when I told my
mom she went and got it and read it too, and we had this
great discussion about it at Thanksgiving break.

Many students assert their independence by holding on to their
new discoveries, however, protecting their new turf and emerging
self from any infringement by family—perhaps fearing the pull back
to an earlier, more passive academic self. Spending an evening discussing the pros and cons of environmental regulation or public
funding for the arts can be exhilarating extensions of classroom
learning—cherished private moments with fellow students. To question, to challenge, to explore established values are crucial steps in
the educational process. But these new ideas are still unformed, and
to share them with parents may open them up to criticism or scorn.
The freshman daughter of two New York attorneys explains:

> I was brought up with the idea that you have to be able to
> back up your opinion with logical arguments, even about
> small things. So now, when I'm changing my opinions
> about things I think are important, like politics and art,
> I'm not ready to talk to my parents about it yet. It's not
> that they'll jump down my throat or anything. I just want
> to be clearer about what I think so I can talk to them on a
> more equal level.

Students frequently appreciate it when their parents express
interest in their academic life, and it is not unusual to hear students
complain about parents who fail to do so. But no matter how
well-meaning and interested parents are, some will discover that
their children do not want to talk about their courses. They want
their parents to respect their need to keep this and other parts of
their lives to themselves.

Not all students will find all, or perhaps any, of their freshman
classes intellectually stimulating. A scenario familiar to many parents is one that starts with a student's phone call home complaining
about one or more courses. Parents may have an instinctive reac-

tion: they may be angry—at the child or the school; they may be disappointed; they may worry that their child is at the wrong school or taking the wrong courses; they may resent complaints when they are making sacrifices and spending so much money. The reality is that parents know little about what is actually going on and can't fix it no matter how much they wish they could. What parents can do is listen empathically and encourage their son or daughter to think of ways to improve a less-than-perfect situation. They might encourage the student to talk to an advisor or to the professor directly and to begin investigating the course options for next semester.

Whether or not they talk to their parents about the academic side of their freshman experience, freshmen all struggle in one way or another with the gaps between expectation and reality. Initially, they may walk into intimidating surroundings, ranging from cavernous lecture halls where they are sentenced to anonymity to small seminar rooms where there is no place to hide. The professor, who the view book suggested would be a friendly sort who would get to know you on a first-name basis, may instead be a distant figure standing behind a lectern and speaking into a microphone.

A Cornell student wrote in a parent newsletter about a freshman class she had attended "where the overflow of students went downstairs to watch the lecture being broadcast simultaneously on a special circuited television—Psychology 101—to more than 1600 students." And a freshman at Emory said, "Big classes were a real shock. You're nobody, not even a face, to the professor. In high school people knew who I was."

Large lecture classes are usually interspersed with small discussion sections led by TAs (teaching assistants), most of whom teach to support their graduate work, which is their first priority. A Berkeley senior recalled the first class she attended her freshman year: "I knew I was in trouble when I went to calculus and the teacher didn't speak English." Foreign graduate student TAs, whose command of English is limited, may be the only available resource to people in a large, popular introductory freshman course.

This situation is by no means unique to Berkeley. A survey conducted for the Mathematical Association of America revealed that

45 percent of the total number of classes in leading math departments are taught by TAs or part-timers, and one-third of math TAs are foreign-born. More than half of the foreign-born TAs at a well-respected midwestern engineering school failed a spoken English exam. Though many schools are now taking steps to ensure that their TAs have adequate language skills, the fact remains that a disgruntled student who complains about not being able to understand the teacher may be dealing with a real and common problem. Although a parent's instinct may be to get angry along with the student, it is more useful to acknowledge his or her anger and then turn to brainstorming some ways to cope with the problem. Students may decide to seek help from upperclassmen or fellow students or to get a tutor from the campus learning center. The student will have to be resourceful to find the best possible way to make the most of the situation, and it is helpful if parents encourage and support that resourcefulness rather than try to take over the problem.

Not all freshman classes are so impersonal. Even large schools such as Cornell and UCLA offer freshman seminars with as few as fifteen students. Although designed to introduce freshmen to the process of intellectual inquiry in an intimate and nonthreatening way, this format can be frightening in its own right. Many students find these small classes intellectually challenging and personally warm and inviting, but the expectation to participate in class is intimidating to some. The atmosphere of open inquiry and multiple points of view can be confusing for the less intellectually developed student who is searching for the right answer, and may conclude that "It's better not to say anything unless it's something brilliant."

Occasionally, freshman seminars are taught by the stars of the faculty. At Princeton, full professors teach these small seminars, attracted by the enthusiasm and openness of first-year students. David Schoem, Assistant Dean for Undergraduate Education at the University of Michigan, expresses the delights of working with his first-year seminar on Jewish identity:

> Freshmen are very passionate. They really want to learn and
> find out answers and think through questions. It's their first

taste of college. In that sense, it's very exciting. They have not been intellectually socialized as to how the discipline thinks about issues, so they bring a whole range of questions.[1]

A University of Michigan freshman, an Indian student born and raised in Zambia, describes her freshman seminar, "Writing about Cultural Communities, Ethnicity, and Imposed Categories." As part of her course work, she explored her own aspirations and background, and the seminar became a transformative experience for her:

Every time I wrote, I realized the people who had influenced me. By the end of the course, I felt a sense of wholeness. I knew I'd had all these experiences, but I never realized that's what I really am.

At some schools, such as Grinnell, every student participates in a freshman tutorial designed to develop research and writing skills. Freshman seminars are often noted for their innovative topics or interdisciplinary approaches to more traditional fare: "Freedom and Authority," "Cross-Cultural Views of Adolescence," "Contemporary Civil Rights Movements," to name just a few. Many schools have adopted a course model known as University 101, developed by John N. Gardner at the University of South Carolina. These classes are designed to introduce freshmen to skills and resources that ease the transition from high school to college. It's not unusual for these seminars to become an important part of the student's life, evolving into a support group, an anchor of sorts for the freshman who feels adrift in an otherwise turbulent academic and social sea.

Opportunities for freshmen to take courses unavailable in high school are enticing—anthropology, philosophy, astronomy, management, marketing, communications, engineering graphics—a smorgasbord of new academic treats. But for some, the course title that suggested an unknown, exotic realm in actuality turns out to be a bore. "*This* is philosophy?" one student moaned after three weeks of reading Plato. Somehow philosophy had brought to mind groups of eager and intense students questioning the meaning of life—*their* life, not Plato's.

And introductory psychology classes are filled with young men and women who had anticipated dealing with the complexities of their own fascinating developing psyches, only to find themselves studying color wheels to learn about perception or mazes and rats to learn about conditioning. "What about people?" they lament. Typically, the introductory courses are just that—introductions to the basics of a discipline, exposing students to the inevitable frustrations that accompany first encounters with challenging materials.

"All classes look great in the catalog, but what goes on in the classroom is another story," sighed a cynical freshman two weeks before finals. His harsh comment can be attributed, in part, to his negative frame of mind at the time, but there is more than a hint of truth in his remark. All students learn that even the most wonderful courses have moments of tedium, that you have to memorize symbols and data and struggle with new methodology before you can use them creatively.

Most freshmen are surprised and confused by the level of sophistication that their professors expect from them. Moving beyond the more literal mode of high school, they are expected in college to be able to present and support complex arguments. Students who arrive at college secure in their ability to read and write well find that now they are being asked to read more actively than they did in the past and to write not just reports, but analyses. They struggle with learning how to think and write critically, how to synthesize material, how to make connections between facts and theories and between different concepts in different courses. Many of them find it very difficult to make the connections; others are excited by these new demands.

A Cal Tech sophomore recalls:

> The problems in math and physics were on a different level, a higher level than what I was used to. The problems were much more intricate. You had to know the principles; you couldn't just go to a formula. It was frustrating but stimulating to see if you could achieve a new level.

Students discover that scholars disagree with each other and that they must begin to rely on their own opinions, supporting them

with coherent logical arguments. A brochure written for parents of
Cornell University students describes an important transition freshmen have to make:

> Students who knew how to produce the "right" answers in
> high school are often confused and frustrated to find that
> the techniques which helped them succeed in the past are
> no longer adequate. After the first round of prelims, they
> will wonder what the professor is "looking for." But some-
> how or other, they will have started learning how to learn.

Professor Linda Salamon, former Chairwoman of the Association
of American Colleges and Professor of English at George
Washington University, explains that this transition is at the heart
of the educational enterprise:

> The overall goal of the undergraduate education is to
> shake students out of complacency in the set of ideas and
> values with which they have grown and teach them a rel-
> ativistic view of the world—to teach them that there are a
> lot of different perspectives on any given subject, that the
> power of the intellect is to imagine a point of view, to cre-
> ate a perspective on an idea, and that the job of a young
> educated person is to have opinions of his or her own.

A dean of liberal arts describes a scenario she typically encounters
with freshmen:

> Three students came in to see me because they were
> unhappy with the grades they had received. They had
> been asked to keep a journal, giving their reactions to
> major texts in American literature that they had read—
> Thoreau, Melville, Emerson, Hawthorne. The professor
> had said, "It doesn't matter *what* your opinion is." He just
> wanted a reaction, a reasoned response. He had written on
> their journals such comments as: "Good idea, can you give

specific examples? What about the text gives you this opinion? Don't just say you don't like Transcendentalism. You have to engage the idea of Transcendentalism, and if you don't like it, that's fine, but you must do so on the basis of a reasoned argument."

We are trying to help the young see what argument is, what evidence is, how to support an opinion. This is our principal goal, whether it's taught in history or philosophy. We're teaching different subjects, but this is the constant subtext: a level of analysis and an understanding of where intellectual authority comes from—how to have confidence in your own views.

Professors who teach freshmen are often deluged with questions about procedures and expectations. "All students want direction," said one professor of political science. "Freshmen just want a lot more direction than the others. They want to be safe, to be sure they are doing things right. And they really expect that there is a right way and a wrong way to do everything."

Students may work industriously, putting in long hours spinning their wheels—often on the wrong track. They compare notes with their peers and reinforce each other's ignorance, raising each other's anxiety level as well. They study for tests, trying to memorize an overwhelming amount of facts and figures, often concentrating on the details without a grounding or conceptual understanding of the theory. This can be a disaster, particularly in the physical sciences. Students are often engaged in what one bemused provost calls "intellectual bulimia—stuffing themselves with volumes of factual material and then regurgitating it back for the professor, maintaining for themselves little of nutritional value."

Many freshmen complain about ambiguity, and about professors who do not follow the syllabus. No longer required to do daily assignments as they were in high school, students are both relieved and unnerved by the freedom. A professor of French at a midwestern university describes the typical behavior of her freshman students:

My freshmen are faced with long-term assignments and projects, many for the first time. When they are assigned a book, they ask, "How many pages a night do you think I should read?" For instance, when I assigned *Madame Bovary* to my third-level French class, I told them we would be discussing the book one period a week over an eight-week period. The freshmen in the class asked me which pages they should read for each class. They wanted me to be directive and tell them exactly what they were responsible for. I, on the other hand, want them to dig in and make discoveries for themselves at their own pace.

Without the routine of daily assignments and regular feedback about their performance, many freshmen feel adrift academically, especially during their first semester. When parents ask midway through the semester how students are doing in their courses, they are apt to answer, "I don't know." Students may be trying to evade the question, but more often than not, they really don't know. Or what they know is limited to their scores on a few tests or papers and is based more on their own hunches than on someone else's feedback. College may seem deceptively easy the first few months. Rarely is anyone checking on how thoroughly students are doing their work or how much progress they are making on long-term projects. Some students welcome this newfound freedom to set their own rhythm and pace, while others find it difficult to function without external motivations and rewards.

Freshmen may put in many hours studying inefficiently. When they work inefficiently, they ask themselves, "Am I just plain dumb or inefficient? If inefficient, should I take the time to get organized, or is that a waste of time? If I take the time to get organized, how do I do that?"

Students find that they have to read some assignments two or three times just to understand them. But if they were to read everything two or three times, they'd never get through the semester. There are other assignments that they have to skim. A lot of freshmen don't trust themselves. They have to learn when to read things over, when to skim, and when to skip, and this takes time.

A junior majoring in English recalls:

> In high school, if a book was assigned and you were told to
> read it, you had to read the whole thing. And almost
> always, you just read it once. In calculus, you just did the
> problems you were told to do. When I came here I realized
> sometime during freshman year that it was up to me to
> decide how many problems to do, to decide if I had done
> enough problems to grasp the material that was being cov-
> ered. Sometimes it might be enough to do three.
> Sometimes I'd have to do ten. It was hard to adjust to hav-
> ing that responsibility—to letting go of that old high
> school idea of just doing what the teacher told you to do.

Learning how to manage time is the biggest academic hurdle of all.
Procrastination runs rampant among freshmen. Faced with the challenge of new disciplines and the heightened expectations of college
faculty, many students fall into the trap of perfectionism. Hesitating
to hand in papers or assignments until they are "good enough," they
fall further and further behind—sometimes ending up with a failing
grade or an incomplete. Students also procrastinate as a way of resist-
ing courses they don't like or rebelling against authority of any kind,
and end up sabotaging themselves. Some find the brinkmanship of
last-minute cram sessions and all-nighters exhilarating, but a steady
dose of these eventually takes its academic and personal toll. Some
find it difficult to be motivated when they are unsure of their academic goals. And some students procrastinate simply because there are
so many distractions, and they have not learned to resist the full
range of seductive inducements to play now and work later.

In addition, their lack of experience with college-level courses
makes it difficult to schedule study time. So much of what they are
being asked to do is a "first." A junior looking back on her freshman
year comments:

> Things always took longer than I planned. I was always
> frustrated. I had no idea how long it would take me to do a

particular task. If you've never written a twenty-page paper before, how can you know how long it will take you? Plus, a lot of kids grow up having their own space to study, to play music, or to be quiet. In college, it's hard to find a place to do any of those things. You have to write the kind of papers you've never had to write before, under conditions you've never had to deal with before.

And a sophomore at Princeton reflects:

My freshman year computer science course taught me the relative value of time and grades. They teach you to program here by sheer volume. I learned there was a limit to the amount of time I was willing to put into it. My time was worth more than a grade.

For those whose identities have been closely tied to their academic success, the reality of competing with others as bright or brighter than themselves is a stunning shock. For those students who see the world in polarities, even an A- or a B+ is seen as a failure, a blot on their past 4.0 record and their future GPA.

Many students feel a responsibility to parents and to whole communities who have encouraged them—and the humiliation and sense of failure at not living up to these expectations can lead to a general lack of self-regard. A freshman at Yale lamented, "No one here feels special anymore. Kids need to know that they're still special to their parents, even if they're getting C's."

Whether or not they have excelled in the past, students worry about how they will be judged in this new setting. Will they lose the "specialness" they felt in high school, or will they once again move to the top of the pyramid? Will they finally get it together and do well after years of just getting by? Will they be found out as frauds and fail for the first time in their lives? Will they waste their parents' money by getting C's instead of proving their investment was worthwhile by getting A's? Will they ruin their GPA and be blown off the track to professional or graduate school?

The pressure to excel comes from families, graduate schools, financial aid offices, professors, and peers; and often the greatest pressure comes from students themselves whose fragile sense of self-worth is tightly bound to external confirmation. In the academic domain, this confirmation takes the form of grades. From the mother of a University of Chicago freshman:

> When she first went to college, Elise was very glib. She'd call and say she didn't know why people had so much trouble adjusting. Then one night in the middle of first semester, she called home crying hysterically, which was out of character for her. My first thought was—she's pregnant. But no, that wasn't it. She had gotten a D on a test. The issue was her loss of identity as a high achiever.

Grades are an indicator of a student's academic success. And there is no denying that they will eventually influence students' chances for acceptance to graduate and professional schools and slots in corporate training programs. But parents who gauge their youngster's total college experience simply by looking at a list of letters miss the complexity of the educational enterprise. Professors, after all, have different goals in mind when grading. The same paper may receive an A from one professor and a C from another. There are, to use the student lingo, "bite" and "blow off" courses; studio, lab, and reading courses; courses that are graded on a curve and others that are pass/fail. Most students would agree that grades mean little out of context.

It is not unusual for students at even the most selective colleges to have a rocky freshman year. Deans and advisors often explain to parents that freshmen are likely to perform at a lower level than they did in high school. Each fall they make a common plea for patience and understanding and urge parents of entering freshmen not to put undue pressure on their children.

Unfortunately, some parents exacerbate their children's anxiety about performance, which is often high to begin with, by putting pressure on them to do well in everything. This attitude not only creates undue stress, it may inhibit students from taking academic risks; they may stick to courses in which they know they will get high grades, missing opportunities to take a course from a particularly brilliant teacher in an unfamiliar discipline or avoiding a quality class that is known to be difficult. Students benefit from their parents' encouragement to challenge themselves; those who know that Mom or Dad will be there if they temporarily fall on their face will have more courage to stretch their intellectual horizons.

Karen Tidmarsh, Dean of the Undergraduate College at Bryn Mawr, states:

> Most frustrating of all is when parents have sets of expectations that are totally out of sync with the college's philosophy—when they say, "I expect you to have a GPA this year of such-and-such if I'm spending this much money."
>
> The GPA may have nothing to do with the ability of the student or reflect the learning that's taking place. These parents decide a standard and take the most artificial one available, and hold it over a student's head. We make every effort to deemphasize grades—no Dean's List or Phi Beta Kappa.

And a Smith College professor notes:

> I'd like to hear more parents inquire about what excites their daughter rather than what grades she is getting. They always seem to want to talk about grades. And the questions I'm asked on Parents' Weekend are almost always numerative: How many students on Dean's List? How many in academic trouble? How many go on to graduate school?
>
> Students are paranoid about their transcript. They assume that it is going to follow them wherever they go. They would be amazed—and are—how few people ever look at it after their student days are over.

Grades can be a barometer, however, when they are viewed in context. They can be a catalyst for discussion between students and parents. They may represent growth and progress, discipline and hard work, or innate talent. A sudden drop in grades may indicate emotional, social, or chemical dependency problems. Grades may soar and plunge as students fall in and out of love, as they become absorbed in campus activities or worry about problems at home. Grades that are consistently low may indicate that a student is taking too many courses or inappropriate ones. They may suggest that a student is feeling pressured to pursue a particular discipline or even that the student is at the wrong school.

When parents respond to a student's grades with accusations, expressions of anger or disappointment, or simple bromides such as "Get down to work," the conversation is over before it has begun. The opportunity is lost to find out what these symbols really mean. Too much emphasis on grades, even high grades, can be disconcerting to students, and a parent's balanced sense of perspective is appreciated:

> Academically, I'm a hard worker—always done three days early. I'm challenged more at Haverford, but I'm doing as well as I did in high school. I hate talking about grades. As soon as you say them out loud, they become someone else's property—parents' and grandparents' accomplishments. It's nice to keep it quiet and feel kind of smug.

> My mother always gives me perspective on things. Every time I say I'm failing, which she knows I'm really not, she says, "C is for celestial; D is for divine."

> I was so homesick first semester, I got really into my work. All I did was study, and I got straight A's. My parents were thrilled. Second semester I started to feel more at home. I made friends and got involved and my grades dropped. My parents wondered what was wrong.

Parents of freshmen are often shocked to learn that since the passage of the Family Educational Rights and Privacy Act of 1974, more commonly known as the Buckley Amendment, they may not have access to their son's or daughter's grades. Colleges take a variety of approaches to the question of access and usually explain their policy in parent or student handbooks. At some schools, students have the option of signing a waiver that allows their grades to be sent home to parents. As one student said:

> We have to sign a thing, saying I will let my parents see my grades. But if you don't sign it, your parents will get a letter saying something like, "Doctor and Mrs. W: Your son, Nicholas, doesn't want you to see his grades." So it's a catch–22. My parents are so offended by that. They're paying all that money and they think they damn well better see my grades.

And the father of a current freshman exclaimed:

> We couldn't believe it. We're paying $18,000 a year for our son's education, and they have the gall to say they won't send his grades!

If grades have been a battleground upon which students have felt bruised and thwarted by parents in the past, then the Buckley Amendment may be one more weapon they can use to assert some power in their struggle. For students who feel comfortable discussing grades with their parents, this barrier may never even become an issue, since conversations about their progress are shared regularly. One young woman, whose parents are divorced, said:

> My dad has always pressured me to get straight A's. I'm afraid he'll pull me out of school. That's my biggest fear. I don't tell him my grades; I lie through my teeth. I tell my mom everything. She can deal with anything I tell her. I think most students deal with grades the way I do. If a parent puts on lots of pressure about grades, they just don't tell them the truth.

Freshmen are bound to get discouraged at various points during the year and question their ability to succeed. They may complain of stress and exhaustion and call home hoping for sympathy and support. Parents should realize that some stress is part of any college experience. If a course is not difficult, if it is not stretching the student, it is probably not a very effective one. The whole purpose of taking a course is to be challenged. But when stress is paralyzing, it is detrimental. Parents can help their children deal with discouragement and stress by listening, by asking them to describe what they are doing, and by acknowledging that what they are going through is tough.

Specifically, they also might ask them where they are studying and how they are dividing their time. Spending hour after hour trying to study in a noisy residence hall with one eye on the social scene outside the door is rarely effective. When challenged to think of alternatives, students often come up with imaginative options, such as finding secret study niches in an Asian Studies library, campus art gallery, or departmental lounge. And upperclassmen are usually happy to pass on some tips, enjoying the chance to demonstrate to freshmen the wisdom of their years.

A lot of students work themselves into a froth and call home before they have even tried to get help. A parent might assist by encouraging the student to seek out help from a professor or TA, to try to get a tutor, or to take advantage of the academic learning center or other academic support services that exist on most campuses today. Some students have too much pride to ask for assistance, and parental encouragement may stimulate them to take the steps they need to get help. It is more difficult to get academic assistance on some campuses than others. Students may have to be persistent, but if they seek out help in enough places they will almost always find it.

Advising programs on a lot of campuses fail to measure up to their descriptions in the admissions literature. In many instances, advisors are faculty members saddled with what they consider an unrewarding bureaucratic task. Knowing little about departments outside their own, and caring even less, they take a laissez-faire approach and sign students' schedule cards no questions asked. Students may need to look for other resources on campus—peer advisors, upper-classmen, counselors, and deans, for the academic insight and advice they need.

Students who do have good advisors often turn to them first when they want academic assistance. One faculty advisor who takes her job very seriously explains her frustration when parents interfere with the advising relationship:

> When parents override a decision by a student and an advisor, it undermines the advisor and the student. For example, as a freshman advisor, I helped a student decide to drop a course in midsemester. The fifth course added pressure that wasn't necessary. The student wasn't organized enough to handle everything. His parents told him it wasn't appropriate to be a quitter, and they refused to let him drop the course. It made the student furious and frustrated, and it tainted our relationship. Ever since then I've been nervous about advising him.
>
> Even in crisis situations, generally I prefer the student to let me know rather than have the parents call.
>
> If parents sense, however, that their child is having a difficult problem and know that he or she won't talk to anyone, then—and only then—the parent might want to intervene. There have been times that I found out things after the fact and wish a parent had called—not to be directive and tell me what to do, but to say, "I'm concerned. My kid is in what looks like a bad situation."

Freshmen don't really expect or want their parents to solve their academic problems, but they do want them to care and to show that they are interested. A University of Vermont student's comments seem representative:

> I looked to my parents for support a lot freshman year. I needed to know that it was OK to tell them I was going through a hard time. I felt there was no way they could

help me specifically. It didn't work when I asked for help with specific problems, because the specifics were all joined together in one giant process—sometimes it felt like one giant mess.

What helped was to hear them show interest—show that they had faith in me. It was important to me that they be concerned that I wasn't doing well. I needed them to be calm, to listen, not to lecture. They were terrific, and that really made a difference even though I had to work things out for myself on campus.

Throughout all the struggles and triumphs of the freshman year, students are sorting out what part academics are going to play in their lives. Will they devote most of their time to their studies and shoot for the top of the class? How important is academic success? What is academic success? They jockey for position with their peers and measure themselves against their own expectations.

Many who started the year with clear goals find themselves not nearly so certain in May. Others have discovered new intellectual passions and are beginning to look toward the future, wondering what they will make of it all. Armed with new ideas and abilities, they spend enormous amounts of time thinking about who they are and who they are becoming. Nothing looks quite as simple as it once did.

THE COLLEGE SCENE

I needed to find the ground of my own personality. I'd spent too much time just being a student in high school, doing the things that people told me. Then I came to college and there was no one paying attention to me; I didn't have to answer to anybody. All of a sudden, I just felt afloat. Schoolwork didn't seem as important to me as becoming responsible in a different kind of way, finding out what kind of fabric I was made of, finding out what I could do—not just on paper. And that goes for relationships too. What kind of friend was I capable of being? How responsible can I be as a friend? There were a lot of things happening to me, and most of it wasn't what my parents seemed to care about. It had little to do with my courses, and it was being denied by the official reality of the institution.

Caught in the web of his parents' and the college's reality, this introspective Northwestern senior looks back at his freshmen year as a time when his primary learning took place outside of the classroom. He speaks of his frustration at not having his reality validated by the adult world around him. The college environment provided him with opportunities and choices beyond his expectations and beyond the experience of his parents' generation. But where was the official sanction for, or recognition of, the many days and nights spent dealing with these out-of-classroom decisions and dilemmas?

The college scene is often chaotic, exciting, and overstimulating, from time to time depressing and deflating, leading to bouts of intense introspection or episodes of bacchanalian abandon. It is a rich tapestry of relationships, activities, and possibilities. And these are competing perpetually with the classroom experience for the student's attention and physical and emotional energy. The dearth of structure and rules results in an abundance of choices and, at first blush, seemingly endless—and joyous—freedoms. But freedom brings with it the burden of personal responsibility and all the attendant anxieties and possible consequences of difficult decisions.

Roommates, Friends, and Lovers

I just can't concentrate. There are three of us rooming in a room meant for two and now Beth's got a boyfriend who spends the night almost every night. There's no privacy; I have to go to the bathroom to get undressed—to say nothing of the fact that they're having sex a few feet away from me. And my other roommate says I'm a prude because it bothers me. Am I a prude? Is there something wrong with me? Am I immature? When I sit down to study, all I can think about is how I'll handle it tonight when I go back to the room.

For most of us, our home is our sanctuary, the one place where some privacy can be found, where the rules and customs are known, if not always adhered to. At home, a loud stereo might provoke a parental request to lower the volume or an equally loud but familiar argument with a brother or sister. But in a college residence hall, the stereo's owner or the roommate who borrows things unasked is barely an acquaintance, and students may be inhibited about asserting themselves with neighbors and recently acquired friends.

Parents are often shocked, dismayed, and angry to discover that the burden of change lies with their child, the one whose rights are being infringed upon. "We're paying for that room; there must be a policy about other people living there. Why don't they do something!"

The prevailing philosophy on college campuses today encourages young men and women to solve their own problems with little intervention from authorities. To live with a total stranger on a floor with all new acquaintances provides numerous challenges and opportunities for learning assertion and problem-solving skills. Residential life personnel usually act as coaches or facilitators of these interactions, only intervening after other avenues have been exhausted. As a result, students may spend a great deal of time trying to handle day-to-day interpersonal problems with their roommates and other residents of their floor.

Likened to an arranged marriage, college roommates, two strangers matched by little more than their smoking habits and sleeping schedules, come together in a very small space that becomes the bedroom, study, living room, retreat, and playroom for each. When it works well, which is more the exception than the rule, students have a companion, company for dinner, someone to let off steam with, an instant cure for the first month's loneliness, and the potential for lifelong friendship.

Students find themselves living with roommates from different cultures. "At times they misunderstand each other simply because their backgrounds are so different," says Janet Loxley, a counselor at the University of California's Irvine campus:

> Even in the initial getting-to-know-you conversations, they may unwittingly offend each other. For instance, black and white students may tend to talk openly about their families. But Asian students may think it's rude to inquire "What does your father do? How do you get along with your sister?"

Sometimes differences in personal habits are more problematic than differences in backgrounds. A young man from a rural community in the South and a cosmopolitan New Yorker may suit each other well if they both like to go to bed early and keep their rooms neat. But a student who has always had her own room may find it difficult to share space; and her roommate, one of six children, may be intolerant of her complaining. They may make awkward attempts at discussions about letting each other know if something bothers them. Some schools even have structured exercises for roommates to do together to help ward off tension. But most students will struggle with the disagreements that are inevitable when two people live together in such close quarters.

An attractive, impeccably dressed freshman at the University of Pennsylvania's Wharton School recounts her first impression of her roommate:

> My roommate seemed very strange, tiny, glasses, braces, no makeup. She wore only army fatigues, and I was totally intimidated by her—and found out later that she was of me. We were very accommodating and compromising— otherwise it would have been a big hassle to change rooms. Much to the surprise of both of us, we eventually became great friends.

But lifestyles can be so different that accommodation is difficult. This Carnegie-Mellon freshman describes his frustration:

> I need my sleep, and I'm a very light sleeper. He's a night person and a fine arts major, and he keeps the light on

doing his projects late at night. He says he has no other place to go, because all of his materials are in our room, but I just can't go to sleep with the noise and the light. It's finally gotten to the point that I'm barely speaking to him.

Or consider this vivacious freshman from the University of Texas:

Every time I come into the room, she's here staring at the TV. I've tried to be friendly, but she's sullen and uncommunicative. And she obviously doesn't like my friends, so I feel guilty whenever I have someone in the room. At first I kind of felt sorry for her because she seemed depressed, but now I'm just fed up. I want out.

And accommodation may raise fundamental questions of autonomy and compromise. How much of myself am I willing to give up in order to live peacefully with someone else?

We got along though we were so different. We had different friends and lifestyles. She'd go to parties; I'd stay in my room and play my guitar or visit with a few friends. We painted our room together and that bonded us, and we put silly things on our door, like "We both throw up when we eat scallops, we have so much in common." I think she thought I was odd, but she liked me. But parts of me would disappear in order to get along with her—maybe to avoid conflict. Parts of me were dormant. I guess her side of the room influenced me.

Issues of competition arise as students measure themselves against this live-in rival:

Why does he always have a girlfriend, and I can't get anyone to go out with me?

■

Her parents give her anything she wants; she has so many fantastic clothes. I have a part-time job and wouldn't have the time to shop even if I had the money.

◼

I study constantly and get C's. He parties like an animal and gets A's.

◼

She's like a size 2 and keeps boxes of cookies in our room for days. I'm always on a diet, and having that food in the room and looking at her skinny body drives me up the wall.

These are the daily problems confronting students as they return home to the only private space available to them. Most schools place freshmen in doubles or suites, and with the current popularity of residence hall living, three students are often squeezed into a room meant for two. Those who do have singles, and are outgoing and confident about initiating contact with students in neighboring rooms, are delighted to have this special place of their own. For more introverted students, single rooms can exacerbate the isolation and loneliness they already feel. One problem is traded for another.

Throughout the freshman year, parents are likely to receive unhappy phone calls about roommate and dormitory crises. They may range from "He keeps messing with the things on my desk!" to "She's talking of suicide and I don't know what to do." Or from "She's the biggest slob!" to "He comes home drunk several nights a week!"

Parents often react to these calls with a for-or-against response. Some rally round with a familial Greek chorus, fanning the flames by getting angry along with the student. Or they call the residence director, the dean of students, or the president demanding a solution. Others, recalling sibling battles, may respond with a sarcastic "Well now *you* know what it's like to live with a slob!" or "What did you do to provoke him?"—responses that tend to end any communication, leaving students feeling that their one lifeline has been cut.

Many parents speak of their frustration and feelings of helplessness, the bubble of this carefully chosen, expensive superschool burst by the reality of a difficult living situation and no administrator clamoring to fix it. Tossing their developing independence aside, some students plead with Mom and Dad to intervene so that they can rid themselves of the problem and get on with their lives. Under the circumstances, the temptation to do so is compelling, but this is a significant opportunity to encourage independent thought and action. College administrators agree that learning to live in a world full of differences is one of the most important lessons of the college years.

The most helpful parents are those who listen, acknowledge their child's feelings, and allow him or her to generate some options. Suggestions can be offered tentatively, as just one of several possible solutions, and students should be encouraged to seek out resources on campus such as counselors or student life personnel, who deal with similar situations routinely.

Parents can show support in more tangible ways as well. Survival kits of earplugs, eyeshades, or a Walkman to block out sights and sounds can provide a lift for a student. These are simple gestures, but powerful reminders that those back at the home front care and send their support.

Often students help each other out or come up with their own solutions. One young woman, who spent several months grappling with the problem of a roommate with a live-in boyfriend, rebuffed her parents' suggestion to talk to the RA. Rather than stir up a potential conflict, she resorted temporarily to what current college students term "sexile":

> I knew I had to live on that floor for the rest of the year, and I didn't want to tattle to the RA and have my roommate and her friends angry at me. I had some really good friends who lived at the end of my floor—and on the nights when Randy was spending the night, I took a sleeping bag and slept on their floor. I did ask my RA to let me know of any room openings, and I moved second semester. It's funny—I was miserable at the time, but I'm sort of glad I went through it. I gained a lot of confidence just having to figure it all out.

And these comments from a woman at the University of Michigan:

> My roommate had a lot of problems; she was bulimic, and
> she talked about it all the time. I was becoming more like
> a parent than a friend. I got too entangled—and at times,
> I needed to get away physically. My father told me to take
> her to the clinic to talk to someone, but I didn't. I needed
> to do it my way.

In some cases, parents may feel so concerned about their child's
well-being that a call directly to a professional on the residence staff
is warranted. A dean of freshmen cited this example:

> We had a student who was being harassed by his suitem-
> ates. There was vandalism, theft, something was even set
> on fire. The student told his parents about it, and they
> told him to report it to the proper people in the residence
> halls. The parents had researched the proper procedures
> and encouraged their son to go through the appropriate
> channels. But he was unable to carry that out himself. He
> just wouldn't do it, or maybe I should say couldn't do it.
> The parents realized that, and they took over. It was
> important that they did what they did.

Calls of this nature are most effective when they are collaborative
rather than accusatory in spirit, in spite of the frustration and anger
parents might feel. A dean at Barnard reminds parents that "we are
partners in this enterprise, not adversaries."

Friendships with roommates, floormates, and classmates begin to
take shape in the first few months of school. Sorting out who will
eventually emerge as good friends is part of the student's search for
identity and becomes an important focus for freshmen who are, in
fact, re-creating their lives in this new environment. There is a
sense of promise and potential—an exhilaration accompanying the
possibilities for new friendships with so many different kinds of people. At the same time there is a sense of profound loneliness and

loss—an empty space left by old friends for whom no explanations are necessary. Students move back and forth between these two emotional states, now thriving on the excitement of new friendships, now retreating into times of quiet reflection and longing for the comfort of old, solid relationships.

After three months at Carleton, a young man made the following observation:

> Social life here is chaotic. So much is going on in reality and in your mind all at the same time. You're searching to have different levels of friendship—intimate, close, and just plain acquaintances. You spend time hanging out with lots of different people at once. You look for people like you think you want to be—punk, intellectual, or whatever. And all the while you're questioning whether you want to make new friends at all or if that means turning your back on your high school friends.

And an Amherst freshman asserted:

> I had friends I'd met at a summer program, and they were really intellectual and my roommates weren't at all—that was a schizophrenic thing. My roommates didn't get along with these other people, and I didn't know who I wanted to be with, and it was upsetting.

Perhaps this is another way of sorting out "who I am" questions—am I an intellectual or someone who likes *People* magazine and the Los Angeles Dodgers? Can I be both? Can I be friendly with different groups of people without losing out on both?

Some students find the identification with a group a secure substitute for missed family and friends. With their identity in such flux, it is not unusual for freshmen to stumble into a group based simply on its proximity. An Oberlin freshman, who had been adamantly disdainful of drug use in high school, found himself within three days of his arrival at college a member of a group of students who defined themselves by their marijuana use. As he reflected on his choice, it seemed almost arbitrary:

> Our floor quickly divided up into three or four cliques for the year. One clique was into country music and Karl Marx. My clique smoked marijuana a lot. We played a lot of cards. We were really into games of any kind, mostly head games, I'd say. Our conversations would be really twisted sometimes and manipulative. Then there was the third group—the musicians. Half of them were homosexuals and the other half straight. And then there were some who hung out in limbo and went from group to group.

Students speak of their floor as a family—often traveling in packs, eating together, or going to movies or local hangouts as a group. Young people who come from fragmented families seem particularly drawn to the bonding that takes place on dormitory floors. They refer to individual friends by name, set against a backdrop of characters on their floor spoken of in the student vernacular as "geeks" or "psychos," yet with a tinge of affection, as if describing eccentric but beloved extended family. Some who felt like outsiders in high school may experience a new sense of belonging in this accepting, inclusive group.

The diversity of the college campus is apparent in the microcosm of each residence hall floor. Students who have traveled the globe share space with those who have just left home for the first time. Some have been living "on their own" for years; others are tightly bound to parents and siblings and feel the stress of breaking away. Students who own BMWs mingle with those brought up in factory towns and inner city ghettos. Some students arrive on campus wise in the ways of sex, drugs, and alcohol, while others have been sheltered and are inexperienced. Whether sophisticated or naive when they arrive, almost all students will be exposed during the course of the freshman year to the problems of eating disorders and clinical depression, to alcohol and drug abuse, to unfamiliar religions and cultures, to gay men and women. Students become familiar with the intimacies of people's lives in a way that they probably never will again outside the confines of family and very close personal friends. Many learn an appreciation for differences from these close associations that will last a lifetime. Certainly, there is a loss of innocence, and with that loss, a new maturity borne of questioning and introspection that is often painful.

For many students, this environment is more disorienting than stimulating. Seeking the comfort of a familiar group identity, they may turn to Greek life or a religious, cultural, or political organization—a more homogeneous group whose identity is clearly associated with their family values or perhaps just the opposite. Some may find at a later time that this group has become confining, but at first it provides a feeling of stability to counteract the sense of uprootedness of the first semester:

> Initially, the people I hung out with and found I had the most in common with were the more conservative. I took a turn toward a more conservative religion than my family's. My father's comments to my older sisters at college had been, "Are you studying and did you go to church on Sunday?"
>
> To me, it was, "Are you studying, and did you go to a Lutheran church on Sunday?" Ultimately, I left the conservative church and went back to the Lutheran. As I became more comfortable, I started hanging out with a more diverse group of people.

■

> When I first got here I tended to hang out with a group of kids who were real involved in the Black Student Association, and I got involved too. I missed my friends from home and my culture. It helped knowing that group of kids. One of them, a senior girl, was like a mentor to me.

Students also form friendships through the camaraderie and absorption of shared projects—working on the newspaper, singing in the choir, playing on the soccer team. Especially on large university campuses, joining student activities provides a shortcut to finding others with common interests.

These shared experiences may offer moments of sheer delight. "It was like a Mountain Dew commercial!" exclaimed one student after a trip with the Outing Club.

"Sometimes we stay up most of the night to get the paper to press on time," said another freshman. "I feel closer to the paper staff than to any other group of people on campus."

In the midst of all the people and activities, loneliness is as normal to the freshman experience as the common cold, mononucleosis, and the flu. Whereas most students feel lonely some of the time, there are others who are truly isolated and without friends. These are often students who lack social skills and have dealt with social isolation throughout their adolescence. Hoping that college will make a difference, they may project their unhappiness onto the school, complaining that "these are not my kind of people." Some students who were loners in high school discover a whole new world of peers with common interests and talents that may not have been available to them before. But more than likely a young man or woman who has not been able to form friendships in earlier years will have difficulty once again. Most colleges and universities provide free counseling or group experiences that deal with shyness or social skill building and support the development of the total student.

Cross-gender friendships are prevalent on today's campuses, a primary outgrowth of coed residence hall life. Though parents often worry about the repercussions of coed living, students are more likely to treat the members of the opposite sex on their floors as siblings, replicating the close relationship of missed family members or perhaps enjoying the companionship of a "brother" or "sister" for the first time.

A young man who had just completed the first three months of his freshman year earnestly described to his parents the advantages of coed living:

> It lessens the tension between the sexes, and it eliminates all the locker room talk there was in high school. It makes for much closer friendships.

Some of these friendships do move into romantic relationships.
The intimacy of shared late-night conversations about everything
from future dreams to past traumas may lead to an intimacy borne of
sexual and romantic stirrings. Developmentally, these are often
healthy, affirming relationships, having grown out of caring and natural ties, but they bring up new questions and anxieties. What will
this do to our friendship, which is so precious? What will happen if
or when we break up? Will it mean too much togetherness?

There are some students who move quickly into romantic relationships, often for the first time. There may be an intensity about
the involvement that suggests a mutual dependency more than a
mature sexual relationship. These partners may cling to each other
and provide a secure haven that keeps them from engaging fully in
their new environment.

A University of Miami junior recalls:

> I began dating a graduate student the first week of school.
> I spent all my time with him and never got to know any-
> one. I barely even knew the people in the room next to
> me—I was just never around.

Most of these early relationships don't last much past freshman
year, but they are still a vitally important part of the student's world
and developing sexual identity. Some parents, suspecting that this
may be just the first in a sequence of "serious relationships," dismiss
it or minimize it. A freshman at Earlham describes her frustration
when she calls home for support about her rocky relationship:

> At times when I call, they've tried to lessen what I'm saying.
> They think they're being really nice. They'll say, "Oh it's not
> that bad," and it *is* bad. I don't need to hear that. When
> they're good, they legitimize my feelings, but when they try
> to diminish a problem, I think they don't want to cope with
> the fact that their daughter's going through a rough time.
> All I want is some support and concern, not "Oh, it's just a
> college romance." It's not just a college romance. I'm having

a nervous breakdown—don't you care? I'll end up calling my sister, but I like calling them first.

Some of these relationships challenge parental values as students become involved with classmates from different religions, races, and cultures. A freshman of Catholic descent, and the first member of her family to go to college, refrained from telling her parents about a relationship she knew would upset them:

He was from Pakistan. They're going to kill me if the guy I marry isn't Catholic. If I told them I was involved with someone who's Islamic, it would just petrify them. They have a lot of racial prejudices. I just didn't want to inflict that on my relationship with them.

Students often talk about feeling torn and guilty, facing the dilemma of how to remain loyal to family while making independent decisions that are in conflict with established family norms. Sometimes these conflicts come as a surprise, as they did to a young woman from Philadelphia during her freshman year at Penn State:

I had met a guy over the summer who came to visit me in October. We decided to go to an inn for the weekend. It was a big problem with my parents. My mom was my rock and had always been so liberal and accepting. And now all of a sudden she was uptight about my spending a weekend with a guy. I learned something; I tested my boundaries and got to my mom's limit. When I was little and had an argument with a parent, I would end up thinking they were right. This time I felt they were wrong. She sounded like a bumbling idiot—this strong, liberal woman. I had always looked up to her. It was painful for me.

Unwittingly, this young woman had tested her mother's limits and run smack into a conflict. She stumbled into the need to make her own value judgments and to establish her own code of behavior.

Sex, Drugs, and Alcohol

Throughout the freshman year students face many puzzling moments of personal decision, confronting previously established values, taking risks, and making compromises—all moments that sap energy and time and often provide fertile soil for spurts in personal growth. What are the unwritten rules of conduct in this place? Am I supposed to lose my virginity now that I'm in college? Am I supposed to pretend that I haven't lost it? Do I spend the weekend with my boyfriend in spite of what my parents think? Do I say yes to pot and no to coke? Do I go along to the fraternity parties where the action is, even though I hate them, or do I look for alternatives out of the mainstream?

Consider the dilemma of today's college freshman whose development has not progressed much beyond seeing things as either right or wrong. These young men and women are left to their own devices in a place and time when the rules about drinking and drugs are often confusing and unenforced and there are few norms about sexual behavior.

Many freshman who "acted out" in high school and are experienced with sex, drugs, and alcohol reexamine their earlier choices within the new context of college life. With the freedom to do as they choose, some continue to experiment, stretching the boundaries to their institutional limits. Others, with no parents to bump up against, are not as involved as their classmates in the experimentation that is part of the freshman scene. The high school "boozer," "druggie," or "mover" arrives on campus without labels; fellow students carry no expectations, and there is a chance to try out a new identity. "It is," said one student, "a whole new ball game."

Some students, who have lived in highly structured and restrictive environments at home and arrive at college with little experience, go haywire when they are left with no external constraints. Lacking internal controls and a sense of moderation, they experiment and try everything—usually to excess. As one young woman puts it:

> All of a sudden you can drink as much as you want, have
> sex with whomever you want, and do whatever drugs your
> heart desires. Your parents aren't there to check up on you

and no one is telling you what to do. You are sleeping in a
room where you can bring a guy or girl home and your
mom is not going to hear you. She's 300 miles away. That
changed everything for me completely. You have complete freedom here. You can go to your room, his room—
that made such a difference about sex. I went overboard
with it. It was a blast, but sometimes I wondered just how
much freedom one person could handle all at once.

Struggling to establish their own identities and to separate from
their parents, some students take a blatantly rebellious stance. Their
behavior sends a message that they are different from Mother and
Dad; they are establishing their own moral turf. They may even tell
their parents about their exploits. They call home and say, with the
typical hyperbole of college freshmen, "Oh I'm totally out of it. I got
completely wasted last night," or, "I've been partying all week." One
student described how much she liked to tell her mother shocking
things. When asked why she enjoyed doing so, she replied, "Because
Mom can't do a thing about it. She has no control over what I do."

Others try to hide their behavior, and their parents don't have a
clue as to what is really going on. One Princeton student described
what he called "a college student's nightmare—having your parents
call when you're stoned":

I remember having had several exams and coming back to a
friend's room across the hall from mine and getting stoned.
My phone rang, and I stumbled to it. It was my mother. It
was the middle of the afternoon, and I was totally incoher-
ent, and I knew it. The next day, my oldest brother called
me because my mother had called him and said she thought
I was studying too hard and would he talk to me. We had a
good laugh when I told him what happened.

Actually, most parents don't know what is really going on, and
unsettling as this may be, it is a necessary part of the separation
process. Students need privacy and an opportunity to establish their

own limits and values. They need to experiment and handle the consequences. John Gardner, an Associate Vice Provost at the University of South Carolina and founder of the National Center for the Study of the Freshman Year Experience, urges parents:

> Look at college as a laboratory for testing behaviors. Students have to figure out who they want to spend time with, what and when they want to eat, drink, and smoke—how much they want to sleep, socialize, and study. As students experiment, they are testing out the consequences of their behaviors. If they can't learn in an unfettered way, they'll test the same things out later when the stakes are much higher, when there aren't the built-in safety nets that exist in college.

There are times, of course, when students truly want their parents to be there for them or even to intervene. They send out signals that they are in trouble—a series of depressed phone calls home or aloof calls of the "everything's fine" variety; they may sound spacy or uncommunicative. Their grades may drop suddenly or their weight may change dramatically. They may be spending a lot of money they can't account for.

The Director of Student Activities and Orientation at a southern university comments:

> Parents need to look for signs, but they shouldn't jump to conclusions. If they have built a relationship through high school, they need to maintain it. Parents should confront their children in a positive way—express concern, not hysteria. They should ask about friends, about the weekend, about eating and sleeping. They should show that they care, but not interrogate.
>
> I think parents should confront their children if they find things that indicate drug use. They should take the time to explain their concern but not cut off communication with a barrage of accusations. They shouldn't make assumptions but should ask open-ended questions and listen. When parents know that their child is abusing drugs,

they should seek professional help either at home or at a counseling center on or near campus. They shouldn't try to handle that kind of problem themselves.

A young woman who is now a sophomore at an East Coast university found her parents' intervention during her freshman year particularly effective:

One time last year my parents called me, and I was just really hung over. I wasn't bragging about it or happy about it, but that's just the way it was. I was in bed, and I said, "Look I can't talk to you right now. Let me call you back."

When I called them back I was fine, and they didn't mention it. But then I did get a letter that said, "We are really concerned that at 12:30"—or whatever time it was—"on a Sunday morning, you're hung over." And that was perfect! It didn't feel like they were bugging me. It was more like—"Hey, buddy, we're really worried about you." They were sort of acting like concerned friends.

I think I was relieved when my parents said something. I was already a little worried about myself. When they brought it up, that opened up a chance for us to discuss what was going on. We talked about it when I got home, and I don't know if it was a direct result of our talking, but I'm partying a lot less this year and have things much more under control.

Some parents have a tendency not to say anything, and then you start to wonder, don't they care? How come they don't say anything? I'm not sure how parents are supposed to know when there's really something wrong. But I think they should follow their instincts and at least say they're worried. They shouldn't ignore it.

Many students who choose to experiment with sex, drugs, and alcohol are motivated by the desire to be part of a group, by a search for intimacy with their peers. There is a compelling camaraderie that develops as students come together over beer or to share a joint while

they listen to music and talk. Students often divide into groups according to their preferences in alcohol and drugs. The word gets around
campus about who does what: one sorority is known for girls who
"drink booze hard-core," a fraternity is "into coke—it's part of the budget for the spring formal." One group "drinks and smokes pot and sits
around playing head games," referring with pride to pot and hallucinogens as "the intellectual drugs" and with disdain to the heavy use of
alcohol or cocaine as the "drugs of the rich kids who are destructive
and into the proving-you're-a-macho-man kind of nonsense."

Each group has an identity of its own, and as students wrestle
with self-definition, the choice of a particular group reveals more
than a simple preference for one substance over another. The lure of
friendship and intimacy is powerful:

> I hang out with a small group. We smoke quite a bit. Dope
> is an interest in itself—a social activity, and it brings
> about a state of mind that definitely is going to bring you
> together. And when you're with people who are smoking,
> a lot of times you'll do something together, like you'll
> smoke and go to a movie and then get together afterward
> and talk some more.

◼

> I'm kind of attracted to a crowd in the dorm next door.
> They hang out together and drink vodka and Kool-Aid
> and play Pente. They're sort of pursuing me, but I'm not
> sure yet whether I want to spend a lot of time with them. I
> may have had enough of that.

◼

> People who smoke pot on campus know everybody else
> who smokes pot. You get to know a lot of people that way.
> We hang together. It's a self-protecting kind of culture. It's
> not the kind of thing that's broadcast.

◼

> I don't drink and I don't want to hang out with people who do. When I go to a party I sip a little beer—just enough so I feel kind of mellow. I call it "drinking for buzz maintenance."

Drug usage tends to be more private than alcohol and usually takes place behind closed doors. But on most campuses today, alcohol is everywhere. No matter what the college's official policy is, students are very resourceful when they want to drink. On weekends, parties seem to erupt spontaneously, and a keg is usually the main drawing card.

All students are affected when their hallmates or roommates overindulge. Said one freshman:

> In high school, I was used to seeing friends drink too much at parties. But I just went home to my nice quiet house. Now I have to deal with the rowdies in the hall every Friday and Saturday night. Sometimes just to get to the shower I have to step over the bodies of the kids who passed out.

Many students are overwhelmed by the party scene and the constant inducements to participate. A University of Michigan freshman admitted that she had a lot of anxiety about this part of college life.

> I was scared 'cause I hadn't been a big party girl or sexually active. I found a lot of others in the same boat. Things move a lot faster than in high school, and since we all live in such close quarters, we see a lot more. I saw a lot more drugs than in high school. I could walk down the hall and smell marijuana. I never did start smoking dope, but a lot of my friends did—and I was surprised to realize that I liked them anyway—that I was much less judgmental than I had been in high school.

Some students drink moderately or don't drink at all, and many of them say that they don't feel the overt peer pressure they felt in high school. "No one will make fun of you if you don't drink," explained one student, "except during something like fraternity hazing. But there is a kind of self-imposed pressure. If you feel shy or awkward in the first place, it's kind of hard not to drink if you're at a party."

But for large numbers of students, the ethic is one of "work hard, play hard"—go to the library during the week and "get wasted" on the weekend. For many, drinking is a way to blow off steam, to get rid of social inhibitions, to prove that they are grown up. It is an integral part of their culture and inextricably tied with their social life and their sexual behavior.

Though the sexual revolution appears to have peaked, there is still pressure on both men and women to be knowledgeable and comfortable with sex. Rarely are sexual encounters between college students as spontaneous, smooth, and carefree as their parents might think. Almost no one is immune to the agonies of sexual growth. Students worry about sexual attractiveness and performance, about finding a private place, and about the future of their relationship. They worry about the dangers of sexually transmitted diseases and how to integrate these clinical intrusions into their lovemaking. Those who choose to remain virgins throughout their college years may question their own desirability or their sexual identity. "If everyone else is doing it, why aren't I? Is it simply that I'm not interested in sex without love, and I haven't fallen in love? Maybe there's something wrong with me." Those who feel sure of these choices based on moral or religious values may have to cope with the stigma of being different. And with the additional pressures brought to bear by the fear of AIDS, these decisions are more complex than ever.

In spite of the decline of sexual stereotypes, there is still more peer pressure on a man who remains a virgin than there is on a woman. And many women are now the initiators of sex, so that some young men find themselves saying no, which is incongruent with their messages about manliness and may cause them to feel off balance and bewildered.

Issues of confusion over sexual identity are also common among college students. The Dean of Arts and Sciences at one southeastern university comments:

This struggle often interferes with academic achievement. Students are sent to me because of academics, and then they start talking. They are not sure about their sexual identity; they can't talk to their parents; some of them feel uncomfortable going to gay groups. What I do is listen. I'm not sure what parents can do, but I think they should know that many students are questioning their sexuality. Their own kids may be, and certainly they will be exposed to other kids who are.

Although homosexuality is far more open and aboveboard than in earlier generations, the stigma still remains. "Coming out" is usually a long and agonizing process. Some gay men and women who are clear about their sexual orientation before they come to college still have anxieties about how they will fit into this new environment.

A student's evolving comfort as a sexual being goes hand in hand with his or her total maturing process. One young man about to graduate looks back on that evolution with a new perspective and insight:

My friends were mostly guys freshman year. At first it was like oh, wow, college! It went from girls and sex were something illicit, like drugs, or like alcohol, just going out of control and being really stupid and insensitive about it, to incorporating sex more and more into our personalities—having more respect for other people—respecting other people's lives and the way they behaved and learning how to live with people.

I lived in a suite freshman year, and definitely we had problem times about that sort of thing—complete lack of respect for the other people around, for what people would think. Like a group of us would be hanging out in the living room and a couple would come in and not even say hello, just go straight to the bedroom, and the next thing, we'd hear the bedsprings and a lot of noise. That changed over time. People became a lot more conscious of other people and were able to be sociable about incorporating sex into their lives, becoming more social human beings.

■

Bombarded with new freedoms and responsibilities, at a time when they are trying to figure out who they are and how they can live on their own, freshmen behave in ways that are often disturbing to their peers as well as their parents. Their exhilaration is mixed with confusion, their experimentation tempered by responsibility. They are trying to incorporate new people, activities, and interests into their lives. They're expanding their academic horizons and learning new ways to learn.

So much seems to be happening at once. At times they appear very certain of who they are and what they think; at other times little about them seems to be integrated.

A dean from Macalaster College reflects on the freshman experience.

> The freshman year is about separation from family and home. It's about the questions "Who am I?" and "How do I fit in?" It's about maintaining one's ego in a strange environment, learning to live with a roommate and handling freedom and responsibility. It's about making friends and finding a niche.

For parents, too, the freshman year is a rite of passage, a passage to a new relationship with their sons and daughters. The *Harvard Parents' Handbook* describes the essence of this major shift:

> For parents, the freedom freshmen enjoy can be hard to accept. So can recognizing how little you can now appropriately and directly do to shape the daily round of your son's or daughter's experiences or his or her lifestyle choices, curricular or career plans. . . . A young person is setting out on his or her own life's course. Don't try to hold the course you set and have been sailing together for seventeen years. It is very hard to sail a ship with two pilots. Come along, by all means. But keep in mind that it is a new voyage, someone else's voyage. This way college can be the shared and happy embarkation it ought to be. . . .

IN AND OUT OF YOUR LIFE

CARRIE HAS THAT "NEW YORK LOOK." HER clothes are from secondhand shops; they're always artfully arranged, never look studied, but seem a natural extension of her cameo face. She walks with assurance, her shoulders back, eyes straight ahead; she appears to know where she is going. A senior at Yale, she's a talented artist and enjoys exploring the rich resources of her hometown, New York City. She feels close to her parents, who have always supported her personal style and encouraged her independence.

It is obvious that Carrie's mother takes great delight in her daughter. She reminisces about Carrie's rocky start freshman year, and the unexpected ups and downs that followed:

> Carrie finished high school early and took courses at a college in the city in place of her senior year. She seemed ready to go away to school. In fact, she seemed more mature than most 18-year-olds and entered as a sophomore. My husband and I drove her to school. I remember that she was anxious and obviously disappointed by the posters of puppies and kittens that her roommate had already put up, but by the time we left, she seemed to be

cheerfully settling in. John and I drove home thinking, This is it, we're on to the next phase of life.

The phone calls came as a surprise. There were lots of them, and they were always late at night. John slept through most of them, and I would listen for what seemed endless hours to her unhappiness. There were many tears and many tales of poor courses and loneliness. She was in one class with all seniors, the result of sloppy advising. It was way over her head, but she refused to change.

Finally, when she came home for Thanksgiving, the dam burst. She became nearly hysterical, and the three of us talked most of the night. When she finally went to sleep, John and I decided, This is not worth it; we'll withdraw her from school, send her for therapy, and she'll go to school here in the city.

The next morning when I began to tell Carrie what we had decided, I noticed the slightest flash of disappointment on her face. It was so tiny that only a mother would have seen it, and I knew instinctively that we were wrong, and that she was strong enough to get through this. She needed us to encourage her, not come to her rescue. I took a chance and said, "Carrie, this is all bullshit. You will go back. You can do it."

She looked shocked and relieved all at the same time. The next day she returned to school on the train. And now she's a senior and will probably graduate with honors. That first trip home was the turnaround. But it was also just the beginning. At times it's been a roller-coaster existence. Carrie has been in and out of our lives in ways we never would have predicted three years ago when we blithely dropped her off in New Haven.

Throughout the freshman year and continuing through the rest of the college experience, young men and women move in and out of their parents' lives, often in fits and starts as crises or triumphs occur. When students become upperclassmen, the quantity and intensity of contacts usually lessen as they shift their support systems from home to school and become more adept at discovering resources for themselves. But the vicissitudes of life at home and at school bring unexpected turns of events, and the reentry of parents and children into each others' lives can be awkward and unsettling, as well as comforting and confirming.

During the course of a year, students experience losses and traumas and may turn to their parents for support. Parents, too, go through their own joys and sorrows, and occasionally will be the bearers of painful news from home.

For students who go to school a short distance from home, there is a sense of continuity as they drop back in for a quiet weekend, a family celebration, or a quick fix of TLC. Their parents, within a short drive of campus, may occasionally drop off a basket of fruit, post a brief note on the door of their child's room, or take their child's friends out for a much appreciated good meal.

But continuity of this sort inevitably diminishes for those who go to school far from home and whose contacts with family are reduced to vacations, occasional visits, and sporadic phone calls or letters. The experience of both students' and parents' lives during these years is reduced to images, frozen in time and often distorted and misunderstood like snapshots viewed out of context.

The impact of such slices of life reverberates across telephone wires every weekend as parents take stock of their children's progress, happiness, and success—measuring their tone of voice and the contents that spill forth against an imaginary norm. How powerful these 10-minute calls, three-page letters, and e-mail musings are, pouring out the emotion of a particular moment. Exuberant accounts of recent events, successes, or a general sense of their child's well-being can brighten up a parent's day. On the other hand, complaints, distresses, disappointments, and depression are delivered in shrill staccato or flat, gloomy conversations that interrupt peaceful Sundays at home or invade an already overburdened parent's domain.

A successful surgeon, the father of four, acknowledges that on Sundays, when he and his wife routinely speak to each child at various locations across the country, "At that moment we are only as happy as our least happy child."

But what of the hours before or the days after his phone calls? Is his daughter who sounded sad or distraught rejuvenated an hour later? Is his son's happy voice genuine or a reaction to an unspoken but imagined request to sound good-humored because Mom and Dad cannot tolerate sadness or depression?

A substantial number of students speak of protecting their parents from their disappointments and problems—some because they don't want to burden their parents who are sacrificing so much for their education, some because they are protecting themselves from their parents' lack of understanding and support.

> My dad made it very clear that he didn't want to hear from me when I was complaining or depressed. He's got all kinds of problems with his wife and stepdaughter, and if I sound down, he just gets mad and I end up feeling worse. So we have these stilted conversations because I have to pretend everything's fine.

■

> Every time I call home depressed, my mom either starts sounding depressed herself, or she says maybe I should come home, like I obviously can't handle things. That's the last thing I want to hear.

When students are feeling down, parents often react too quickly; they have difficulty assessing from afar how much this depressed phone call or letter reflects the totality of their child's life. A Californian at Boston University explains how frustrating it is when she simply wants some support and understanding, but her mother overreacts and responds as though her bad moments are the whole of her experience:

> I'll say one thing on the phone, like I'm tired or down, and my mother makes such a production of it. She spends the whole day picking tangerines from our tree and wrapping

them up individually to send to me. She encloses a note, telling me she's worried about me, and my sister tells me that's all she and my dad talk about for three weeks.

And a freshman at Trinity College in Connecticut has difficulty communicating her low times to her mother without getting what she considers an overreaction or an underreaction:

> My mom is such a stoic. She just says, "You're fine," when I'm sick or depressed. It hurts her so much when there's something in my universe that she can't cure. All I want her to do when I'm depressed is to recognize it. . . to validate it. So when she says, "You don't sound too bad," I'll say, "You're not listening to me. I'm really, really down." And then she becomes convinced that I'm suicidal or deathly ill and starts calling every day. "Hi. Just calling to see if you're still alive."
> I can't just have a cold. She either thinks it's nothing or it's mono for sure. All I want her to say is, "I'm sorry you have a bad sore throat, I know how miserable that can be."

Many students admit that they call home when they want to complain and tend to share their good times with friends:

> There's only so much you can complain around here, because everyone complains so much. I have four papers due. My friends' attitudes are, "So what!" They'll be bitching about their own heavy load . . . so you call home for pity.

Even when students do attempt to communicate both the ups and the downs to their parents, they find it impossible to capture the day-to-day pleasures of their new world in such brief sketches. A Pomona student explains:

> I feel like my parents only know what upsets me, like when I call home and say I'm failing something or I had a fight with my roommate. But when I say I went to a party last

night and had a lot of fun, I don't think they have any idea
how wonderful my life is here . . . how wonderful my friends
are. I think my life is pretty rich, and I'm very secure. This is
more of a natural environment than even being at home was
for me. I'm much more in my own element with people I'm
comfortable with and have a lot in common with.

I have two separate worlds. I have another life here that's
as full and complete as my life was at home. They're separate
and distinct. I'm made aware of it when I talk to my parents.
Even though when I was home they didn't know a lot about
my life. We were close, but I didn't tell them very personal
things—they saw it; they saw people I spent time with.
When I talk to them on the phone now they really have no
conception of what my life is like. It's so disconnected.

And for a Bryn Mawr student from India, the physical distance, as
well as the cultural differences implicit in her college experience,
highlight the sense of disconnectedness:

I've always shared everything with my parents. They're so
far away now, I can't call them and tell them about everything. Especially when the work gets underway, I don't
have the energy to sit down and write. What it would take
is a ten-page letter every week. It's impossible to let them
know what my life is really like here, so it tends to be post-
cards or notes to my sister, letting them know that I'm OK.
I realize I'm going to get out of here after four years without
their ever having seen any of the rituals or the friends or
anything that's become such a part of me at this point, and
they won't ever know that, and that's hard, but there's
nothing I can do about it.

I'm used to communicating with my mother on a very
adult level. I am a friend to her. I'm the eldest, but once I
came here I became her little girl. All she can think of is
taking care of me. So this very intelligent, interesting
woman—all she can say is, "Are you all right? Are you

drinking your orange juice? Are you praying every day?"
That's the extent of our conversations. When she writes,
she writes as to a child.

The fact is that college students *are* no longer a regular part of their
parents' lives. For most students the reality of the ever-widening gap
between their experience and the world of their parents is fraught with
conflicting feelings. Young people, as well as their parents, struggle
with letting go. At times college students revel in their separateness,
keeping the delights and traumas of their lives at school to themselves.
At other times they long to share their college world with the family at
home, even as their worlds inevitably become more separate. Heady
moments of independence and the adventure of expanding horizons
give way to wistful desires to be taken care of and nurtured.

KEEPING IN TOUCH

How can parents keep in touch, yet still affirm their sons' and daughters' growing adulthood? There are a number of recommendations
that students make again and again when they are asked what they
would like their parents to do. Almost all students claim that they
want attention and support from their parents—but not unsolicited
advice. They want mail; the contents don't seem to matter as much
as the simple, tangible connection to the life they have left behind.
They want care packages, and they talk with childlike delight about
receiving bundles of food at exam time and inexpensive decorations
for their rooms at holidays. They appreciate phone calls, but not
early in the morning. Most prefer to talk on the phone to one parent
at a time, and especially enjoy private conversations with siblings.

Students talk also of their frustration with parents who call "only
when they're angry," and the pain of rejection by parents who
always seem too preoccupied to communicate at all. They dislike
getting caught in the middle between divorced parents, and sometimes can't remember what they told to which parent.

Many say they love it when their parents make their plane reser-
vations home for them at the end of the semester, when they are

overloaded with exams and papers. These same students, however, complain when their parents are "too helpful," sending immediate replacements for lost sweatpants or gloves, without being asked to do so, or sewing buttons on as soon as they arrive home for vacations. Though college students resent intrusions and parental attempts at control, they long to be understood, and contrary to their public claims, most of them do care what their parents think:

> When I call home excited to tell that I'm doing some-thing independent, and I just want to tell them, and they give me advice, it's deflating.

> I wish my mom would be more in tune sometimes with what's going on with me. Mention my friends by name in letters; say hi to them so I know she's hearing what I'm telling her. I have my friends here, and she doesn't know as much about them as I'd like her to. That's hard. I guess it's part of growing up.

> Phone calls are very important to me. It's important that I have their approval, and even if they don't approve, it's important to have their understanding. They're not going to approve of everything I do, just like I don't approve of everything they do. We're different people with different ideas about things. But I want them to try to understand where I'm coming from, and why I'm doing what I'm doing.

> A lot of times you get the idea that professors don't believe in you. It's important for parents to let you know they care and believe in you.

> I called home full of complaints last night. Mom just lis-
> tened and listened. At one point she said, "Isn't growing
> up a bitch?" That was just great!

Students want to be kept informed about the changes at home,
from the superficial alterations in the household decor to more substantive changes in the health and well-being of family members.
They are particularly vehement about being told about major crises
and feel betrayed when parents, hoping to spare them, withhold
information. "I want the privilege to worry over someone I love,"
one young woman exclaimed angrily after learning of her father's
serious illness when she arrived home for spring break. "It's a violation of trust not to tell me. I'll always be anxious about what might
be happening that I don't know about. And it makes me feel very
isolated and remote from everyone at home. What I know about, I
can handle."

Though students make it clear that they want to know what is
going on, parents still have to wrestle with how much to say and
when to say it: Can the news wait until exams are over or is it important to tell her right away? Can I let him know what is happening
without burdening him with details and my own anxiety? Should I
call some official at the college? How can I use the system that is
already in place to provide support during this troubled time?

One mother received the traumatic diagnosis of a malignancy and
impending surgery several days after her freshman daughter's arrival
at William and Mary. Her sensitivity to her daughter's needs in the
midst of her own crisis helped to ease this difficult time:

> Amanda went to school early for preseason hockey prac-
> tice, so she was in an empty dorm with just her head resi-
> dent. I told her I wanted her to tell people what was going
> on at home, and she agreed to talk to her head resident. I
> called the head resident myself and also her coach, the
> two people I knew she was having the most contact with.
>
> She wanted to come home, but I said, "No, you need to
> get started." I suggested that she come home in early

November after the surgery, after people had flocked around, and when I knew I'd need cheering up.

In their concern for their children's happiness, parents may unwittingly focus on their vulnerabilities. When the father of a young woman who has a tendency to procrastinate keeps asking her if she has had a productive week, or a shy young man's mother asks repeatedly if he's made any friends, the student's attempts to cope independently are undermined. By constantly bringing up a sensitive topic, the parent is sending the unspoken message "I'm worried about you and don't think you can manage on your own." The student may become more anxious or, in an attempt to break the parental bond, engage in the very behavior the parent is worried about. A sophomore at Emory comments:

> Everyone in our family has a weight problem. Before I came here my mother teased me about the freshman 40 instead of the freshman 10. When there is a weight problem in your family and the last thing your mother says before you go away is "Watch out for the freshman 40," that's really not a good thing.
>
> When I first got here I was paranoid about food. The first few weeks of school my mother asked at every phone conversation, "How is your weight doing?" Parents should be careful, because the number of bulimics at school seems to be amazingly large.

Parents may wonder why at times their children seem so accessible and at others, so distant. Moments of understanding and tenderness between them are treasured by both. And yet, as parents and children temporarily bridge the gap between their worlds, their sense of connection is tenuous. Although comforting to students, it can also feel threatening—a flashback to earlier times of childhood dependence.

Sometimes after periods of intense and intimate contact with parents, students pull back abruptly. Ambivalent about their own ability to be independent, they act out this ambivalence through bouts of silence or antagonism. They may stop calling or writing for weeks on end and be unresponsive to family attempts to communicate, claiming uncharacteristically that they have nothing to say. Some fight their separation battles on an intellectual level, haggling with parents over the phone about politics or values, testing themselves and establishing their autonomy. Some retreat silently in an attempt to extricate themselves from the knots that bind them to an alcoholic family member, or from battling parents who are vying for their allegiance. Or, finding it stressful to switch gears abruptly from being an independent college student to being the kid in the family, some decide to stay at school over brief vacations such as fall break or Thanksgiving.

Students may seem unpredictably elusive and remote for months at a time when college life takes them into realms never experienced by their parents. A young woman whose parents live in a working-class Irish enclave and have never left their home state talks about feeling guilty and frustrated as she tries to share with them the diversity of her college friends and the travels they have enjoyed together. Another student returns to his depressed neighborhood in East St. Louis and tries to imagine what it would be like to bring his neighborhood friends and college roommates together. He often feels like a stranger in both worlds, but he can't explain any of this to his parents, who wonder why their formerly gregarious son is suddenly so quiet.

A lesbian from an upper-middle-class competitive and traditional Long Island community deliberates over how to stay close to the family she loves and admires while rejecting their community and lifestyle. Though she goes to school less than 200 miles away, she rarely goes home, but worries that she is hurting her parents as she wrestles with redefining her relationship with them.

And still another student, from a Puerto Rican immigrant family, talks about the anger she felt toward her parents, especially during her freshman and sophomore years, because they didn't understand her life. She resented what she considered their limited aspirations and their attempts to limit her. She withdrew from them emotionally and physically. Now, as a senior, she has come to a renewed appreciation of her parents and realizes that if they had-n't done certain things, she never would have gone to college, that her own life would have been much more narrow. After a painful withdrawal, she has reclaimed her past and reentered their lives.

WHEN SOMETHING GOES WRONG AT SCHOOL

The unexpected bombshells from campus that suddenly invade the daily routine of a family back home range from bouts of homesick-ness to serious illness. It is not easy for parents to assess the severity of a problem from afar, but students do send them signals and clues, some of which are indirect pleas for attention.

During the first few months of school, homesickness calls are rou-tine interruptions in many homes. In most cases, they eventually wane, only to erupt once in a while at particularly stressful times. A Colorado College freshman explains:

> In the beginning of school, I called my parents every day. I was very homesick and I felt like I needed to talk to them. I felt a tremendous void inside of me, and by talking to them I was able to fill that void. After about a month, I got into the pattern of school. I don't call them nearly as much anymore. Before, I loved talking to them. Now, I don't have as much to say to them, and when we're on the phone, I am easily distracted by others around me.

A divorced mother of five recalls her middle child's grueling first semester:

> At first she called nightly wanting to come home. I told her she couldn't, but could come for a weekend. She cried every night. She was really scared and kept telling me she missed the rainbows in her room and that she wanted to stay with me forever. I finally told her she could call two times a week unless there was an emergency and after the first semester we would talk about whether she would stay.

> She made it through the semester . . . we both did; it was
> tough. By second semester she had made a commitment to
> stay and had three and a half pretty good years after that.

There are, of course, the few exceptional cases that deans and counseling centers deal with each year when the rupture of leaving home is simply too great and the panic increases with each passing day. With the help of college administrators and counselors, parents and their children may have to come to the disappointing, but not irrevocable, decision that a student should go home. Most youngsters will be able to separate from their parents eventually in their own way and at their own pace, some with the additional help of therapy. Many return to college after a year or two of either working or going to school closer to home.

It is bound to be difficult for parents when their children come home unexpectedly. This sudden switching of gears throws a wrench into the whole family system. Parents may feel let down or burdened by having to cope with their children's problems on a daily basis. While trying to provide their children with emotional support, parents are likely to be struggling themselves with a sense of remorse as they question what went wrong. This return to the fold certainly was not part of the original plan when, full of dreams and expectations, they sent their children off to college.

As they try to separate, young adults often test their parents' limits in painful and destructive ways. The more emotionally dependent they feel, the more dramatic the rupture is likely to be. "In our darkest moments, we felt vilified as parents," said one mother whose daughter left school abruptly during her freshman year. "We turned to our friends for support. It was comforting to be told that we were just human, that we'd done the best we could."

From the father of a student who returned home halfway through his first semester:

> We had to keep letting Josh know that we cared about
> him. He got an apartment near where we live. He was
> belligerent and very hostile. When we heard from him

we had to listen to the melody, not the words. The
melody said, "I need to know you're around." The words
said, "I don't need you."

We all got into family therapy. It was important for us
to have an outside person to bring us together when the
ferment was so chaotic.

During the course of their college careers, all students inevitably
face bouts of minor illness. When they become rundown and suffer
from colds and the flu, they understandably miss the comforts of
home, the privacy, chicken soup, and coddling they may have been
used to. They are likely to call when they are feeling their absolute
worst, seeking a bit of mothering. The first time this happens, the
parents may be caught off guard. The mother of a Creighton
University freshman says with a smile:

> The second or third week of school, he called and said,
> "Mom, what do you do for a real bad earache?" What I
> wanted to say was, "You put the phone down and wait for
> your mother, and I'll be there in four hours."

Of course, she didn't say that, but told him instead to go to the
health service, which on all campuses is equipped to handle common
illnesses and injuries. Some students simply need—in addition to
expressions of sympathy—a bit of encouragement from their parents to
use these services and to take responsibility for their own well-being.

The calls that all parents dread are those that bring news of a
child's serious illness or accident. Most parents expect the college to
keep them informed of serious medical problems. The notion of
what constitutes something serious, however, is a matter of opinion.
It's not unusual for parents to find out about episodes such as a
rollerblade accident or a case of mononucleosis long after the fact.
They may be upset by this, but as one health service director
explains, "Students are in the process of passing from dependence to
independence, and we try to foster that."

If students are coping well with the problem and have not been hospitalized, most colleges will not call home on their behalf. They may encourage students to do so, but will treat them as adults.

When students do encounter serious medical problems, parents face the difficult situation of having to place their trust in unfamiliar medical caretakers and their child's own ability to follow through. In the course of the academic year, a certain number of students will have to be hospitalized with either a physical or psychological illness. Dean Anne Schroer-Lamont of Washington and Lee firmly recommends that one or both parents come at such times, unless the hospital stay is brief and not traumatic. Many students are hesitant to ask, but usually want their parents with them, even if they don't say so directly. This is a time when parents can cooperate with administrators to give the support and encouragement a student will need. Adjustments will have to be made; perhaps a lighter course load or leave of absence will be in order. When a serious accident or illness temporarily sends a college student back to childlike dependency on parents, it may take a special effort for the family to separate again after the student has recovered.

Less dramatic than hospitalization, but equally demanding of a parent's attention, are students' comments, either direct or indirect, that they are worried about their own behavior. Students who hint at or tell their parents of eating disorders, alcohol and drug dependency, and other self-destructive and compulsive behavior want their parents to respond. They don't want them to panic or nag, but to know they are in trouble and to take them seriously, as this student from Ohio State asserts:

> It took me two years to get up the courage to tell my mother that I was bulimic. By that time I was frantic. She hardly responded—kind of blew it off—and never mentioned it again. I'm not sure if she just couldn't handle it or if she really just thought it was a phase and didn't realize how serious it is.

Another student, a sophomore at Columbia, describes her parents' head-on approach:

When I came home over break, it was obvious that I had
gained weight and wasn't keeping in shape or doing any
sports like I usually do. And during the first week I was
back, I was hung over two or three times. My parents were
really worried about this drinking thing with me to the
point where they made me see somebody about it. They
sent me to my doctor, who discovered that I'd gained 12
pounds, which is a lot on a small frame. He also said I had
an iron deficiency, which can happen from drinking.

Maybe I was lucky that my parents picked up the signals, and that my doctor discovered I had anemia. Once
my doctor figured out what was going on, I talked mostly
to him. When my parents and doctor intervened it was
kind of like I was pulling back from being totally responsible for myself. I guess I wasn't doing a very good job of it.
There had to be some help.

Doctors in college clinics see an abundance of symptoms related
to stress. When a student comes in four or five times complaining of
headaches, stomachaches, or sleep difficulties and no organic problem surfaces, the physician is likely to view the symptom as a func-
tional problem and may talk with the student about it, perhaps making a referral to a counselor or psychiatrist for evaluation.

Psychological concerns are often insidious, developing over time
and perhaps not clearly troublesome until well under way. College
students are often mercurial; they may use the word *depressed* when
they simply mean tired or lonely, and they tend toward hyperbole,
especially when describing their own moods. So it is particularly difficult for a parent to distinguish normal ups and downs from psychological distress that needs attention.

Just as parents are beginning to relax and enjoy the pleasure of
thinking about their son as an independent, capable, well-func-
tioning adult, they receive a frantic phone call from him—now
anxious and frazzled, having lost all sense of perspective. Or they
get a disturbing late-night call from a despondent daughter who is
questioning the meaning of her life. After a sleepless night, the par-

ents anxiously call back the next day only to find the same daughter about to leave for a touch football game, irritated by their overreaction.

Brief episodes of depression and anxiety are common among college students. Most will feel the extreme pressure of some aspect of college life sooner or later: always another book to read, another paper to write, another exam to take, another set of problems to do—it never seems to go away. Add to this a broken love affair, disappointing grades, the threat of losing a scholarship, being rejected by a fraternity—all losses that take their toll. Most youngsters will cope with their fears and disappointments and, given the time to grieve for their losses, will pick themselves up with remarkable resilience. Letting go of dreams, coming to terms with one's limitations is, after all, part of the reality of being an adult. But losses may be particularly powerful at this stage of development. Noted psychiatrist Robert Arnstein comments on this phenomenon in his book on suicide and depression in adolescents and young adults:

> The developmental issue of separation may be especially important in vulnerability to a depressive disorder. Depression is often precipitated by a loss or separation; because loss and separation are part of psychological development at this life stage, a late adolescent–young adult may be peculiarly vulnerable to depression. There are several events that are characteristic of this period. First, going to college may be experienced as a separation from parental ties; and, although this is presumably a desirable step in the process of development, not everyone is emotionally ready and some may be overcome by depressed feelings. Second, romantic attachments and detachments are frequent occurrences in this period, and the detachment phase may be especially painful for the late adolescent. Although pain probably always accompanies a loss, the superimposition of the actual loss of an attachment to parental figures may multiply the feelings of depression and lead to a state of hopelessness.[1]

Dr. Arnstein's observations may help parents to understand the intensity of some depressive episodes when there seems to be no momentous precipitating cause. Why does a young man become suicidal when he gets a C in physics? How can the ending of a two-month fling bring on such feelings of worthlessness and hopelessness? These are the young people who don't bounce back from their bouts of anxiety or depression, but who continue to sink deeper into a period of increasing despair.

Janet Loxley of the University of California at Irvine's counseling center acknowledges that many of the typical signs of depression may simply be normal behavior among college-age students. Changes in eating and sleeping patterns, withdrawal, low energy, and flat affect in conversation are a few of the common symptoms that may or may not signal trouble.

Dr. Loxley believes, however, that if parents notice a cluster of these kinds of changes in their child's behavior, they should pay attention:

> In addition to the other patterns I mentioned, a marked change in hygiene, not just long hair or weird clothing, is something I'd be concerned about. Other things of note are forced cheer—trying hard to look happy—a sense of apathy and lack of interest in peers, waking up early and not being able to go back to sleep. Contrary to what some people might expect, depressed people are unlikely to be sitting around crying all the time. It's more subtle than that; they often just demonstrate little energy or interest in the world around them.
>
> If parents are concerned that their son or daughter is depressed, they might start by asking a simple open-ended question such as "What's going on?"
>
> When a kid says to a parent, "It's not going well; I don't have friends," the parent wants to make the kid feel better fast and is tempted to say things like "Don't worry. It will get better." Or "I know how you feel. I went through the same thing. Everyone does."

What the kid needs instead is to know that he or she has been heard, that the parents heard that these things are problems. A parent might say, "I'm not 100 percent sure, but you sound kind of depressed to me. Do you want to talk about it?" Let the kid feel as though he has some room.

Dr. Loxley believes that it's fine for parents who are worried about a noncommunicative and seemingly depressed child to call up a housing official or dean and tentatively express concern, though their son or daughter will be initially displeased by their intervention. But parents shouldn't try to get the university officials to collude with them without telling their child. Dr. Loxley asserts:

> It's one thing to call the head resident in the dorm and say, "My daughter has been sleeping late every day, and I want to make sure she's up by eight each day—and don't tell her I called."
>
> It's a totally different matter to call and say, "I'm not certain that there's a problem, but I'm concerned about my daughter and told her I was going to call you. I'd appreciate it if you'd keep an eye on her and encourage her to use whatever resources you and she think might help her."

Depression is a complex topic, and its causes are still being debated. College students, whose identities are shaky to begin with, live in a highly charged and demanding environment. Some bring with them the added burden of family problems; some may have a predisposition to depression. It's no wonder that depression is the most common psychological problem among college students.

As a result of the dramatic improvement in psychopharmacological approaches to treating depression, an increasing number of students suffering from this disorder take antidepressants that allow them to function well in college. When students go off their medication and then call home for help, parents are faced with yet another challenge.

The mother of a freshman describes a phone call from her daughter a month into college:

My stomach dropped when I heard her say, "Mom, things aren't going so good. I really want to come home. You know that I'm not a student; in fact I really hate school. I should have never come here. I'm not going to classes. I can't do this without you pushing me out the door." (She had in fact slept through her first exam.) "I miss you. I miss the dog. I'm not going to make it. Please let me come home."

As Caroline spoke, I held my breath so I wouldn't let on to her how scared I was. I listened, asked lots of questions, and tried to let her vent her worries. She had taken herself off her antidepressants the week before the phone call. I had to somehow convince her to go back on her meds, to respect her desire not to have "these chemicals in my body," and to help her regroup. We talked for a long time. She bought my metaphor about first semester being like making waffles. (You sometimes burn the first waffle, but you don't throw out the batter; in other words, you are just learning about this college business, not to mention all of the adjustments, so don't give up yet. You'll screw up, but so does everyone else.) I let out my breath by the end of the conversation. She said she would go back on her Zoloft. I cried when I got off the phone.

A number of students suffer severe psychological illnesses that require them to be hospitalized, and some eventually have to leave college. This is devastating to parents and activates intense feelings, from guilt and self-doubt to anger and resentment. These families suddenly find themselves catapulted into a world of mental health professionals that may be foreign and frightening. Parents are encouraged to learn as much as they can about the illness and to reach out to friends, counselors, or clergy at such a draining time so that they can get support for themselves and still be emotionally available to their child.

Phone calls bringing news of unexpected traumatic experiences are likely to catch parents off guard. The father of a University of Virginia sophomore tells of his helpless feelings when he and his wife received a phone call from their son in the middle of the night:

Jay had gone to Washington to visit some of his high school friends at Georgetown for the weekend. On the way to a concert, they found themselves in the midst of a crowd running toward them, so they ran back to their car. Suddenly, they were kicked to the ground by several policemen, their hands forced behind their backs, hand-cuffed, and Jay found himself with a gun pointing at his head. After much physical and verbal assault, they were let go when it was clear that they had been innocent bystanders. But the trauma had taken its toll.

When Jay called he was clearly shaken, and we felt so helpless not being there with him. My wife wanted to pack up his things and bring him home. I told her this could have happened three blocks from us, and we can't protect him from it. Although Delores answered the phone, Jay just wanted to speak to me. I think it's a gender thing. There are certain things kids just are more comfort-able talking to the parent of the same gender about.

He worried about upsetting us. I was glad that we had inculcated into our kids that no matter what happens, we may not like it or what you may have done, but we are your parents and we need to know.

It helped us to talk to the parents of the other kids and to our pastor, and it helped Jay to talk to his friends. But when he was still feeling down several days later, we suggested that he also talk to someone at the counseling center.

It was important to take care of what we could—con-tacting the police, the university president, an attorney—to get some control. I told Jay, "It's not guaranteed that we'll get results, but we'll do what we can do, and then you need to get back to the normal pattern of your life at school and remain focused."

When Jay went away to college, I knew that something was likely to happen. These things happen to us and our loved ones all the time. I thought it more likely that he might be picked up in a small town or driving on a back street. This incident happened because he was in the wrong place at the wrong time, but also because he is an African-American male. I had told Jay of the fun times I used to have visiting my friends at other colleges, and then this happened. It ruined what should have been a happy time.

Remaining steady in the face of frightening or heartbreaking news draws upon all of a parent's resources. When a son calls to report that he has been in a car accident or a daughter describes a sexual assault by a date, parents may respond out of their own anxiety rather than in ways that would be helpful to their child.

Though date rape and crime on campus are common topics in the headlines, nothing really prepares us to handle these situations when they happen to our own children. Startling evidence of our sons' and daughters' vulnerability is likely to stir up all of our most protective parental instincts. We're thrown off balance ourselves—frightened, sad, and angry about what has happened. We'd like to think that there's some way we can prevent something like this from ever happening again. And that's when we start asking the kind of questions that one student labeled the "Why did you? Why didn't you?" variety.

A young woman who had been forced to have sex with a classmate after a party explains what happened when she finally got up the nerve to call home and tell her mother about it.

The first thing my mother hit me with, after she asked if I was OK, was "Why was he in your room? Were you drunk? Was he drunk?" I was raped, for God's sake!

And then I had to deal with my father, who called me back that night and wanted the name of the guy. He wanted to call the dean and find out what the college was going to do about it.

They just didn't get it! At that point, I didn't know exactly what I wanted, but I knew I didn't want to be blamed or rescued . . . just listened to and supported. I needed someone to help me figure out what *I* wanted to do.

Having experienced the helplessness, violation, and betrayal of date rape, a woman needs to regain control over her life—to make her own decision about reporting the incident or pressing charges. It's not unusual for a woman to wait weeks or even months before she labels an act of unwanted intercourse as rape, and it may take even longer for her to reveal it to someone else. Recovery from rape, or indeed from attempted rape, is a long process. Most campuses now employ counselors who are specially trained to help students who have suffered this trauma.

When a young woman calls home to talk about what has happened to her, parents can help by encouraging her to use campus resources. Though times such as these may stretch us to our emotional limits as parents, our children need us to listen, not judge; to be patient, understanding, and supportive.

The director of the University of Michigan's Sexual Assault Prevention and Awareness Center offers parents the following advice:

> The first thing you should do is take two deep breaths, and then tell your daughter you have faith in her, and that you're really sorry this happened. Emphasize that it's not her fault, and that the decisions about what to do are hers, and that you'll support her through this.
>
> Then I think you should go get support yourself. The feeling of helplessness, especially for parents who live far from their daughter's school, is overwhelming. Supporting your daughter through this is very painful, and you're probably going to need help.
>
> In addition to counseling and support from friends, I highly recommend Linda Ledray's sensitive and informative book, *Recovering from Rape*.

Students often respond intensely to the problems and tragedies that occur around them. A fellow student's attempted suicide, a rape, a fatal accident—any tragedy that powerfully shatters the illusion of invulnerability that cloaks the lives of college students—is likely to create ripples of distress throughout the campus. "I used to feel so invincible," said one student after the death of a classmate in a car accident. "Now it's never going to be the same again."

College faculty and administrators are on the alert when there is a suicide on campus. Such an event triggers thoughts of suicide in other students, and there is often an increase in attempts during the weeks following. Though many colleges don't report—or even keep—suicide statistics, suicide has been deemed the second leading cause of death among college-age people.

Students react, also, to the losses their classmates suffer. When one student's parents decide to get a divorce, his or her friends may start to feel anxious about the relationships of their own mothers and fathers. And when the parent of a classmate becomes seriously ill or dies, intimate friends, and even acquaintances who happen to live in close quarters, feel the reverberations of the loss.

Some students become so enmeshed in the problems of their friends that they feel virtually taken over by a sense of responsibility to them—more responsibility than they can realistically handle. Although students can often help and support each other through difficulties, some problems require professional intervention. In their concern for each other and desire to be helpful, young people are often unable to set appropriate boundaries. When parents become concerned about their child's overinvolvement with a depressed or suicidal friend, they might point out that their child's constant availability may be keeping the friend from getting the professional help that is actually needed.

WHEN PARENTS VISIT SCHOOL

Visits to students on their own turf have the potential for bringing new perspectives and delights—if parents are sensitive to their child's needs and agendas.

Some parents choose to visit on Parents' Weekends, specially planned occasions orchestrated to show off the college at its most hospitable. Others opt for a visit that fits more easily into their child's schedule or one that coincides with a particular event involving their youngster, such as a football game or a musical performance.

Most freshmen look forward to showing off their new home, new friends, and new selves to their families. They may look like the same young people who left home so recently, but the first few months of college seem like an eternity to them and they'd like their parents to take note and understand their lives. They may act surprisingly remote at first, suddenly feeling the vulnerability of their emerging independence. Or they may take charge, frenetically trying to introduce their parents to everyone and everything on campus.

A freshman at Bowdoin describes how she felt about her parents' first visit to campus:

> I was nervous and excited when my parents said they were coming for Parents' Weekend. I wanted to show them my world, to show them where I go biking and where I take people on admissions tours. It's my home. I wanted them to see it and like it.
>
> I wanted them to meet my friends, but not for too long—like I didn't want them to hang out in my room. I wanted them to see the faces behind the names I'd been talking about. But I was used to acting a certain way and kidding around with the guys next door. I was afraid Andrew and Rick would do something embarrassing in front of my parents—or that my parents would tell a dumb joke or tell a story about when I was little. At first it felt kind of weird to suddenly have all these parents around. But it all worked out fine. We kind of got back together as a family and had a fantastic time.

Not every freshman is this enthusiastic about parental visits. A senior from the Midwest recalls:

> My mom kept asking me about Parents' Weekend freshman year. And I kept putting her off. I guess I just wasn't ready for her to come visit yet—maybe because I'd only been there a few months, and it still didn't feel like my

place. I wasn't sure what I wanted, but she must have picked up my uncertainty, and I'm grateful for that. She waited until sophomore year to visit, and by then it was great to have her here.

Bubbles can burst when parents comment on the state of their child's room or clothes or shaggy hair. The weekend can turn sour if the visiting parent demands instant maturity and constant attention. Students expect to be able to continue their studying and social lives when their parents are in town. A delightful dinner together may deteriorate if parents are disappointed or angry when their child leaves for a party soon after the coffee has been served:

> I learned the hard way that Parents' Weekend didn't mean that Doug would be with me the whole time. He had a paper to work on, and he slept in for the parent breakfast Sunday morning.

◼

> Tom and I realized that just as we had some rules and expectations when Heather came home for vacations, she had expectations of her own for us when we went to see her. We decided ahead of time that we were going to try to tune into her agenda instead of sticking to our own. For example, we were hoping to go to a class with her, but that clearly and emphatically was not OK with her. Once we got past the initial awkwardness, I felt almost euphoric seeing her in her world. I got a new sense of how in charge she is, of how much she feels at home there. Before we went I had questioned whether we could justify the cost of the trip. Now it's a high priority for us to visit her at school once a year.

Both divorced and married parents talk about the particular pleasure of a solo visit to campus. A woman who recently spent a day with her son while on a business trip to Boston reflects:

I ended up going on a long afternoon walk with Dan and his girlfriend, making a couple of stops along the way for ice cream and a cappuccino. Then Dan and I went biking along the Charles and topped off the evening at his apartment, where he cooked dinner and his apartment mates wandered in and out. The music was blaring and the phone kept ringing, and I soaked in the whole scene in a way that just wouldn't have happened if my husband had been with us. When I came home and told Steve about our day, he was jealous and decided that he's going to treat himself to his own visit sometime during the year.

Students who live off campus talk with pride of sprucing up apartments and cooking meals for visiting dads and moms. It's an opportunity for them to show off firsthand another step in their growing competence. Although visits to college are wonderful opportunities for students to share their world with parents, most students still take great pleasure in old standby parental pampering, such as a care package from home or a special dinner out for them and their friends.

WHEN STUDENTS COME BACK HOME

Visits home and long-awaited vacations often crystallize the changes taking place across the miles. They evoke questions about relationships and highlight a student's growing independence and separation. They may be particularly complicated for the large number of students whose divorced parents live in different households, sometimes in separate cities. Even parents who have worked out custody and visitation arrangements long ago may suddenly find themselves locking horns over where their son or daughter will spend vacations.

And if parents divorce while their child is away at college, the student has to grapple with questions of allegiances at the same time he or she is trying to separate. It is a difficult combination. In the turmoil of their own distress, parents often minimize the blow of this news to their college-age children and may be surprised by the emotional fallout. College students still define themselves as part of a family, and the rupture to that family unit is usually a major jolt. They may be angry at their parents for splitting up, and although they may act cool about the whole situation, parents should not assume that their external reaction represents what they are feeling inside. It is important for parents to keep their antennae out for emotional reactions and to refrain from involving their child in their own conflicts.

"I've seen parents pull at a kid like a Gumby doll," said one director of residential life. "One kid who didn't want to face making the choice between the two of them went back to his home town for Thanksgiving and checked into a hotel with his brother."

A move to a new city can also be wrenching for college students, especially at vacation times. It makes separating more complicated and often has more of an impact on a youngster living away at school than parents realize. College students are at loose ends when returning home for vacations to a city without friends or familiar landmarks. Family rituals and traditions provide a sense of continuity and may be particularly important at such times. But young people may feel displaced when parents are their only link to this alien community. At a time when they are trying to separate, coming to a new home may throw them into an uncomfortable position of dependence. They may be testy or restless; they may want to leave and return to familiar places and high school friends. A sensitive and understanding parent will be flexible about vacation plans to accommodate this conflict.

A junior whose divorced parents have each moved twice since she started college comments:

> The worst time was freshman year when my mother moved out of the house I grew up in. I felt like a visitor when I went home. My mother's next move was to a whole different part of the country. After that move I did a lot of visiting over the vacation; I went to my boyfriend's house. My parents didn't care, but my grandparents did.
>
> Moving is a pain in the neck. Most of my stuff at my

mother's place is in boxes. Things that are real important to me are here at school. School is more of a home than my official permanent address is.

Home is wherever I am at this point. In a lot of ways it's at school 'cause that's where my closest friends are. If anyplace really feels like home, it's where my grandparents are. I think of them as family and spend part of each of my vacations with them.

The first vacations of a student's college career are usually the most intense for everyone involved. Students and parents, eager to see each other, feel an unfamiliar tentativeness as the family comes together again. A junior at Tufts recalls:

I didn't go home until Christmas freshman year. It was really awful. I remember lying in bed crying the first night and thinking, Sara, you're not the same Sara who left here. I had come home with a bad cold and I was up half the night feeling terrible and confused. The next morning, Mom looked at me kind of sad and asked why I wasn't happy to be home. She looked so let down.

Another student remembers wandering around his house, thinking, I'm supposed to be different, but I don't really feel different. And from the father of a Colby freshman:

We picked Andy up at the airport the day before Thanksgiving, and after the initial greetings and hugs, he just kept staring at us. As he got in the car, he looked at it and said, "Wow, our car—our same old car." He kept making remarks like that about all the familiar landmarks on the road back home, fast food restaurants he had frequented, even gas stations—anything he'd ever had any connection to.

His first few hours at home, he kept walking around the house, noticing every detail. He kept saying how quiet it was, and how weird it was to have all this space for four people. It was like he was trying to drink it all in, like he was trying to convince himself that it was all real. It took a while before we could just settle in and be with each other.

When students return home, most of them expect to find everything just the way they left it, as though time had stopped while they were gone. They prefer to find their rooms untouched and their siblings and parents just the way they always were. Yet they also want their parents to recognize and respect that they have changed, that they have been living on their own and have become more independent. All this calls for a sense of balance—not to mention a sense of humor. And it is the rare family whose members do not find themselves trying to renegotiate relationships and expectations during these weeks between semesters.

Young people look at their families with the discerning eyes of outsiders, seeing, sometimes for the first time, qualities and dynamics they had never noticed before. They may be disillusioned at the less than perfect scene they see; it is likely to have been idealized during their months apart. Or, after observing the way their college friends or roommates interact with their families, they may appreciate aspects of their own home life that they had previously taken for granted. They cast disdainful glances at household changes, even simple improvements.

The mother of a Yale sophomore recalls:

> When Jeff came home freshman year, he was taken aback to find we had a computer and a microwave. He joked about it and said, "Hey! I'm the one who's supposed to go away to college and change, and now you've come into the 20th century." We've had a family myth that we're not a technological family. That was part of Jeff's identity and we took it away from him.

Some students react by being outwardly critical of family habits and patterns that have long been taken for granted: Why do we have to eat dinner at such an uncivilized hour? Why don't the women of this family stand up for themselves? Why do we have to go to church? So what if you and Dad are divorced—can't you at least be civil to each other?

They often bait their parents with newly learned, but as yet unintegrated, bits of philosophy and social consciousness. They bristle at parental attempts to control their comings and goings, their behavior, or their schedules. Having been used to the independence of college life, yet feeling uncertain about their adult status within the context of the family, they may take rigid stances and balk at any suggestions offered:

> It hadn't entered my mind that I'd have to ask to use the car or answer so many questions like "Where are you going?" "What time will you be home?" "Who will you be with?" "Call if you're not home by twelve-thirty." It was a chore.

> Can you believe it? My mother started getting upset about my shoes being left on the stairs? I mean, who cares!

> It's so weird after being independent to go home and have to be a son. What do you mean, clean up my room?

> My freshman year winter break, it was ten or ten-thirty at night, and I wanted to go out and get some coffee, and my mother said she didn't think it would be a good idea. We live in suburbia, not exactly dangerous. My mother said, "It's kind of late." I said, "It's ten-thirty. Are you insane?" And I walked out the door.

Parents may find it tricky to strike a balance between respecting their son's or daughter's emerging independence and wanting to run

their household with some degree of order. They may need to mod-
ify some of their old rules in light of the increased freedom their
child has become accustomed to. Everything becomes even more
complicated when divorced parents have conflicting sets of guidelines in their separate homes. Each family has to negotiate its own
set of expectations, but as one freshman dean says:

> There's bound to be some tension about rules and what
> needs to be said and done. Students are used to coming
> and going without reporting to anyone. I think it is fair for
> parents to expect the same things from their children that
> they would expect from a courteous guest. It's reasonable
> to expect them to pick up after themselves, and let you
> know whether or not they will be home for dinner and
> approximately when they will be in at night.

Students, too, talk of setting new guidelines with their parents
after having lived away from home. One young woman describes
how she convinced her mother to respect her need for quiet in the
morning:

> I'm really in a foul mood when I get up. Unless it's an
> emergency, I'd rather not have people talk to me, and that
> was something I'd gotten used to at school. My roommate
> and I had made quiet pacts and didn't say a word to each
> other for the first hour we were up. When I told my
> mother I wanted to do that at home she was surprised, but
> it worked out OK.

In some households there's a sense of self-consciousness about
how to reenter each others' lives. Students describe parents who
suddenly treat them so much as equals that they lose the special
quality of their relationship:

> All of a sudden I'm just another person in the house. My
> parents think I want to be treated as an adult, like their

> equal. I'm tired of all this independence. I really needed to go home to my mom and have her be a mom. Instead she wants to be my pal.

Others say they feel smothered and long for more parental recognition of their evolving independence:

> I want my parents to treat me as an equal. They baby me and don't seem to realize that I don't want them to do everything for me.

And one young man tells with an amused grin how his parents, each trying to welcome him home, acted like caricatures of their good intentions:

> I went home to a nursemaid and Buddy Hackett. My mom started washing my clothes and folding them for me. My dad started telling me dirty jokes, slapped me on the back, and said, "Hey, you want a beer, kid?"

By their very nature, vacations are times of relaxation and pleasure, and many people approach them with anticipation and heightened expectations. Parents who take their cues from their returning college offspring report delightful moments of rediscovery and joy. Recognizing that this is, in fact, their son's or daughter's vacation, not theirs, they take pleasure in watching their youngster get together with friends and do not mind when he or she spends endless hours just unwinding around the house.

But as students arrive home geared up for rest and reconnecting with high school friends, many parents have their own, very different agendas—fantasies of special family outings, three weeks of unscheduled time for productive summer job-hunting, intimate moments alone with a maturing son or daughter. Such expectations are a trap and may lead to disappointed parents and resentful offspring.

Some parents save up their serious conversations for vacation times; they have plans of heart-to-heart talks with their child about excessive

partying, poor grades, summer plans, or, perhaps the most stressful subject of all, their child's future. All of these are legitimate concerns, but
timing is important, and without caution, discussions can become lectures that will turn off even the most receptive young person.

Often a simple open-ended question such as "What's happening
in your life?" or "How are things going?" gives students just the
opportunity they've been waiting for to talk about what's on their
minds. A young woman from Scripps remarks:

> It's tricky. I want my parents to know about my friends and
> what's going on with me, but if they ask too much it might
> feel intrusive. I think the best thing is for parents and kids
> to take some of the time when they're together over vaca-
> tion to try to catch up.
>
> Anyway, over vacation my father made the biggest
> move he's ever made. He said, "So what's going on?" I let
> out a big sigh of relief and said, "I'm glad you asked. Let
> me tell you."
>
> We talked about four or five of my friends at school,
> including the guy I was dating, and we had never done
> that before in the year and a half I had been there. We
> had discussed what courses I was taking and the extracur-
> riculars, but we hadn't discussed social life, which is a big
> part of my own life. It's difficult to have those kinds of
> conversations over the phone. For me it was the ideal situ-
> ation; my mom and sisters had gone to the movies, and
> Dad and I were sitting by ourselves. It was just the two of
> us, and it's easier for me to talk to my parents one-on-one.

Some students plan to talk to their parents about issues of major
concern during vacations rather than by letter or phone. A gay student from Iowa describes the painful process of coming out to his
father during the winter vacation of his sophomore year.

> I'd always known I wasn't attracted to females, but I kept
> praying it would change. I kept hoping when I got to col-

lege I'd start over and things would be different. I did become very attracted to someone, but that someone was a male; I realized I couldn't fool myself anymore.

My mother died when I was in high school. My Dad and I have always been very close—which, by the way, destroys the stereotype about homosexuals having cold, distant, or absent fathers. I wanted to tell him, and I knew eventually that he would accept it, but I was still worried about his reaction.

During Christmas break, I got my courage up and told him. Initially, he was very accepting, calm, and support- ive. He said, "You're my son. I still love you. Nothing changes. I just want you to be happy."

The first time I became involved with someone, however, he reversed a bit. He was very upset that I was comfortable with it and that I was really planning to go ahead and live my life this way. I hesitated bringing my friend home at spring vacation. After several phone conversations, my dad seemed to have become more resolved. He said, "Of course, come home and bring him. If he's someone you care about, I want to meet him."

This young man acknowledged that he had the "near-perfect coming out" and that many of his friends went through a much more traumatic time. Some have been banished from their families; the parents of others desperately try to find ways to "cure" their chil- dren through psychotherapy, religion, or by actively encouraging heterosexual relationships. And still others pretend they do not know and make it clear they do not want to talk about it. All of these negative responses lead to alienation and distancing between parent and child.

The student quoted above was sensitive to the shock and pain his father would go through. Both father and son had built a strong foundation of trust and communication, which allowed them to get through some tension-filled times and to become closer. They recog- nized that these first awkward conversations are part of an ongoing process—a process that began long ago with their evolving relationship and will continue as each moves through his own difficult journey ahead.

Parents often need information and support when their children confront them with the news that they are gay. Students find it encouraging when their parents take it upon themselves to become informed. *Beyond Acceptance* by Carolyn Welch Griffin and *Coming Out to Parents* by Mary Borhek are among several sensitive and informative books on the subject. And the national self-help organization Parents and Friends of Lesbians and Gays (P-FLAG) has groups in all parts of the United States that have helped provide information as well as support for those in need.

For many parents, vacations are a bittersweet time. Just when they thought they had gotten used to a quieter household, it fills up again with the music and laughter and exuberance of college students. Their children's friends drop by to reminisce about their childhood capers and share tales of their current college exploits. Suddenly there isn't enough milk in the refrigerator and the phone rings every five minutes as plans for the evening are made and remade. The dinner table crackles with the excitement of newly discovered passions, academic and otherwise, and everything seems a bit livelier than it had been. Of course, the dinner table is also the setting for the replay of sibling bickering and volatile outbursts about trivial matters: Who gets the car tonight? What TV shows do we watch? What do you mean by borrowing my sweater without asking? For most parents, however, the squabbles, the McDonald's wrappers in the car, and the pile of towels on the bathroom floor seem a small burden to bear compared to the joy of reconnecting as a family.

"But," says a Wisconsin mother of a sophomore and a senior, "even though it's great to have them back, there's a certain sadness. You realize that it will never be the same again; they are not totally home. They have a whole different world that is part of them, and they are only temporary visitors."

And indeed, most parents find that as their children progress through their college years and become more separate, their visits home take on a distinctly different quality. Students' eagerness to return home and reconnect with family and friends freshman year typically gives way to a more tempered reentry in the years that follow. Many say they don't feel as though they really belong anywhere. School isn't home, and home is no longer the center of their lives.

A Hawaiian woman whose only child attends the University of Santa Clara in California found herself facing a whole new level of adjustment between her daughter's sophomore and junior years:

> It hit me during the summer that this may be her last summer home, the last time she'll be with us for a whole three months. The reality is that there are very few jobs here, and she probably won't be coming back here for a long period of time again.

Students may return less often or set clearer boundaries of separateness when they do come back. Sometimes their behavior is confusing, sometimes humorous, and sometimes painful. Many go through periods of strident distancing before they can reconnect comfortably with their parents on more mutual terms.

The father of a sophomore describes a discrepancy between the way his son relates to him over the phone and the way he wants to interact when he comes home for vacations:

> Kevin calls a lot from school when things aren't going well. He calls to complain about courses or girls who gave him the cold shoulder, almost anything that's on his mind. He describes how he's feeling—if he's depressed or anxious or questioning what he's doing there.
>
> Then when he gets home, all the things he needs to talk to us about when he's at school suddenly seem not to be issues anymore. But of course they still are. It's just, I think, that he feels safer talking about them when he's at school. We can be a long-distance sounding board. But when he's in our house, he might be swallowed up by us. It's too threatening. He's very quiet here, and I think we need to respect that.

■

And the mother of an in-town student who lives in the residence
halls reports:

■

> When Abby was a freshman, she used to come home every
> week to do her laundry, and she'd spend a lot of time talking
> to me. She said the washing machines weren't very good.
> This year she's a sophomore, and she never comes home to
> do her laundry. It's funny; they're the same washing
> machines as last year.

A divorced mother of two describes the abrupt change in her
older daughter's behavior during the summer between her junior
and senior years:

> Libby used to tell me everything. Sometimes I worried
> that she was too dependent on me as a confidante. Her
> father left home when she was 13, and she and I had some
> rocky years together. Anyway, we were very close. But last
> summer when she came home it was as though she put a
> curtain down between us. She barely spoke to me. I knew
> she'd been going through a hard time at school, but she
> didn't want to talk about that or anything else. It was
> really a strain having her around all summer and getting
> the silent treatment. But I kept telling myself that there
> was a method to her madness, that she really needed to
> pull back from me.
>
> Now that she's back at school, we've had a few good
> talks over the phone. It's not the same as it used to be, but
> at least we're talking again.

As students mature, they increasingly look at their parents as separate people, not just Mom and Dad. After a long absence, they may
see signs of aging they had never noticed before. They shed their self-

absorption and begin to feel more empathy for the stresses and struggles of their parents' lives. A young woman, a junior at Washington
University, observes:

> I've noticed changes in my parents lately, especially my
> dad. I think he's changing as he's watching his parents get
> old and is responding to things differently. My dad is going
> through the kind of changes my mom went through a few
> years ago when her parents died. Right now my dad's
> mother is very sick and his father is not doing well either.
> In the last six months my dad has had to take over the role
> of taking care of both of them. I think he feels the burden
> of a lot of responsibility. I also think he's analyzing what
> happened in his parents' lives and the way they dealt with
> him. I'm not sure what the outcome of that will be, but
> I've already seen a change. I think he's becoming more
> sensitive.
>   I also think he's feeling very pressured, watching his
> parents get old before his eyes, and sometimes I feel some
> of that pressure. For instance, if I come home from school
> with an incomplete, it feels like a disappointment to him.
> I think he needs as few problems as possible. I think he
> needs nurturing. He's having to nurture his parents and
> his kids, and I think he needs some of that nurturing back.

The pleasures and pains of parenthood are highlighted during the
periods throughout the college years when children reenter the
household. There is the joy of seeing a child develop—listening to
her describe the way she is going to improve the school literary magazine, or watching him explain to his little brother what archaeol-
ogy is and why he is so excited about it. It is rewarding to see evidence of burgeoning intellectual capacities and self-confidence,
which may have been apparent in letters and phone calls but bring a
more poignant delight to parents in the course of daily interaction.
  When children return home with problems, however, their disappointments and pain become part of their parents' day-to-day exis-

tence too. It hurts to see a child in the throes of misery from a broken romance, or filled with self-doubt, or struggling with a weight
problem. It is more difficult to separate your pain from theirs when
they are at home; their unhappiness is a constant presence.

And parents are reminded, also, of bothersome traits in their children—traits that had faded temporarily from their memories in the
glow of eagerly awaited letters and phone calls from their distant
college offspring. They may find themselves worrying about behaviors they hadn't thought about for a while and wondering, "How can
this budding engineer consistently leave the gas tank on empty and
never replace the toilet paper on the roll?" Or, "She doesn't know
how to lose an argument. How will she ever sustain a relationship or
hold down a job?"

Parental anxiety often gives way to renewed attempts to control,
to take another stab at trying to "set this kid on the right track." In
their more rational moments, parents know, of course, that such
attempts are doomed to failure.

As students move through their college years, their early experi-
ments begin to turn into commitments—and these commitments
may be in conflict with parents' own dreams and values. The
mother who was amused by her son's "granola stage" freshman year
now has to come to terms with the fact that he has decided to
become a forest ranger rather than a lawyer as originally planned.
The father who hardly gave a second glance to the silent, sulking
boyfriend his daughter brought home freshman and sophomore
years begins to wonder if he is going to be a permanent fixture in the
family. As they decide who they are and how they want to live their
lives, students make choices about their majors and careers, about
religion and values, about sexual preference and intimate partners.
When they return home, these loaded issues leap to the forefront
and parents come face-to-face with the essence of letting go.

SOPHOMORE SLUMP AND THE YEARS BEYOND

Did you feel when you first came to college that it was all so new and exciting, such a big change from home? By spring it began to be a little routine, and this fall here you are taking these courses and it's much the same and you don't really know what you're here for and you don't know why you're taking these courses rather than any other courses. You're sleeping a lot, but still always seem to feel tired. Maybe you're just blowing off—sitting in the library, staring at the same page for 40 minutes; maybe you're going out and eating pizza when you know you should be doing your problem sets, but you just can't focus your attention.

"That sounds like me," a bewildered sophomore responds, wondering how his dean knows so much about his lethargic state these past few months. This dean of a highly respected and academically rigorous university is not a psychic, nor does she have informants waiting in the wings. She has just described the common phenomenon known as "sophomore slump" to a student she had summoned to her office for a discussion about a failing grade.

The sophomore slump doesn't always happen sophomore year;

some experience a similar state during the second half of their freshman year or when they are juniors or seniors, and some don't experience it at all. But the sophomore year has particular characteristics
that make it an unsettling time of self-doubt and vulnerability for
many students.

What has happened to the energetic and enthusiastic freshmen of
just a year before? What has happened to their intense and often
quixotic responses to the college environment, that beckoning
world with new intellectual vistas and few social restraints? One
might expect the second year of college to be a repetition of the
first, perhaps a bit more stable since the sophomore has the advantage of knowing the ropes. The sophomore slump, though a common colloquialism, comes as a surprise to both parents and their
children.

Sophomores return to school without the anxiety and hoopla of
orientation that launched them the year before. Most are happy to
be back and eagerly seek out friends and old haunts. They bask in
their sense of belonging as they watch the glassy-eyed freshmen
stumble by. Once school is under way, the peaks and valleys of the
academic year—marked off by exams, vacations, and traditional college events—are reassuringly familiar. But the second college year
presents new choices, new responsibilities, and new problems to
solve. The world of the college sophomore is substantially different
from that of the freshman.

Sophomores, no longer the new kids on the block, are responsible
for themselves in ways they weren't the year before. They don't have
a freshman advisor holding their hands while picking courses. They
are expected to know the system by now, and they are often embarrassed to let others know when they don't. No one is eagerly showing them how to use the library or computer center or guiding them
to the remote corners of the campus. Campus groups are no longer
clamoring for their membership; and everyone assumes that sophomores know from their own experience what it means to belong to a
particular fraternity, team, or club. No one assigns them a roommate; the choices and the consequences are their own. If they don't
get along, they can't chalk it up to a glitch in the computer match-

ing system or the misguided whims of the residential life staff. They may feel both comforted and confined by their friends from the previous year, but the potential for making new friends no longer seems unlimited. And intimate relationships may suffer the strain of unexpected changes after a summer apart. Some sophomores, especially in large, overcrowded universities, move off-campus into apartments, undertaking a whole new range of tasks and responsibilities.

As one administrator put it, "No one is loving you up anymore, whether it is the RA, an advisor, or your parents; and at the same time you're betwixt and between in your academic life."

Academically, sophomores know enough to recognize how little they know. Though they are developing the tools that will allow them to do more creative work later on, they wonder if they will ever be able to master anything—whether they have what it takes to be as competent and knowledgeable as the juniors and seniors they admire. They haven't yet delved into the meat of the substantive specialized courses, and in many schools they are still relegated to large lecture classes. If they haven't picked a major and affiliated with a particular department, they have no academic home. The few who have collected enough advanced placement credits to move into upper-level courses may have difficulty competing with juniors and seniors who already know the academic ropes and can handle what one dean refers to as the "rapier cut and thrust of the classroom discussion and the put-downs that accompany it." These gifted students find their upper-level courses stimulating, but may feel like failures and question their abilities, perhaps for the first time.

The freedoms that sophomores celebrated the previous year haunt them now. The choices still seem endless—choices of courses, friends, and activities; choices of politics, religion, and lifestyle; choices of taking time off, transferring, or spending a year abroad. But they think more about the consequences of their choices than they used to. Making one choice means relinquishing others; choosing means taking responsibility for the choice. All the while, time is running out. In most colleges and universities, by the end of sophomore year, students are expected to choose a major, and the pressure of career choice is not far behind.

THE SLUMP—MORE OR LESS

I felt like a character in the roadrunner cartoon—you know, running frantically full speed ahead, straight off of a cliff—and that awful moment when he looks down and realizes there's no ground under him—that he's just out there by himself in the middle of the air. That's how I felt most of sophomore year.

Forging ahead with enthusiasm and eagerness, students may discard—though often temporarily—the values their parents hold dear. Now, as they are pressured to make decisions about their own futures, many become aware of the void that is left. Though some youngsters attend religious or culturally homogeneous institutions that confirm their family values, the majority of today's college students are surrounded by diverse points of view from their classmates and professors. They are exposed to many so-called right answers, all backed up by rational arguments. How can all these answers be true?

Many sophomores question not only their parents' values and choices, but the very possibility of making rational choices at all. As they move beyond a dualistic view of the world, one idea seems as worthwhile as the next. They feel off balance and disoriented; nothing seems solid. Seeking answers, they find only questions: "Why am I taking this course?" "How can behaviorists and Freudians both be valid?" "I always thought physics was great, but why is physics better than philosophy?" "Why am I at this school?" "What difference will it make if I stay or transfer?" "What is the purpose of education?" "What is the meaning of my life?"

They describe their experience as "tenuous," "arbitrary," "meaningless." They describe themselves as "fragmented," "seasick," "rootless." Frequently, students look inside themselves and feel lost and immobilized. Their reactions range from hedonistic escape to existential angst.

A Brandeis student recalls:

Sophomore year everyone collapsed—or at least my friends and I did. It was a year of questioning. What's the point of doing anything in life? What does it all mean? What is this all about? "Being and Nothingness" was the name of the game.

Parents may be taken aback by unexpected phone calls from a normally upbeat child who is suddenly questioning the meaning of life. The mother of one sophomore recalls:

> Madeline called at midnight talking about God and death. She's taking a course about aging and death, and she was distraught. After 45 minutes of listening, I finally told her I just had to get some sleep. I suggested that she talk to someone there—a chaplain or counselor—and I'd call her the next day after I got home from work.

When asked about his sophomore year, a University of Chicago student responds:

> All through my sophomore year I was unhappy. I was losing sight of what it all meant. It was kind of a masturbatory philosophical question, because there really wasn't any answer to it. It was just, where am I headed—what does this mean? I got so wrapped up in trying to solve that one that I neglected the present. I was real unsure of myself. There weren't a whole lot of black-and-white standards to deal with. Nothing was concrete.
>
> It seemed like I was spinning my wheels with schoolwork. Nothing seemed to make much difference. I would turn in the token paper for the token class, making the points that they grade on. It wasn't doing me any good. It just seemed really trivial at the time, like a big spoon of cough medicine that everyone has to take at some time.

Some students, such as this young man, become paralyzed by their own introspection. Caught like a gerbil continually spinning the wheel in his cage, they may try to alleviate their anxiety with numbing devices: drugs, alcohol, or a series of meaningless sexual liaisons.

Some look outside themselves and impulsively grab hold of a group or ideology for support—a fraternity, a women's center, a political group, or, for a few, the rigid structure of a cult. Others, aware of a general malaise but unable to pinpoint the source, decide to transfer or take time off, hoping to find solutions elsewhere. Even those sophomores who continue to be actively engaged in their studies and social environment are often caught off guard by periods of confusion and disenchantment.

A young woman from Ohio, now a vibrant and self-confident junior, looks back on her sophomore year:

> I had done really well second semester freshman year, and I came back to school thinking, I know how the system works now. But it was a real struggle. I thought, Now I'm just going to sail through with A's and B's the whole way. But I took classes I had no background in—a computer class, accounting, Spanish. They were all tedious and time-consuming, and I felt very inadequate. Spanish was the first class I ever took where I studied and didn't see results. The only thing that kept me studying was the fear that if I didn't, I was going to fail. At one point, that almost sounded better. If you fail, at least you can say that it's impossible, that you just can't do it. If you get C's and D's you always question if you could do better.
>
> I had already decided to major in English, but I had a bad experience in the first E. Lit. course I actually took. My professor's comments on my first paper basically said, "Learn to write or get out." I felt outclassed because there were a lot of seniors in the class. I felt there was a gaping hole between what I needed to know and what I knew. I went to talk to my professor, and he wasn't very reassuring about it.
>
> On top of this, I had been invited to participate in a Women's Leadership Training Institute. We met monthly and it brought up a lot of issues I was ready to deal with. Thank God for WLTI! But it also brought up problems in a

relationship I was in. I became angry at my boyfriend as I became more aware of things. I started thinking, I'm a woman first, what does that mean?

I started looking at what I wanted to do with my life. And how does my English major fit in? I think I spent the year saying, Is this what I'm cut out for? Does this tap into some wonderful resource I have in me, or am I just going to struggle along like this the whole way? I remember feeling tired a lot.

In the midst of all this questioning, students wonder whether the financial commitment they and their parents are making is worth it. Financial sacrifices and the specter of loans to be repaid weigh heavily on students who feel unmotivated and unproductive:

My sophomore year was a very tenuous time for me. I was very frightened. I was afraid I was drifting apart from my friends at home. I wasn't quite sure where I was going, what direction. I had no solid ground to pin myself to intellectually. I was aware of time flying by. Tuition was going up each year. What did I have to show for it?

Some sophomores who don't feel the unsettling ennui of the slump describe an almost manic sense of excitement that can be unsettling in its own right. Each new course they take uncovers another academic possibility, another world waiting to be discovered. They ask themselves, "Is this the department I want to settle in? Is this the subject I want to master?" Or, stimulated by the interests of their classmates, they take up one hobby after another—playing the guitar 5 hours a day, then turning with equal intensity to ultimate Frisbee or lyric poetry.

A sophomore at Dartmouth describes her second year there as "fantastic," but adds:

Sometimes my head is reeling from all the choices. When I look at the catalog before registration I get excited—and confused. There's so much I want to study. My parents probably think I'm nuts each time I call home with a different idea about what I want to major in. Right now I'm into philosophy—18th century. And I love Italian. Maybe I'll combine that with art history and spend time in Italy next year.

While all this is happening at school, students continue to loosen the ties to home. Loyalties shift from family and high school friends to college friends, suitemates, and lovers. Though new connections are beginning to replace the old, sophomores often talk about feeling lonely and adrift. They describe their feeling as a sense of aloneness in the world rather than a dearth of friends.

Many college students live in a world devoid of meaningful contact with adults. As sophomores they are unlikely to have developed close relationships with faculty, which are usually the prerogative of juniors and seniors who have immersed themselves in seminars and research projects of their major department. Even in small schools that pride themselves on their accessible faculty, underclassmen are often too shy and intimidated to seek them out. It is not unusual for sophomores to go through the whole year without ever having an intimate conversation with someone over 22 years of age unless they take the initiative to connect with head residents, deans, faculty, student activity advisors, or chaplains.

Disturbed by a feeling of rootlessness, students reach out to one another. Friendships that were formed freshman year may begin to deepen and thrive. Some unravel, however, as students continue to develop new interests and venture forth from the pack:

> I moved into a suite sophomore year. We were all good friends, and we thought, This is going to be so much fun living together. And the first two weeks were fun, but then each person got singled out—"Be mean to Sue week." It was a mess. We had a huge fight at the end.
>
> We'd been so similar freshman year. We were all freshmen in the same boat, all gained 10 pounds, all were

homesick. We came back and we started to choose majors and meet more people and expand our circle of friends, and we didn't like each other's friends or the habit of smoking that one picked up—a lot of petty things, but we were establishing our own identities. Sophomore year I started solidifying the me that people know and the me that I know.

Longing for intimacy and continuity as well as new adventures, many students talk about their dashed expectations. From a University of Pennsylvania sophomore:

I thought when I started my sophomore year, Now I can choose my roommate and where I'm going to live, and I know people. It's going to be great. But I found out things were pretty much the same. I wanted to meet new people, do new activities, study in new places. I was intimidated by people already having friends. The friendships I have here seem so artificial and unsatisfying. I haven't really found something yet that's for me, and the older guys are checking out the freshmen girls now.

Questions of identity and intimacy are intertwined, as young men and women refine their definitions of themselves through their relationships with each other. They treasure the intimacy of being a couple, yet strive to protect themselves from getting lost in the twosome. Particularly when they live in the same dorm, sometimes even on the same floor, students struggle to be identified as individuals rather than one half of a whole. The constant "Where's Becky?" that he hears as he walks down the hall, the guilt that she feels as she moves quickly past his door without stopping in—these incessant reminders echo in the thoughts of committed couples, and as a result, they may start to pull away from each other.

In all arenas of their lives, there is a pressure on sophomores to define themselves and begin to take a stand. Marion Hyson, Professor of Individual and Family Studies at the University of

Delaware, believes that the issue of control is at the crux of a lot of problems students face during sophomore year:

> Many feel little sense of control over their own destinies. They feel trapped by the choices they made freshman year—choices about friends, fraternities or sororities, roommates, and courses. They have to declare a major, but feel constrained by family and social agendas. They are pulled in different directions, asked to make choices and live with the consequences.

Those not ready to make commitments are most vulnerable to the sophomore slump. For some this is an important though painful time. In an article for *Princeton Parents* newsletter, a junior describes the unexpected slump he experienced and the effect it had on him:

> In my case, and I think in most cases, the slump did not result in disastrous grades. Underneath the decent marks, however, lay an academic dissatisfaction and a temporary lack of desire to learn. Curiosity waned, and reading became a task rather than a joy. If I took anything from the aimlessness of sophomore year, it was the insight that comes from having no direction. . . .
>
> In retrospect, it may have been necessary to waste time. For many Princetonians, high school was an intense, harried experience. Freshman year at college is a matter of survival. Total confusion forces new students to be on their toes. Sophomore year is the transition between wide-eyed awe and upper-class confidence. The slump may not be as much a sin as a temporary hibernation, a time for the mind to sleep and to wake up refreshed.[1]

At this vital and energetic stage of life, standing still and feeling stuck can be almost unbearable. Kenneth Keniston, noted author and social psychologist, writes of the "enormous value placed upon change, transformation and movement" by young men and women and their panic "when confronted with the feeling of 'getting nowhere,' of 'being stuck in a rut,' or of 'not moving.'"[2]

In the past, young people projected their desire for motion outward toward social and political causes—the women's movement, the peace movement, the civil rights movement. The restlessness of youth was captured in books and film, from *On the Road* to *Easy Rider*, and in the alteration of self through transcendental meditation or psychedelic drugs. Many of today's generation of students channel their need for movement primarily into collecting academic and extracurricular credentials that will get them onto the fast track of career, status, and power—a world of adulthood that some sophomores fear as the ultimate trap. And so they procrastinate, stagnate, and spin their wheels until they find it intolerable and begin to make decisions.

THE MAJOR DECISION

I declared my English major in September and then spent the rest of my sophomore year investigating it.

I changed from architecture to urban studies and sociology. I'd wanted to be an architect since sixth grade. It was hard to change. It was hard to lose the identity I'd built up over all those years. I didn't tell my parents about it until first semester junior year.

Horrendous, horrifying! Here at Harvard, we call them fields of concentration and most of us change at least six times.

In high school I was president of the computer club. When I got to Oberlin, I hated math. I took an anthropology course and loved it and decided to major in it. There was a lot of pressure from my parents to make a choice, to choose a road. My parents didn't care what I majored in as long as I chose something.

■

Working as an engineer seems great, but I'm not wild about engineering school so far. I love metalsmithing in the fine arts school more than anything else I've ever done here. But switching doesn't seem practical.

The pressure to choose a major starts as early as the sophomore and junior years in high school when students fill out the forms for the Preliminary Scholastic Aptitude Tests. At 15 and 16 years of age, students are asked to indicate their academic and career interests, and the computer code for undecided always seems to be double zero. Most college admissions offices request similar information from applicants, conveying the message that before students even come to college they are supposed to know what they want to study and what career they wish to pursue.

It is not unusual for a parent to apologize to admissions officers on behalf of a child who "hasn't decided what he wants to do yet," as though being open to all kinds of possibilities is some sort of deficiency. In response to this parental anxiety, one admissions officer always asks the parent how old the child is, knowing full well that a prospective college student is likely to be 17 or 18. He then says incredulously, "Well, that seems perfectly normal to me. Most people don't know what they want to do with the rest of their lives when they are 17. Did you?"

There are, of course, those rare young people, driven by their talents and passions, who know they are destined to become musicians or biomedical engineers or entrepreneurs. When one such student was asked by a professor if she still wanted to be a dancer, she looked at him with eyes flashing and said, "It's not a matter of what I want. It's a matter of what I am!"

But such commitment and certainty are exceptional among the young. Despite the careerist era in which we live, most entering college students are not sure what they want to study, and even those who claim they know are likely to change their minds. Dean Anne Schroer-Lamont of Washington and Lee, for instance, estimates that only 15 percent of freshmen really know what they want to pursue. And in a survey of University of Virginia alumni, fewer than 10 percent said they had a very clear direction when they graduated.

But on most college campuses, the mythology prevails among sophomores that "everybody else seems to know what they want to major in and what they want to do for the rest of their lives." Rumors run rampant about which departments are good and what the future holds in store for its graduates. Each campus has particular departments that are held in high esteem by students and others that command little respect. Some schools are stridently preprofessional; others are more supportive of the liberal arts. Everywhere, stereotypes abound. Choosing a major not only means choosing a course of study, it means selecting a niche on campus—assuming an identity as "an intellectual philosopher," "a no-nonsense computer scientist," or "a far-out artist." When students meet each other, one of the first questions they ask is, "What's your major?" And the response elicits a set of assumptions, an initial code for sizing each other up.

A young woman may feel defensive about picking a traditionally female field such as social work or education. On some campuses she is likely to catch flack from her peers who have more respect for the hard sciences and preparation for the high-status professions than they do for the humanities and helping professions. Jokes about majoring in "Play-Doh" or "sandbox" quickly wear thin, and some education and child development students even contemplate changing majors as a result of repeated taunting.

Business and engineering students, too, complain about being stereotyped by their peers in the humanities and social sciences who make assumptions about their motivation: "I get tired of everyone making comments about me going for the big bucks," said a sophomore in mechanical engineering. "I'm in engineering because that's what I'm good at and that's what I like."

In making a decision about a major, students weigh their own interests with concerns about status and image and future opportunities. They may feel pulled in different directions by parents and peers and faculty, all trying to help—all sure that they know what's best for the student.

In an ironic twist of the women's movement, mothers pressure their daughters to stick to architecture or engineering, or other fields that used to be the realm of male students twenty-five or thirty years ago. Urging their daughters to take advantage of opportunities they never had themselves, they may unwittingly present them with a new set of constraints that make independent choices stressful.

Those students who enter the university with a specific and pragmatic career goal in mind pick the major that fits their career choice. That seems simple enough. But often the career goal of an 18-year-old is based more on image than on a realistic understanding of the demands of the course of study and the career itself. When a physical therapy student who wants to help people, but doesn't like science, looks ahead to the long sequence of required science courses, or an engineering student realizes that an aptitude for mathematics isn't necessarily synonymous with an interest in engineering, a change is in the offing. That change can be upsetting, particularly when the student is uncertain about what to study instead. And parents are often upset when their child makes an alternative choice based more on passion for the subject than practical career preparation. Students and parents worry about time lost, about getting "off the track," when time is precious and tuition costs are high.

Premeds who change their minds—and many of them do—often have a particularly difficult time giving up their identity as premeds. Long after they've decided that they're not interested in the studies or the career, or realized that they simply don't stand a chance of gaining admission to medical school, many students struggle with finding new academic and career goals.

Some of these students, referred to by one administrator as "prenatal premeds," had never actually made a choice to be premed in the first place. They may have been successful in high school science, and swept along by the enthusiasm of their teachers and parents, they began to think of themselves as premed. Or they may have come from a family of physicians and merely assumed that they would follow in the family tradition. When these students decide to change, they are taking a big step in separating from their parents and asserting their independence. Unfortunately, some parents make it difficult for them to do so. Perhaps finding it painful to give up the dream of "my child, the doctor," and failing to separate their own goals from those of their son or daughter, they refuse to accept the impending change of plans. Some parents respond with accusations or sighs of disappointment; others go as far as threatening not to pay tuition for any course of study except one leading to medical school.

A former premed describes her change of heart and her father's subsequent disappointment:

> I was a gung ho premed, but I started changing my mind first semester. Competition here was really fierce. I think that little spark in me started to dull, and when I'd go to these classes with two or three hundred people, half had already had AP chemistry, and I was struggling for the first time.
>
> I had a couple of so-called friends tell me the wrong way to do problems before first semester finals. They thought it was funny and said, "Oh well, we're cutthroat premeds." I started realizing that part of my excitement about premed was connected to my father's thrill that I had decided to go preprofessional. I started realizing I wasn't totally doing this for myself. I started looking around and began to realize I'd enjoy and do better in psychology and sociology. And that's what I've double-majored in, much to my father's chagrin. He still keeps telling me I'd make a good psychiatrist.

Many parents, wanting to assure their sons or daughters a secure and satisfying life, exert a tremendous pressure on students to follow a clear-cut professional route. Even parents who simply give offhand suggestions have more influence than they realize. Students often experience their comments as demands. And aside from explicit expectations, there are often implicit family norms. If the parents are successful in a particular field, they set expectations by their example. So do older siblings, whether they realize it or not.

It is not surprising that discussions about majors inevitably lead to the question "What are you going to do with that?" And when the proposed major is a subject like comparative literature or history, the question is often asked with an air of obvious skepticism. Indeed, many students who become enamored of a liberal arts discipline ask the question of themselves.

They are, in a sense, asking themselves the wrong question. Parents might encourage students to ask themselves instead, "What kind of an impact will these studies have on me? Who might I become, how might I view the world, and what skills might I develop if I begin to master this particular discipline?"

During her tenure as president of Bryn Mawr College, Mary Patterson McPherson urged parents not to worry if their daughter calls home and says that she is going to major in Latin, or any other subject:

> In my view, it doesn't matter a hoot what your daughter majors in. What matters is that she loves the subject; that she can work creatively and freely in it; that she's learning what we have to teach her. And what we have to teach her is not content. We teach her approach, methodology. We're honing her faculties, her skills. We're letting her find her intellectual strengths and measure her own weaknesses, and it doesn't matter what we're doing it in. And the fact that she does it in Latin may mean she'll be a much better lawyer or a much better doctor, which many of them go on to be anyway, not professors of Latin, though excellent professors of Latin are needed as well.

Nevertheless, students tend to attach enormous importance to choice of a major. They are reluctant to believe it when their deans or advisors tell them that there is no right major and that in most cases their major will not determine their career. In a University of Virginia survey of arts and sciences alumni, seven out of ten reported that "no matter what their major, the broad educational background of liberal arts was much more important on the job than any specific educational training."[3]

As a dean at George Washington University comments:

> It really doesn't matter what students major in. But it's important for a student to major in something. An important part of intellectual development is beginning to have some sense of mastery over a body of material, to be able to get your arms around a discipline. You get a sense of the variety of analytical tools that are brought to bear in this discipline, the kinds of questions it asks and those it doesn't. With luck, with good faculty, you learn some of its mistakes and dead ends.
>
> You can get that kind of sense from English, political science, or geology. You'll get some idea of causation, some sense that things can be divided into component parts. In any discipline, you will learn to make reasoned judgments, to develop fundamental intellectual skills—to analyze, synthesize, and express yourself. What we are giving students is power, the tools to teach themselves a new subject during the rest of their lives, the ability to approach a new mass of material and say, "OK, how do I start?" That's the real-world skill that a major is all about.

Some students are comfortable with exploring. They may take a long time to decide on a major and enjoy the academic journey. Others are so anxious about making their choice that they are reluctant to experiment. Says University of Delaware professor Marion Hyson:

> Many of our students find it hard to justify to themselves or their parents the value of taking anthropology or musicology. I wish they could see that the period of time they're settling on a major is not just spinning wheels. They're developing skills of pursuing certain kinds of inquiry and self-expression. As sophomores, some start to make connections in their minds between fields of studies and disciplines. That can be very exciting in itself.

For some students, however, lack of a focus is so uncomfortable that they may find it hard to concentrate on their studies. They complain about being unmotivated and may consider leaving school. They desperately want to make a decision, to have a goal. One dean suggests that these students invest in temporary choices. She urges them to "try out" their interests and tells them:

> If you think you're interested in psychology, try it out. Get into it. Really get into it. Take several psych courses. Work in a child development center. If you don't like it, come back and we'll talk about it. Negative choices are terribly important. Being able to shut doors is just wonderful. Sometimes when we close doors, we open others. Sometimes when we narrow the perspective somewhat, we can move on.

With all this talk about majors, it is important to remember that a major usually constitutes about a third of the courses a student will take in college. For most students, especially in liberal arts, there is plenty of opportunity to plan a curriculum that complements and supplements the courses in the major department. More students today are choosing double majors, or a combination major and minor. They are combining business and English literature, French and international development, sociology and computer science. They are straddling the humanities and technology; they are pursuing their intellectual passions and practical skills.

Most colleges and universities, mindful of the liberal arts/preprofessional dichotomy, have introduced numerous opportunities to combine the two. Internships and cooperative education programs offer students hands-on experience while still in school. And career-related part-time and summer jobs supplement many students' traditional academic fare.

A junior math major at Duke who was actively involved in the performing arts had no idea what to do after graduation until she stumbled upon a summer job in the education department of a major symphony orchestra, and loved it. Arts administration seemed to combine her organizational skills and facility with numbers with her interest in the arts. Upon her return to school in her senior year, she was able to gain administrative experience by doing an internship with a local dance festival and producing the campus fall musical rather than acting in it. By using her imagination and initiative, along with the resources of the university and community, this young woman was free to immerse herself in the intellectual challenge of higher mathematics while developing marketable skills for a career in arts administration.

This kind of inventiveness is increasingly common among today's students. An English major who capitalized on her experience as an orientation leader eventually wrote a handbook for parents' orientation and was sent to the National Orientation Directors' Conference by her college. A student with a double major in Spanish and international relations interned one summer at the International Trade Administration in Washington and was invited to do research for them the following academic year. An economics major who took a year off to work at the Chicago Stock Exchange returned to finish his academic work while interning in the production department of a public television station.

The anxieties that students feel about entering the job market can't be dismissed. For those whose academic interests lean toward the humanities and social sciences, internships, jobs, and student activities provide a means of developing career-related experience. These opportunities free students to pursue majors that truly interest them and to make an academic commitment.

MORE DECISIONS

It was February—cold and bleak outside. I was cooking a pot roast when the phone rang. It was Betsy calling from Skidmore.

"Are you OK?" I had just talked to her two days before.

"Yes, fine. But I forgot to talk to you about a few things." She sounded exuberant. I relaxed.

"I've decided about next year, but I don't think you'll like it."

So much for relaxing.

"Instead of spending my junior year in England"—she plans on majoring in English—"I want to go to Italy and study art. I talked to someone in the Syracuse program and she loves it, and you get the language training and live with an Italian family."

I was both jealous and concerned.

"It's your choice, of course, but you've always had so much trouble with languages, and what about your requirements for your English major?" I hated my words, which were bursting her bubble.

"I'll take care of that. Don't worry. And another thing—spring vacation? I could come home or stay here and ski or Les invited me to New York to stay with him." Was this the time to mention that she still hadn't gotten a job to pay for her living expenses? Better leave it alone.

"I think I want to work on a ranch this summer."

"What about the camp job you interviewed for?"

"It's not enough money, and I really want to work on a ranch."

"Did you have any particular ranch in mind?" My mind was beginning to swirl and the pot roast was burning.

"Well, no, but I'm talking to people."

"You'd better check that out soon, because if you wait you'll end up like last summer."

"What was wrong with last summer?"

"You didn't make much money and you were bored with your job."

"I was not!" The exuberance was definitely gone.

When I hung up the phone I was wondering where I went wrong.

When I repeated the conversation to her father, he said, "Terrific. That's Betsy! England was safe. Italy's an adventure—the same with this summer."

He responded to her spirit. *I* kept placing barriers in her way.

And by the way, she did go to Italy, she never mentioned
the ranch again, and she came home for spring vacation.

This is one mother's account of a typical conversation with her
sophomore daughter. Overwhelmed and disconcerted by her daughter's
barrage of options, she was reeling by the time she hung up the phone.
Although she thinks of herself as a supportive and encouraging mother,
her instinctive reaction had been to pull back in face of the onslaught
and to point out all the potential pitfalls of her daughter's list of possibilities. Not a particularly helpful response, but one that many parents
succumb to at some time during their child's college career.

Sophomores often call home with an ever-changing set of ideas
and plans that may seem like the "whim of the week" to their bewildered parents. Just as parents have gotten used to the idea that their
son is going to spend second semester in Washington on a political
science internship, he calls home and says he has scratched that
idea and is now planning to stay at school and switch his major to
Spanish. Last week's request for permission to take a semester off
turns into this week's decision to transfer to a larger school instead.

Summer vacations are also filled with possibilities. Today's career-
anxious students want to fill their résumés with meaningful summer
experiences, and many eschew the traditional jobs of the lawn care
and lifeguard genre for positions in banks and research labs or pursue
exotic alternatives such as picking fruit in the south of France or
canning fish in Alaska.

The plethora of choices that face today's college students is often
overwhelming to their parents as well as themselves: from summer
internships in Africa to a semester at sea; double majors and joint
degrees; stopping out and dropping out; a year abroad or an
exchange at another university; graduating in three years or a fifth
year of undergraduate study; staying put and making do or transferring to a different school.

Many parents assume that their child will go off to college for four
years, pick a major and stick with it, come home and work in the
summer, and graduate at the end of the fourth year, moving directly
to graduate school or a professional job. But just as the typical

nuclear family of working father, housewife, and two or more children represents only a small fraction of the population, so too the typical linear progression through college is more the exception than the rule. Many of today's students are approaching their education with a creativity that reflects their own needs and the demands of the society in which they live.

Stopping Out

"Stopping out" is not a euphemism for dropping out or running away, but a viable alternative for many students who want to spend a semester or year away from school. A student may take time off, or stop out, for any number of reasons—to find an academic focus or sense of purpose, to earn money, to contribute something to others, to get experience that will be valuable later on. Although the most common time for stopping out is during the junior year, students may decide to take time off at any time in their college career.

Many colleges and universities have begun to acknowledge these periods of time out in an institutional way. A Williams College handbook for parents states:

> The college urges that such time off be for the duration of an academic year and hopes that it will be spent positively and planned constructively. Such time away, perhaps as a period of reassessment and self-evaluation, often proves more beneficial than a half-hearted commitment to academics.

Parents may view the decision to take time off as a failure, a deviation from the norm. And those parents who feel constrained by the financial and emotional obligations of their middle years may find it difficult to listen with patience to the many enticing choices their child is contemplating. When parents haven't taken a vacation in years because of college expenses or obligations to an aging parent, their son's or daughter's dilemma about whether to spend a year in Germany or to take time off to prospect for gold in California may seem like a frivolous indulgence.

In spite of her father's skepticism, a sophomore at Brown exudes a dazzling sense of possibility as she describes a string of alternative routes for the coming year:

> My dad denies this, but I think he and my mom have an ownership philosophy. You know, "We're paying for your education . . . ," "When you're living in our house . . . ," "Because I'm your father, that's the reason."
>
> I feel they're not supportive about what I want to do and don't take it seriously. I wanted to go abroad with the American Field Service for a year after high school. They didn't want me to. I'm definitely going to do something different after my sophomore year. I go crazy when I feel like I'm just a student and not "living." It's so frustrating. I'd like to take a semester at home at Case Western. I know Cleveland and I can integrate being a student with my volunteer work in the community. Or maybe I can go to Bryn Mawr. I almost went there and I'd like to see what it would be like. I'd like to drive or bike across the country. I'd like to go to Central or South America. I'd like to have a significant job.

This young woman, excited and unfocused, needs a calm and patient listener who might help her begin to channel her energy. She may not yet realize that there is no best answer, but in finding the better answer she will learn to make commitments and to live with the regrets of roads not taken. She will certainly be more motivated to follow her own path than one chosen by her parents.

Parents who came of age in the '60s or '70s might be tolerant of their children's plea to stop out if they plan to devote themselves to a cause. But most students today are not leaving school to rally for or protest against anything. Many feel the personal pressure to succeed, to produce, to be responsible, to pay off loans, but are not quite ready to face such grown-up commitments. Some, like the woman above, see their education through a wider lens and want to grasp opportunities that are now available to them. Many have a hard time articulating why they want to leave. Using the college-age vernacular of "splitting to get my head together" or needing time to "hang out," these young people often turn parents off before any discussion begins. Their own language trivializes whatever legitimate insight lies behind it. "At more than a thousand-dollar increase in tuition each year, he can go 'find himself' after he finishes!" one father exclaimed.

Parents who give an unqualified no to a request for time off, without an opportunity to explore alternatives, may stymie their child's growth inadvertently rather than encourage it. A job or internship is just what some students need to find the sense of direction that eludes them on campus. For others, merely having unpressured time for reflection is enough for them to become refreshed and clearer about their personal and professional goals. There is, of course, a fine line between bumming around and doing nothing, and pausing for some time to gain self-understanding. Financial pressures are of concern to most families, and a student who is serious about taking time off should be prepared to grapple with the dollars-and-cents aspects of this decision. By assuming financial responsibility, even through a mindless job, students enjoy an increased sense of independence while stepping back from the academic world to get a new perspective.

A University of Michigan student describes what happened when he took a break from school and moved back home:

> Living at home this semester really hasn't been the big exclamation point in the book of life by any means. Living with my parents again is a weird thing. From their point of view I came home because I had something I wanted them to help me out with. I think they thought I'd be sitting down and talking to them for hours at a time. They were apprehensive; they worried about me. But I just wanted to get a job and hang out by myself for a while. I needed to clean out my system and get reoriented—to stop and think. A degree is something to work for; it's not an end in itself, but it does figure significantly. Like you have to do the work in order to get it. I'd been kind of missing that crucial point.

> When I was at school, I really didn't spend much time

by myself except when I was sleeping. At home, when I'm not with my family, I'm on my own. It just gives me a lot of latitude for thinking and ironing out things—coming up with new ideas and perspectives. It's a good feeling to wash all this excess off the top of your skull. I'm enjoying it. I like figuring out things about myself. I think stopping out was probably the best thing I could have done. I'd go as far as to recommend it to other people who need to clear the air. There's no social stigma attached to it.

Setting aside time for thoughtful face-to-face conversations about taking time off can clarify the issues at hand for both parent and child. And without such discussions, parents may find that their attempts to direct their son or daughter on the traditional four-year path backfire.

A senior in his fifth year at a midwestern university recounts his experience:

I wanted to split school to get my head together, and my parents wouldn't allow it, which was a stupid mistake on their part. I wish I would have been able to convince my parents to let me do it, but they simply wouldn't listen. I felt definitely that I wasn't able to take advantage of what the university had to offer and what they were putting their money down for. It was just not the right time for me. I was just too messed up. There was a lot of time that I wasted in college being stoned. Being in school was a kind of ideal model for them. My parents have the idea that everybody finishes college in four years. But it wasn't happening. I didn't finish some of my courses and had a bunch of incompletes. I blew the stuff off, and I felt bad about it. But I thought it was stupid that they had this idea about the number four.

Last year I finally laid it on the line with them. I told them I wasn't going to graduate, that I had more stuff to do as far as the university was concerned. I knew there was a lot more I could get out of it now, and I wanted to go

back. They agreed, and I'm very glad that I came back
here. It's been very positive so far.

Sometimes open, flexible discussions about taking time off lead to
a change of heart on the part of the student. The mother of a
University of Wisconsin sophomore relates:

My son was rooming with someone first semester this year
who didn't like school. He clearly had an influence on
Peter, who called home right after he returned to Madison
in January and said, "I think I'm going to leave school for
a while."

I told him I didn't think it made sense or was practical
to leave school in the middle of the sophomore year. I put
my foot down, knowing that he was probably looking for
some kind of limits at that point. If my daughter had
called and said the same thing, I might have reacted differently. I threw out some options and said, "You might
want to take off next year and work, or try photography,
which you love, or transfer to another school." I tried to
give him reasons for my opinions and some options to
consider. I tried to combine the guidelines with leeway, so
he could eventually make the best decision for himself.

I also knew that, like so many sophomores, he was concerned about picking a major. It had gotten to be a joke over
winter break. Everyone who saw him asked the same question, "What are you going to major in?" He got really fed up
with the repetition of that question, and eventually started
to answer very fliply—to smart off by saying, "Sanskrit" or
some such thing. The truth was he really didn't know.

I suggested he go to the counseling center to talk about
choosing a major. He started to get a handle on his interest, and before long it became quite clear to him that he
wanted to major in journalism. The counselor he talked to
suggested that he start to work on the newspaper, which
he did. After that we never heard any more about his

desire to leave school. We weren't against his taking time off; we just didn't want him to do it for the wrong reasons.

The mother of a Lafayette student who stopped out cautions:

The original reasons they give may not be the real ones. Our son told us what he thought we'd want to hear: "I'm wasting your money; I don't have a sense of purpose."

True, he hadn't been very happy there; he had no idea what he wanted to do, and he had to declare a major by the end of sophomore year. But he also wanted to earn enough money to buy some expensive musical equipment. And underneath that goal was his need to establish his independence.

He lived at home because it wasn't financially feasible for him not to, but he paid much of his way, gas for the car, the phone bill, that sort of thing. He worked two jobs and found them boring. And he missed Lafayette and visited there several different weekends. He began to appreciate college more. And he realized that his college degree is a union card. That's the hard and fast reality, and he doesn't want to go through life without one.

Of course, many parents fear that once their youngster leaves school, he or she may never return to graduate. Although this is always a possibility, most students who do return after a leave of absence perform at higher levels than they did before they left. The change of pace triggers renewed enthusiasm, a sense of purpose, and commitment to their formal education when they return.

The dean of a highly competitive liberal arts college comments:

I think I have never known a case where the student took time off and returned to the same institution and didn't do better. I think they find out it's no fun to work in an unskilled job. They return more mature, with a better sense of who they are and about the world of work.

In retrospect, many parents who had originally opposed the idea look back at their children's time off positively. A Brandeis senior recalls with a wry grin:

> I took a year off—worked on construction for six months and then went to Europe with the money I'd earned. My father was desperate about it. He was so afraid I would never finish. Now he thinks it was wonderful. He tells all his friends about this adventuresome thing I did.

Some students don't finish. A college education is not for everyone, and some youngsters make the decision to turn their sights to other pursuits—part-time study, vocational or technical training, apprenticeships, or opportunities to develop artistic talents, to name a few. Others who feel locked into the university or a particular field of study because of parental pressure may go through the motions of getting an education but, lacking the interest or talent, ultimately fail or leave. For them, college has not been a rich, expansive field of possibility but a confining prison that has rendered them unmotivated and thwarted. Most students who leave school don't make the decision lightly. They still want and need their parents' emotional support at the same time that they long for acknowledgment of their separateness. This is a challenge for parents, who must let go of their own dreams for their child and accept instead the alternative route he or she has chosen.

Moving Off-Campus

Though living in the residence halls is back in vogue, a lot of upperclassmen contemplate moving to an apartment off-campus. At many universities, apartment living has become as much a part of campus life as pizza and beer.

Some students make the move because they have to; there simply isn't enough room for them in the dormitories. Others, discovering that sharing an apartment and cooking one's own meals can be cheaper than the room and board plan on campus, make the move to save money. Some, tired of the lack of privacy in the residence halls, seek space, quiet, and a haven from the constant social scene. Still others crave the independence that apartment living symbolizes and see the move as another step toward the adult world.

Parents who spent four years at a residential college where everyone lived on-campus may be surprised when their son or daughter calls with the news that a move to an apartment is in the offing. The next surprise comes with the mention of a roommate of the opposite sex, since coed living is common off-campus as well as on. Though parents may have difficulty believing it, most of these arrangements are based on friendship, practicality, and serendipity. Women often feel safer and worry less about security when there are men in the apartment. For many, sharing apartment space with the opposite sex simply seems a natural extension of coed dormitory living.

When students who live off-campus talk about their roommates or apartment mates, they are referring to the people who share their apartment. When they use the term "the man (or woman) I live with," that usually means they are in a relationship. Neither arrangement is unusual today. And the difference in phraseology is a subtle but commonly understood part of the campus vernacular.

Sometimes the decision to move into an apartment is based on a student's commitment to a small group of friends. These groups usually come together with high expectations of community and intimacy, hoping to create their own home away from home. Other students who barely know each other join together in haphazard ways, united only by their common desire to share space. They expect little more of each other than basic civility.

All students who make the switch from dormitory to apartment life face the daily challenges of independent living. Paying rent on time, keeping the common living spaces clean, and buying food for a relatively balanced diet require time, thought, and action. At a time when much of their world seems tenuous and unsettled, taking care of themselves in the most basic, pedestrian ways can help students assume more control of their lives.

Many students muddle through and feel increasingly self-reliant. No lecture on nutrition from a parent is as likely to change a student's eating habits as opening the refrigerator once again to find it stocked only with diet soda, beer, and leftover spaghetti. And after seeing their funds erode at the campus cafeteria, students begin to plan ahead and pack lunches for themselves. Arguments with roommates must be worked out without the help of an RA, and students learn to negotiate and share household responsibilities. Seniors often remark that the experience of living in an apartment reduces their pregraduation jitters, that it makes the transition into the real world look a bit less traumatic.

But apartment living requires adjustments that may add to an already overloaded schedule. The freedom of living on one's own is accompanied by the burden of responsibility. And if a student is weighed down with schoolwork, extracurricular pursuits, or a part-time job, the additional responsibility of taking care of an apartment may prove to be too much. Some students enjoy the space of off-campus housing but feel isolated and cut off from college life. They miss the easy availability of friends and the ever-present stimulation that dormitory life provides. The decision about whether to move off-campus has to be weighed in the context of everything else going on in the student's life at the same time.

A vivacious young woman, now in her junior year, remarks:

> I moved into an apartment sophomore year. I had opted for an apartment because I wanted my own room. I'd never had a room of my own. I'm a vegetarian, and I thought meals would be easier for me if I could cook myself, and I wanted the adventure of an apartment.
>
> But I felt really isolated. I met no one. By the end of the year, I was working at a snail's pace in my architecture classes. I had gotten more involved in outside activities, and I was in a stressful, serious relationship. So this year I decided to become an RA and move back into the dorms. The money I save by being an RA takes some of the financial pressure off as well.

Transferring and Other Alternatives

Almost all students contemplate transferring at some point during their first two years of college—some fleetingly, others giving it serious thought. Disappointing classes, broken friendships or romances, the sheer exhaustion of a demanding schedule, all lead to periods of confusion and doubt. A change of scenery, a fresh start, is a tempting solution—a magical "right" answer to a complicated question. The grass and the ivy look greener somewhere else. How do students sort out the inevitable imperfections of their college experience from a legitimate mismatch?

One assistant dean advises:

> It becomes a question of, are you running away from something here—loneliness or confusion—or are you moving toward something that isn't available here. Much of what I ask them revolves around what kind of a person they are and what kind of a person they want to be. Being bored isn't an acceptable answer; it's up to them to change this.
>
> Some students stay simply out of a sense of obligation. They don't do anything to change the situation, and they're the ones I call the "what-ifs." What if I had done this instead? What if I had gone there? Others go through the questioning period and then really make a niche for themselves here. They get involved in the newspaper or a committee, go to lectures, seek out the community at large. They have a successful time.

Sometimes it is clear that transferring will answer a specific need. Discovering an interest in occupational therapy at a school without an OT department, feeling overwhelmed and lost at a large university and longing for the sense of community that a small campus affords, missing the stimulation of an urban center after time spent in a rural setting—these are clearly concerns that can be rectified by going to a different school. But when students speak of transferring to a school that is a rubber stamp of the one they are in, chances are they are seeking solutions that exist right under their noses, or that they are searching for a nonexistent perfect place. Parents can help by asking open-ended questions, listening patiently, and allowing their child to discover his or her own solution.

A New Jersey father talks with pride of his son's growth as he wrestled with the decision about whether to transfer:

> Gordon complained a lot about St. Lawrence. The kids weren't "like him"; he didn't like his classes. He was convinced that he had made the wrong decision and that there was a right school somewhere out there for him; he just had to find it. But his sophomore year he moved into a theme house; it was a political awareness house, and it gave him a niche. He had housemates with similar interests. He also really got into skiing. It was a turning point for him. The school still wasn't all that he had hoped for, but he began to see that he could make the difference.

Parents' reactions to talk of transferring are often proportional to the amount of time they invested in the original college selection process. One mother recalls:

> She came home and said, "I hate this place." I'd been telling everyone how much she loved it. I guess when I think about it, she hadn't really said much.
>
> I was angry. I thought, Here we go again. I'd put all that energy into helping her get into what I thought was the right place, and now I was wrong. I felt one of the reasons she had ended up there was because of me.
>
> I told her, "OK. If you can find a school that will take you, and you make the arrangements, do it." And this time around she did everything herself.

The process of transferring offers another opportunity for a young person to make an independent, reasoned, and informed decision. The mother above insisted that her child take the initiative this time. When her daughter went to a school of her own choosing, she found that she was in for a big adjustment, but one that she was willing to tackle.

Some students decide not to transfer, but opt for a semester or a year in a different setting or different kind of institution. A young woman from Wellesley College was able to look at her all-woman institution with new and appreciative eyes after a year at coed Williams. A Beloit student, feeling confined by her small, sheltered surroundings, chose to study at an urban university on the East Coast and returned from her adventure to enjoy the familiarity and warmth of her friendly campus for the last year. Students have opportunities of enormous variety, ranging from semesters of study with policy makers and lobbyists in Washington to programs in urban education in major cities or wilderness studies at field stations in remote locations. The most popular choice of alternative study still seems to be study abroad, usually in the junior year. It is an option that affords yet another confusing but tempting array of possibilities.

Study Abroad

Bolstered by a spirit of adventure, more and more students are taking advantage of the unique opportunities for international study. The Institute of International Education directory, *Academic Year Abroad 1996/97*, lists over 2300 programs in eighty countries. This is more than twice the number available ten years ago. Some students study in summer and graduate programs, but academic-year programs for undergraduates are available for credit at more than a thousand schools.

The experience of a semester or a year abroad provides the opportunity to enlarge young people's vision of the world, of the United States, and of themselves. It proves to be a pivotal life experience for some, a splendid adventure for others, but it is not for everyone. Before students decide where to go, they face the dilemma of whether to go.

In some cases, the decision is made for them. Many programs and universities require a minimum grade-point average; in certain disciplines, such as engineering and business, a prescribed study in sequence makes it difficult, if not impossible, to take time during the academic year for a credited period of study abroad; language requirements eliminate many underprepared students; family obligations and financial restraints prevent others from going. Meanwhile, for some, especially language or international relations majors, study abroad is an integral part of the curriculum.

For many students, the decision presents a tug-of-war. They weigh the alternatives and ask themselves a lot of questions: Should I grab this once-in-a-lifetime opportunity? If I go, I can't transfer. Should I transfer instead? If I stay, I'll have a good shot at being editor of the paper senior year, or maybe president of the fraternity. Do I want to give that up? Studying abroad will look good on my résumé, but will I fall behind in the job search? Can I afford it? Will my financial aid transfer? What's going to happen to Jane and me if we're so far apart for a year? Do I have the guts to go?

Some students have the misguided notion that study abroad will magically solve academic or social problems, that the stimulation of exotic new cultures will cure the state of confusion, stagnation, or ennui that they are currently experiencing. It's true that many students find study abroad programs stimulating and the catalyst for personal growth, but those who choose them to escape from unhappy circumstances are likely to bring their problems with them or simply postpone them for a time.

Students need not make this decision to study abroad in a vacuum. They can talk to friends, faculty, and advisors, and upperclassmen who have spent a semester or year abroad are usually delighted to share the pleasures or disappointments of their own experience. For information about the programs themselves, they can turn to a study abroad office or an overseas program advisor, who has been designated to provide this service. These offices and campus libraries offer informative books and pamphlets.

All programs are not created equal, and beckoning brochures can be misleading. Study abroad counselors can help point the way to tried-and-true programs or guide the more adventuresome student to apply directly to a foreign university—a less costly alternative and one that promises an integrated experience. Students are often

surprised to learn that some study abroad experiences are less expensive than a year at their home college. These experiences are no
longer the purview only of the well-to-do.

The decision to go abroad stirs up feelings reminiscent of the initial departure for college. Parents, as well as their children, get
caught up in the anticipation and anxiety of the upcoming journey:

> He's refusing to figure out if all the stuff fits into a back-
> pack for four weeks of travel before school starts. He says,
> "I don't need to test. I've got everything under control."
> The last four days, that control has dissolved. He's bounc-
> ing off the walls. His confidence is shaken and so is mine.
> And my husband has been living on Tums.

■

> No, I'm not worried about the terrorists. I'm worried that
> she'll lose her passport or mess up her money or miss her
> train—the same things I always worried about with Nancy.

■

> He is so much more into getting ready for this than when
> he went to college—scattered, but much more organized.
> But he seems like such a naive little kid sometimes. My
> fear is that he will not pay attention to his surroundings
> and something dangerous will happen.

These are the voices of parents as their children leave home
again, but this time for distant and unknown places. Thrown into a
heightened state of anxiety and excitement, families play out the
themes of separation once more, the discordant tensions of disen-
gagement and the unexpected pangs of loss:

> My intense reaction to Christy's leaving for a full year
> abroad in Paris came as a big surprise to me. I thought,
> We've been through this passage when she went to college
> and we weathered it so well. Why am I feeling so much

anxiety and loss? I think it's partly because she's so much more wonderful to be with at 20 than she was at 17. I feel like no sooner had I gotten to know her as a young adult this summer, without so many of the tensions we've had in the past, than she's off again. So I will genuinely miss her. And I also know she doesn't need me as much anymore. Somehow her determination to go on this adventure, so far away, confirms what I already knew—that she has grown up.

Once the initial weeks of study abroad are under way, some parents discover a new relationship with their offspring. Overseas phone calls are outside many students' budgets. When students and their families have access to e-mail, parents are likely to get a day-to-day feel for their child's international experience. Most students don't have this ready electronic access, however, and yearning to share the excitement of their new lives, they discover the art of letter writing. Their letters are often unself-conscious and revealing in ways that long-distance phone calls seldom are. They are full of vivid impressions of places and sights and expressive discoveries about themselves and the world. Paradoxically, the distance of an ocean provides a safe cushion for intimacy.

A UCLA senior from New York reminisces about her correspondence home during her year in Israel:

I could kind of say anything when I was 6000 miles away, and I wrote things I would never say when I was with them. I told them a lot that I loved them and how much I appreciated having this opportunity, which they never had.

And a Miami University junior wrote from Denmark, "Would you please send me any bits of advice for when I get lonely and depressed. Don't worry. I can handle it from this far away."

As the months go by, many parents describe a growing sense of liberation as they experience a new level of separation. The vast distances make it virtually impossible to remain entrenched in a son or daughter's life, and as a result, students are left to their own devices. In most situations, they rise to the occasion.

> As much as I missed her, I also knew that I had very little control or input into her life. I don't know the customs, the rules, or the dangers. I had to defer to the resource people in her program, who did.
>
> I always feel freed up when the kids go back to school after vacations. They may go out partying until all hours of the morning, but I don't know about it so I don't worry. Well, having her in England was like this only tenfold. I didn't speak to her by phone. By the time her letters arrived, they were ancient history. I had no choice but to let her struggle through the hard parts, the loneliness, the homesickness. This was the first time I felt really free of the pull to make things OK for her.

Students' growing self-assurance breeds a new respect from their parents. Young men and women speak of the confidence born of weeks of traveling on their own, of the capacity to manage their own finances in a foreign currency, and of the uphill struggle to master another language—often a lonely and arduous task. A junior in an English-speaking program in Madrid lived with a local family and learned the language slowly and tediously:

> When people talk to me, I have to watch them, their gestures, anything I can pick up. Every time I have a conversation, I first have to translate what's being said into English and then go through it again before I speak. I have to plan out whatever I say, a meal or a favor; it can't be spontaneous. I have to have complete concentration all the time. I'm so tired at night, I just flop into bed.

By the middle of her second semester, however, her confidence had grown along with her competence, and her letters home were joyful:

All of a sudden, everything is beginning to click, and if it continues like this, all those months of struggling and shyness will be worth it to say the least. God, it's the most amazing feeling to achieve something like this and to have fun doing it.

Parents who are able to go abroad for a visit have the pleasure of witnessing firsthand their child's growing language skill, maturity, and cultural immersion. These are treasured times when the tables are turned and their son or daughter becomes a much appreciated and admired guide, interpreter, or art historian.

The students who thrive the most seem to be those who are receptive to the culture, without too many preconceived expectations. An ability to make friends easily, to be uninhibited in trying out an imperfect command of a foreign language, to tolerate occasional periods of intense loneliness—these capacities all tend to enhance the study abroad experience. And those who stay for the full year describe a feeling of mastery the second semester that surpasses the romance and stimulation of the first:

> I've graduated from frenetic energy to lazy relaxation; that is to say, life is much more normal now and I'm enjoying the increasing feeling of *being* a Florentine more than observing the culture as a foreigner as I did last semester.

◼

> After one semester, you can say, I spent a semester in England. After a year, it's like home. You know how things work. You get a much fuller picture.

◼

> I went into an army basic training program for foreign students during the few weeks between semesters. All my Israeli fellow students had already been in the army for two or three years, and I decided if I wanted to understand

them better, I had to do something that was key in their
life. After that, I was much happier second semester. I
made more Israeli friends and could identify a lot more.

Identity issues broaden from "myself as a woman—or an engineering student or an advocate for social causes" to "myself as an
American," an American who has discovered Norwegian roots, an
American Jew committed to the state of Israel, a Japanese-
American devoted to his Japanese heritage, or an American who is
part of a world community. Just as students discover the flaws in
their own families when they see them from a distance, many young
people view the United States through the critical eyes of their new
international friends.

Students return home with remnants of a new culture—a British
accent, the colorful fabrics of a Nigerian wardrobe, a subscription to
the *Jerusalem Post,* or a passion for Chinese poetry. They miss the
friends, families, and lovers who had become a part of their lives in
another land. A student returning from South America recalls:

> I was gone for a year in Colombia, and I had really assimi-
> lated. I had a life there and I felt Colombian. I didn't just
> change countries, I changed identities. The last two weeks
> there were terribly emotional. I couldn't bear the thought
> of leaving my country.

Many suffer culture shock when they are reunited with their families and their friends at school. A senior describes the period of
reentry after spending a year in Norway:

> I felt so totally alone; it was a terrible loneliness until
> October or November. No one could understand what I
> had been through—what my life was like. I was a differ-
> ent person there from who I was when I left sophomore
> year. And when I came back to school, I expected the
> world had stopped because I wasn't here. And to think
> my friends here lived without me, and they have their

friends, and everyone else is doing their own thing, and I don't have my niche anymore.

But more long-lasting than the adjustments of reentry, they return with a new perspective, a worldview that replaces the self-absorption of their earlier identity quest, and a new sense of their own ability to handle life on their own.

COMMITMENTS ON CAMPUS: JUNIOR AND SENIOR YEARS

After getting through sophomore year—it was horrendous—I came back to school with the attitude that I can make it for sure.

◼

I see a big difference between sophomore and junior years. The main thing for me is I know how to solve problems. I know how to dig deeper and find resources. That goes for academics too. I know how to approach academic problems.

◼

Juniors and seniors have made a place for themselves. We've got a major and a definite set of friends we'll be calling up in forty years and asking, "How are the grandchildren?"

◼

I trust my own opinions a lot more than I did freshman or sophomore years. I feel freer to disagree with faculty or drop a class if I want to.

◼

I'm more realistic about what I can and can't do. I've channeled my commitments and don't try to do everything. I manage my time better and make sure I eat and sleep right. Sometimes my work comes second. My main priority right now is the lighting for the spring production.

Junior and senior years are a time of consolidation. No longer trying on a series of roles, juniors and seniors have a more solid sense of
their own identity. Most have settled into a social niche on campus
that confirms who they are and what they value. They have staked
out an academic home in their major department. And now it is
their turn to assume the campus leadership positions they may have
aspired to as freshmen and sophomores.

As they become more aware of their own limits and talents, they
wrestle with trade-offs, with the pros and cons of one choice over
another. Whereas their earlier choices were made in the spirit of
exploration, rebellion, or testing extremes, the commitments of
upperclassmen are those they claim for themselves. Some opt for a
balanced lifestyle, dividing their time among part-time jobs and academic, social, and extracurricular pursuits. Others choose to put most
of their energy into one arena of campus life and narrow their focus.

Those who immerse themselves in academics discover the
rewards of scholarship. Their sense of self-confidence grows along
with their insight and competence in their discipline. They develop
the skills of critical inquiry and delve into research and analysis. No
longer satisfied by the "right answer" of an external authority, they
respond to the challenge of ambiguity. They read original sources
and struggle to form and justify their own viewpoints. They measure
their success in academic terms, and their scholarly pursuits are an
essential part of their identity.

Some "hang out" in departmental lounges, endlessly drinking coffee and testing their emerging skills in discussion and debate with
their classmates. They may become involved in departmental politics or undergraduate organizations that revolve around an academic
discipline. Relationships with faculty change, as students leave
behind the formality of the large lecture halls for the more intimate
seminar rooms of upper-level classes. Some seize the chance to work
as a research assistant for an admired professor; if they are fortunate,
the professor takes on the role of mentor, guiding and encouraging
their intellectual growth.

Although extracurricular involvement is meant to supplement
academic life, for many upperclassmen, what goes on beyond the

walls of the classroom has become their first priority. The sports editor of the college paper dashing to meet a deadline feels a rush of excitement as he joins his coterie of fellow journalists in a common pursuit. No journalism class could measure up to this laboratory of learning. No fraternity bond could be stronger than the one he feels in this community. A junior who had enjoyed singing in a campus choir in prior years now spends many evenings at rehearsals with a small madrigal group and is taking lessons in the flute as a result of her growing interest in early music. As a computer science major, she has found the complexities of sophisticated programming intriguing, but she considers the friends who share her passion for music to be her college family.

Sometimes campus activities give students their first taste of a potential for leadership. Whether their commitment is to a sorority, a religious group, or a service organization, they have the chance to develop lifelong skills and a sense of themselves as people who can effect change. A senior from Portland, Oregon, looks back at the impact that campus involvement had on her:

I joined the undergraduate English society sophomore year. I liked going to its poetry readings and figured I might as well get involved. Before I knew it I was in charge of pulling together a panel for one of the meetings. I had to call alumni and ask them if they'd be willing to participate. I was scared to death calling all those important people. But I did it, and then on the night of the program I introduced them and moderated the panel. It was the first time I thought of myself as a leader, and I liked it. That was just the beginning.

By junior year it all started to come together. I was elected president of the English society and got involved in campus politics. I was invited to participate in a retreat for campus leaders run by the student affairs staff, and I was knocked out by it. We learned everything from assertion skills to how to lead a meeting. I got to know kids I never would have met otherwise. And I got to know the guy who's the director of student activities and he's had a big influence on me ever since. They kept talking about empowerment, and I understood what they meant because I was starting to feel it. Right now I'm running for president of student government. It's the first time in a long time that a woman has run for the top office.

Whether this young woman wins her election is less important than the process that got her there. There is only one student government president at every school, but all students have an opportunity to learn through their involvement in campus and community life.

The journey from the fragmented and disconnected state of the sophomore slump to the engagement and commitments a year or two later is not the same for everyone. But by the time they are seniors, most students have a greater sense of their own competence in and out of the classroom. They know more about who they are and what they believe in. They have found a place in the community that has become their home.

10

THE END IS THE BEGINNING

THE FAMILIAR RITUAL OF DEPARTURE IN EARLY fall—the journey back to campus, reentry one more time—the beginning of senior year. By now it seems natural, this coming and going, this moving in and out of the family orbit. Students casually pack their life's belongings into the back of a car and drive off to school. Or they hop on a bus or a plane with the confidence of those who know where they are heading.

Seniors are at the top of the heap now. They are the team captains and newspaper editors, the leaders of campus organizations, and the enlightened voices in the classroom. Though some revel in that knowledge for the entire year, most are acutely aware that their position is tenuous. At some point they are struck by the realization, "I'm a senior. This is it—the end."

The year is filled with a series of last times: the last convocation, homecoming weekend, basketball game, fraternity rush, winter term, midterm, final. Never will life be quite so ritualized again. And the dawning of the reality that "This is it" brings on a flurry of "last chance" activity. There is a sense of urgency, of time running out. Some students throw themselves into a host of endeavors as they try to make the most of college opportunities. They spend precious time with their circle of friends, hang out with professors, explore the surrounding city or countryside. And with graduation a mere eight or ten courses away, encounters with the academic cata log take on a new significance. As they juggle their schedules, they are no longer just choosing courses; they are relinquishing the possi bility of taking that seminar on Shakespeare's sonnets, or that fan tastic course on film, or that once-in-a-lifetime chance to study with a renowned professor.

Some seniors use this year to take an assortment of courses they have always wanted to take—courses they consider fun. Some fill in their liberal arts curriculum with accounting and computer pro gramming, practical courses they see as an entry to the job market. And others streamline their academic and extracurricular involve ment, focusing on an honors thesis or an engineering final project, a music recital or a drama production. This represents the culmina tion of years of effort, and for these students the sense of accom plishment has a tangible by-product.

A graduating civil engineering student beams with pride when describing the final structural design project that he did with a team of three students:

> We were told by the faculty, "You will design a bridge over the Mississippi River and you will design everything. You will design every bolt, every plate, every girder, every beam, every cable, every piece of cement. You will design the whole thing, and then you will present it to us, and we will tell you if it is good."
>
> This is the one class that pulls it all together. For the past two or three years I've been saying, All this theory, all this pragmatic, dogmatic stuff—as long as I can put out a good structural design project, I'll be satisfied. Now I know I can do this. Look at this bridge! You present this thing, and you have a professional engineer saying, "That's a good bridge."

Linda Salamon, Professor of English at George Washington University, is a proponent of honors theses and senior projects:

No matter what the field, I see value in a sustained piece of work over a long period of time. A research effort and synthesis demonstrates to students, not so much that they can master a particular discipline, but that they can use skills of inquiry, analysis, and sometimes creative imagination as well. It's a culminating experience for students who do it. When they call their parents in the midst of it, moaning "I'll never finish," or "This is a giant monster," parents shouldn't worry. They should just encourage them.

For some students the sense of mastery is not tied to a thesis or particular project; it is more internal, less accessible to public display. They exude a sense of joy in their intellectual development. A Chinese studies major at Middlebury exclaims:

I feel on the top of the world. Academically it is my best year. I feel as though I can do anything. My professors agree with what I say, or if they disagree, I realize I can argue with them. I've taken lots of classes specific to my field, and I've spent a year studying and traveling in China. I don't depend on gut feelings anymore; I can back up what I say with sources and cogent reasoning. Whatever I say has some validity to it. I know I can say something without making a fool of myself.

And a graduating history major, while enjoying the richness of his senior studies, realizes that the end of his college experience marks the beginning of his commitment to learning for the rest of his life:

Since I've found something that interests me, that I want to learn about, this year has been incredible for me academically. I want to take classes on my own until I'm 60 or 80 because now I realize there's so much more to learn, and I'll study because I enjoy it and not because I have to. There's a reason for it. It won't be for a distribution

requirement; it won't be for my major or for my minor; it
will be because I'm interested and I really want to know.

Lacking a crystal ball to predict their future, seniors look back,
sometimes wistfully, often with amazement, at the accrued accomplishments and changing perspectives of past months and years:

> I keep having these total flashbacks of four years. I can
> just picture myself waiting in line as a freshman, not
> knowing what to do next, staring at the map, trying to fig-
> ure it out. I've done so many things, been so many places,
> met so many people. I've done some really crazy things. I
> think about how it's all progressed and how much I've
> matured.

■

> College opened my eyes to life and what happens—good
> and bad. I had no idea how bad things could get—or how
> good—or how different people can be. In high school it
> was almost like a mold that everyone fits into. Last year
> my floor had a lot of international students and I lived
> with people from countries I didn't even know existed. I
> learned about everything from food—like how Latin peo-
> ple don't eat much peanut butter—to how Pakistani peo-
> ple get married, to dances and clothing and a little bit of
> language. It's made me much more tolerant—more open-
> minded. Not many things surprise me anymore.

■

> Somewhere I had this assumption that things would be
> taken care of at this stage—that I would cancel the news-
> paper and cancel the phone service and pack up all my
> personal problems and blithely move on to start life anew
> in another city. All of a sudden I realized that it was not
> going to be quite so simple. I see the complexities of
> things so much more now. It's not that my life is more

complex. I guess I'm just more aware of the complexities. No more good, bad—right, wrong. It's harder this way. My mom says it's all just part of growing up.

Many express frustration, and regrets as well—thoughts of lost opportunity and squandered time. They often describe such thoughts, however, with newly acquired perspective on their total college experience:

> At the beginning of the year and part of this semester, I would kick myself about, oh God, I wish I'd done that, and I did so much wrong in college—but I guess part of growing up is knowing thFere are going to be regrets. There are things you're going to mess up—then realizing why you didn't do things as well as you could have and learning from that.

Some students have to come to terms with the fact that they haven't done well in college. Occasionally, students who've scraped by with C's and D's fail in their final semester. Unable to graduate with their class, they face summer school and an anticlimactic finish. This is a difficult scenario for everyone involved. An academic dean who deals with this each spring reminds parents:

> The student knows this is a failure—it's a failure in the biggest task he's undertaken in life to date. And he needs his parents to be there for him. Parents should remember it's not their own failure.

Senior year is a time of intensity and contradiction—of the highs of accomplishments and the lows of dreams unfulfilled—of the comfort of familiarity and the anxiety of the unknown looming ahead. For many, there is a sense of things coming together, of goals reached, of efforts rewarded. And yet, standing at the top of the mountain, there is scarcely time to admire the view. Self-confidence becomes shaky as thoughts of the future invade the present.

As seniors make forays into the world beyond the campus, the question "What's next?" is never far from their thoughts. Some do internships in a brokerage house or TV station, in a juvenile court or an art gallery, wondering throughout—is this what I want to do next year? For as long as they can remember, their occupation has been student, and September has meant going back to school. But now September conjures up either a blank, a void, or transient images of where they will be, whom they'll be with, or what they'll be doing a year from now. Some hedge their bets and apply to graduate school and for jobs simultaneously. Some become immobilized and do nothing. Still others make a conscious decision to concentrate on school and postpone the search until after graduation.

Although many will eventually seek advanced degrees, the majority of today's college seniors face the tensions and uncertainties of searching for their first job in a period of downsizing and rapidly shifting employment opportunities. Dressed in their interview suits, future bankers and corporate trainees run—or wobble on newly purchased high heels—from an oriental philosophy class to a meeting with a recruiter from Chase Manhattan Bank. They write résumés with on-line career programs and practice their interviewing skills in front of a video camera.

Those aspiring to attend graduate or professional schools write applications and take entrance exams, comparing their scores with an intensity reminiscent of their former bouts with SATs. Those who have no idea what they want to do are sure that everyone else does. Waves of panic sweep over most seniors periodically, sometimes triggered by a friend's job offer—or their own rejection letter.

At just the time that students may be feeling vulnerable and looking to their parents for reassurance, many parents become anxious as well. Instead of providing a calming perspective, they often inadvertently add their own worries to those of their children. Separation issues resurface as they look forward to the end of tuition bills, but wonder if these will be replaced by other burdens, financial and emotional. What if he doesn't get a job? What if she doesn't get a fellowship? What if he wants to come back home to live?

Even those who have been avid supporters of a broad liberal arts
education may get the jitters about job prospects when the end is in
sight. Fathers who had been uninvolved in the brouhaha of "getting
in" four years before suddenly call inquiring about on-campus interviews by major corporations: "I know you don't want to work for
IBM, but perhaps you should have a contingency plan in case newspaper writing doesn't work out." Mothers give unsolicited advice
about how to dress and act in interviews. Parents who just months
before bragged of their daughter's independent travel on another
continent now worry that she will be unable to figure out the next
step in her own future.

Parents who forge ahead as if the job hunt is their own are often
puzzled by their offspring's negative reaction when they call to
announce that they have set up an interview for him with a friend
or client. Others are more subtle, hinting, "I saw a great new book
on résumé writing in the store."

A senior from Dallas describes the added burden of her parents'
interrogating phone calls:

> My parents have been more involved than ever this year.
> They call wanting information: How's it going? How're
> you doing? Have you heard from this school? Have you
> heard from that school? What are you doing this summer?
> Do you have a job? Do you have a place to stay?
>
> It's hard. I already expect a lot from myself. Then to be
> bombarded with questions by them makes it harder. I
> want to say, "Look, Mom, look, Dad, I know how impor-
> tant this all is." They don't seem to understand that I am
> aware, that I do know what's important. I wish they'd say
> stuff like "We know that you're going through a lot. We
> know it's tough." Or ask, "Are you nervous? Are you
> scared?" They seem to just be concerned with the facts.

Although every senior seems to have at least one friend who has
landed the perfect job in the perfect place at a higher-than-hoped-
for salary, the majority of students do not have everything wrapped

up by graduation. It is not unusual for seniors to leave campus after commencement stating, as one student did, "My life is one big *if*. Nothing is solid right now."

"The growth in today's job market is in small- and medium-sized firms that don't recruit on campus," says Jim Case, Assistant Vice President at the American Graduate School of International Management:

> It's a myth that most people work for large multinational corporations. Though students can get started while still in school, and can certainly learn about strategies and resources at their campus career center, most will have to wait until after their diploma is in hand before they can devote adequate time to a job campaign. As all career literature suggests, looking for a job is a full-time job.

The ambiguity and uncertainty of not knowing, however, is frustrating, and students appreciate parents who acknowledge this without trying to rush in and solve the problem for them or prod them into instant action.

Understanding and encouragement does not imply a light dismissal of the problem either. An engineering student who, much to his surprise and disappointment, was without a job at graduation found his parents' buoyant optimism more stressful than helpful: "They don't seem to understand that I'm really scared about not having a job. And it doesn't help when they tell me it's no big deal."

Knowing that they will soon be on their own, seniors are emphatic about maintaining their sense of autonomy. A former premed who discovered Spanish and international relations during her sophomore year called home with excitement when offered an opportunity to do an internship for Amnesty International after graduation—unpaid. Her mother, a nurse, was shocked and mystified at the news that her talented and bright daughter was planning to return home to live and work at a menial job to pay expenses, while participating in an unpaid internship:

To my mom, this internship is kind of a black hole. When I called her and told her about it, there was silence at the other end of the phone. I knew she was upset. To her, it's no payoff for all the work I've done. To me, it is the foundation for moving on to something else. It's very important.

When I switched from premed to Spanish in the middle of sophomore year, that was a hard thing to do because Mom wasn't happy about it. When I went away to Mexico junior year, it was the first major thing I did without her approval. And it was the best year I've ever had.

Now this internship is an opportunity to build a foundation for what I want to do in international relations. For my mom, it's a culmination of all the changes I've made. She's realizing that I'm going to be doing stuff like this forever, and that's hard for her to handle. She doesn't understand the international opportunities of jobs, and what I can do and why I want to travel. My mom grew up in Cleveland and never left; it was an environment where you either went to nursing school or you became a teacher—something traditional with a name or a title. And I'm never going to have that. I don't want to have it. She was divorced and worries about my security. If I'm not something with a title, that's very insecure to her. To me, it's not. To me, it's exciting.

Though this young woman longed to maintain the close, loving relationship she and her mother had always enjoyed, she was determined to pursue her own goals. The week after she called her mother about the internship, she wrote to her and essentially laid it on the line. Her confidence in her own identity, in who she has become, is evident:

I wrote an intense letter, spilling my guts, and said, basically, accept me as I am. I said, Would you like me to come home to the suburbs and become a secretary and live there for the rest of my life? That won't be me. It's not me; it's not who I've become. You sent me off to college to do well, and I have—and I took advantage of the opportunities and I grew, and I traveled, and I learned. And now here I am at the point of graduating. I am who I am because of what college has done to me and what I've done during college, and it's too late now. I can't change that. College is in me.

What a tribute to all college can and should be—the sheer joy of a student's discovery of the expansive world around her and ultimately of her own expanding self. But as parents, we often cringe when it is our own child who is taking the more adventuresome, less traveled path—or any path that differs from our hopes and expectations. We carry our own agendas. A dentist, whose real passion has been an involvement in Jewish volunteer activities, has a strong investment in his daughter's becoming a rabbi. A mother of the '50s drums into her daughter time and again that she should take advantage of today's opportunities for women and not settle for the traditional teaching or social service job. A doctor sees a medical career as the only acceptable route for his son. A bus driver makes sacrifices for the dream of his daughter, the future engineer. But the would-be engineer discovers TV production, and the doctor's son opts for a graduate degree in classics. The dentist's daughter forgoes rabbinical school for a career as a Jewish educator, and the young woman whose mother had visions of law school makes a commitment to medical social work.

Our children will go their separate ways, and so they should. They have become who they are, not who we would have them be. As graduation draws near and students declare their financial independence, both parents and children feel the balance of power shifting between them. Money has, after all, been the one tie that has continued to bind, often unacknowledged but inevitably present in the background.

With plans to enter a bank training program in Chicago, a Hamilton College senior rejoices in the prospect of his impending financial freedom:

I've got my own Visa card now! I have my independence. My folks can give me advice; they always have. But they can't tell me what to do anymore. It's not that I've always listened to them, but up till now there's been this feeling of obligation.

In many families, issues of money are still under negotiation. Some students have put themselves through college and are facing substantial debts. Others worry about building a financial base so that they can go to graduate school in the future. Still others are in the throes of a job hunt. And questions arise for both parents and their children: Who will pay off the loans? Can I retain my independence and live at home? How long am I willing to help subsidize my kid? Who's going to pay for graduate school? If he lives at home, should I charge him room and board?

Each family has to weigh its own financial realities, values, and needs. Those who talk openly about money matters—expectations and limits—avoid disappointment and resentment at a later date. There are, of course, no hard and fast rules. One student who supported herself all through college decides to live at home so that she can pay off her loans. She is confident and secure in her independence, and her parents, who were unable to pay for college, welcome the chance to be of help. Another senior turns down his parents' offer to pay for graduate school, even though he knows it will be several years before he can pay for it himself. He's convinced that the financial ties are too threatening to his autonomy.

By the time they are seniors, most students have stopped turning to their parents for their primary emotional support, and turn first to their friends and lovers. For many, the heart of college life, especially during these last months, centers around a cherished group of friends. Much of their undergraduate experience is tied up in a mutual history of heartaches and treasured memories.

As the school year comes to a close, students are aware of the impending separation from those who have become so central to their lives. They plan outings and weekend getaways; some look forward to traveling together before settling into the routine of a job or graduate school; others hope to keep a thread of continuity in their lives by joining forces to live together after graduation.

They look to these trusted friends for confirmation of their decisions and validation of their identity. An about-to-graduate senior
from the University of Wisconsin confides:

> I went through a stage three months ago of being very
> remorseful about leaving my security blanket, which this
> university has become. My friends know Lisa. They know
> what she stands for, what she does. I'm accepted here. I
> dread going out into the real world and having to reestab-
> lish myself and reintroduce myself. My self-confidence is
> wavering. I've decided to stay in Madison for the summer,
> live with a good friend, and send out applications.

Those whose plans will clearly take them far away from friends anticipate the grieving process that lies ahead. A young woman who intends
to return home to Minnesota before entering divinity school notes:

> Part of me dreads after graduation, when I've left all my
> friends and I go home and get depressed and my parents
> are going to say, "It's not that bad—get yourself
> together"—and I'm going to say, "No, let me be depressed.
> It's OK for me to feel bad."

Those who plan to work after graduation worry about leaving
behind a world in which they have been surrounded by people their
own age—where it's always easy to find someone to talk to about
politics or music or whatever. And there's always something to do—
parties, lectures, concerts. And they're usually free! As the time to
part approaches, they make plans to keep in touch, and joke about
the reunions they'll have in the as yet unimaginable future. Those
who have stayed in close touch with high school friends reassure
themselves that they'll do the same with their friends from college.
A senior on her way to medical school says laughingly:

> I know I'll keep up with my friends here. And I know that
> if I get married, my little kids are going to meet their little

kids. There's no doubt in my mind that's going to happen.
And now I understand that anywhere I go, I'll be able to
make new friends, but that it's going to take time.

The unspoken intentions of romantic partnerships must now be
addressed. Graduation brings a convenient end to some of these two-
somes; commitment was only to this time and place. But for many
students, conflicts of identity and intimacy are brought clearly into
focus at this juncture. Choices are many, and decisions are often
painful and poignant: Should I give up the chance to work on Wall
Street and pick up whatever I can in Ann Arbor while she goes to
grad school? Will our relationship withstand the strain if he's in D.C.
and I'm in Tampa? If we compromise and go to the only law school
that accepted both of us, will we end up resenting each other?

Parents are often surprised to find that couples who appear to be
very much in love put career priorities ahead of personal ones. Old
assumptions about relationships no longer hold true. Women do not
drop everything automatically to "put him through medical school."
Some men make compromises in their own career aspirations to follow the woman in their life. Some couples develop a sequential plan
and take turns making career compromises for each other.

Many young men and women acknowledge that their priority is
to establish a more solid sense of themselves beyond the campus
world before they make a long-term commitment to someone else.
After an intense year-and-a-half relationship, a future graduate student in education finds herself at a crossroads:

> The past twenty years I've been my parents' child, and
> even at college, you're not a full adult. And I'm getting out,
> and here I have a chance to be me, and that's most impor-
> tant. I love Sean a lot, but after twenty years, it's time for
> me now; it's time for me to do what's best for me. And if
> what's best for him is going to coincide with that, well
> that's great, that's fantastic. But he's not the most impor-
> tant thing in my life right now. I don't expect to be the
> most important thing in his life either.

Parents may be caught off guard when they find that their child is making plans to live with a partner. What may look like impulsive, cavalier behavior may actually represent a carefully thought out decision. A senior at Dartmouth explains that his parents were taken aback when he called to tell them that he and his girlfriend were moving to San Francisco together:

> I had intentionally not told my parents much about our relationship. I didn't tell them anything until it was a fait accompli. It ended up being more of a scene than it would have been otherwise. They were very upset because they had no idea how important she was to me. I hadn't told them. In trying to avoid confrontation earlier in the year, I brought on more. I underestimated them. After all, I'm the fifth child, and nothing I could have done would have been a surprise. If I had to do it over, I would have let them know more along the way.

In the midst of all this planning for the future, saying good-bye to dear friends, wrapping up the last round of papers and finals, the pressure mounts. A chemistry major from Puerto Rico recounts:

> This is probably the most confusing time in my life. Everything is up in the air. I haven't heard yet from med school in Puerto Rico or if I have a job here. I'm packing up four years worth of stuff, but I don't know where I'm going to be. I'm still under pressure in one class—a take-home exam I have to finish by tomorrow. My parents have a new house. Nothing's solid, past or future. It's nine days before graduation, and I never thought it'd be like this.

Even those with definitive plans begin to feel disoriented, to experience waves of highs and lows as the countdown to graduation begins. When they finish their last exams, everything comes to a halt. "It's like coming off of drugs," said an engineering student from a highly competitive university:

You've spent four years of intense pressure, day in and day out, and your body has become used to such incredibly high levels of stress. I keep thinking, What do I have to do? What's my homework? I've got to race to get this done. And then I remember, it's over.

His girlfriend added:

I finished up yesterday and I thought, I'm going out to lunch and get drunk. And I'm going to be so happy, and my life is going to be so perfect now.

   We had lunch, and I was kind of let down. It was like—well—I'm going to go home and take a nap now. It wasn't what I thought it would be.

An anthropology major from Minnesota shares his thoughts:

I'm leaving everyone I love here, all my supports, all the people who love me. It's like leaving home all over again.

   On the brink of adulthood, these young men and women retreat to realms of childlike playfulness. "I've done a lot of crazy things with my friends," said a business student in his final weeks. "Nothing harmful. Just absurd. Like walking 6 miles to White Castle for a hamburger last weekend." The campus takes on an air of celebration, a spontaneous round of parties and picnics, barefoot smiling students cavorting with friends among the ubiquitous campus canines chasing sticks and Frisbees, scantily clad seniors lazing in the sun—a week's hiatus before the finale.

   Students put finishing touches on plans for the big day—graduation. Groups of friends make arrangements for cocktail parties and brunches and look forward to introducing their parents to each other on their own turf. For a number of students from divorced families, graduation stirs up the pain of unresolved family conflicts. Some of them anticipate having to orchestrate the comings and goings of parents, stepparents, and grandparents who barely speak to each other. They talk about feeling trapped and resent the burden of having to hold things together on their special day. For many children of divorced parents, however, this isn't a problem. Their parents put their own conflicts aside and come together to share the joy of this milestone in their child's life.

When graduation day finally arrives, the campus is at its most resplendent, lawns clipped and bushes pruned. Instant gardens have sprung up in newly planted flower beds. The carillon rings out familiar tunes, and with luck the weather cooperates to produce the picture-book aura of the admissions office's most enticing brochure.

Parents, some with young children in tow, or with grandparents on their arms, view the proceedings through the eyes of omnipresent video cameras. Reflecting the diversity of the graduating class, assembled guests sport turbans and veils, three-piece suits, cowboy boots.

The students congregate, a sea of black robes and mortarboards. Beneath the solemnity of academic garb, they express their individuality with Hawaiian shirts and shorts, purple sandals and red hightops, sunglasses of every imaginable color. Atop their mortarboards they have taped champagne glasses, pinwheels, a mysterious Chinese symbol, a sign that says, "Hire me." They carry everything from bottles of champagne, balloons, and flowers to a stuffed Snoopy dressed in full graduation regalia. As they line up for the processional, groups of friends join each other, expressing disbelief that this day has finally come. Their irreverent humor hints at their anxiety and belies the formality of the ritual: "I was once a waiter. I can do it again!" "I think I'll pick my grad school by what nifty color robes and hoods they have; I like Stanford hoods myself." "It's with all of you guys that I got my best education. Good luck, we're getting out of here!"

The ceremony starts with a roll of drums or flair of trumpets, followed by the color and pageantry of a medieval academic procession. The music builds to the familiar strains of "Pomp and Circumstance"—guaranteed to send chills up the spine of even the most jaded graduation-goer.

Among the speeches, musical interludes, and conferring of honorary degrees, there are the familiar phrases that invite the assembled graduates to "enter the company of educated men and women." The final words are greeted with cheers, popping champagne corks, tossed mortarboards, and the release of balloons into the sky.

The grandeur and pageantry of this final college ritual is ephemeral; it remains only in memory and faded family albums. What endures is less dramatic and unfolds over time.

In the words of one brand new graduate:

> It's not like right after graduation time stops and you just stand there and look at this big event—and this big white light comes out of the sky and says, "Sandy, you're 21! Look into the past at your life. Look forward at your future."
>
> You just take off your cap and gown, and it's still the quad.
>
> The place hasn't changed, but I have. Four years ago I wouldn't have understood this, but I feel like I'm leaving college with so many more questions than when I came in—and that's great. I know what the questions are and how to go about finding the answers.

As the recessional sounds, our children march out with arms around each other. We stand aside and watch them from a distance, catching a glimpse of the world that has been theirs for four years. We feel pride and joy and tenderness—but we also know that this is their moment, that they are creating their own futures.

RESOURCES FOR PARENTS AND STUDENTS

We've put together the following list of resources as a starting point for parents who want to seek out additional information. We have focused on books, organizations, and Web sites that we and many parents have found useful, including a variety of resources targeted to specific populations and students with special needs. Our list is not meant to be exhaustive. There is an ever-changing body of helpful information available to parents of today's college students. Exploration of many of the resources here can lead to untold treasures on bookstore and library shelves or in the endless links of the Internet and the World Wide Web.

ADMISSIONS AND FINANCIAL AID

We have selected guides written specifically for parents and those targeted to special populations. This list does not include the standard college guides and directories.

On the Internet
http://www.collegeboard.org/
   An excellent Web site from the same people who gave you the SATs. Tips on how to use the Web for admission and financial aid informa-

tion; advice for parents and students and links to many other related websites.

http://www.mit.edu:8001/people/cdemello/univ.html
Alphabetical or regional listing and access to college and university home pages across the world.

http://www.fastweb.com/
The Internet's largest free scholarship search.

http://www.finaid.org/nasfaa
The Web page of the National Association of Student Financial Aid Administrators has timely and valuable information specifically for parents.

http://www.webcom.com/~cjcook/SDBP/hbcu.html
The historically black institutions and related resources, such as: The Black Collegian and The United Negro College Fund.

■

Adler, Joe Anne, with Jennifer Adler Friedman.*Women's Colleges*. New York: Prentice Hall, 1994.

Beckham, Barry, ed. *The Black Student's Guide to Scholarships*. Lanham, Maryland: Madison Books, 1996.

Boyer, Ernest L., and Paul Boyer. *Smart Parents Guide to College*. Princeton, New Jersey: Peterson's, 1996.

Cernea, Ruth Fredman, ed. *Hillel Guide to Jewish Life on Campus*. New York: Random House, 1995.

Clark, Andy and Amy Clark. *Athletic Scholarships*. New York: Facts on File, Inc., 1994.

Dalby, Sidonia, Sally Rubenstone and Emily Harrison Weir. *The International Student's Guide to Going to College in America*. New York: Macmillan, 1996.

Dolber, Roslyn. *College and Career Success for Students with Learning Disabilities*. Lincolnwood, Illinois: NTC Publishing Group, 1996.

Historically Black Colleges and Universities. Wintergreen/Orchard House, Inc. New York: Arco Publications, 1995.

Koehler, Michael. *Advising Student Athletes Through the College Recruitment Process: A Complete Guide for Counselors, Coaches and Parents.* Englewood Cliffs, New Jersey: Prentice Hall, 1996.

MacGowan, Sandra F., and Sarah M. McGinty. *50 College Admissions Directors Speak to Parents.* San Diego: Harcourt Brace Jovanich, Publishers, 1988.

Mitchell, Robert. *The Multicultural Student's Guide to Colleges: What Every African-American, Asian-American, Hispanic and Native American Applicant Needs to Know about America's Top Schools.* New York: The Noonday Press, 1996.

Money Guide: Your Best College Buys Now. From the editors of *Money Magazine.* 1996 edition.

Peterson's *Choose a Christian College : A Guide to Colleges Committed to a Christ-Centered Campus Life.* 5th edition. Princeton, New Jersey. 1996

Peterson's *Colleges with Programs for Students with Learning Disabilities,* Editors: Charles T. Mangrum II and Stephen S. Strichart. 4th edition. Princeton, New Jersey, 1994.

Weinstein, Miriam. *Making a Difference College Guide.* San Raphael, California: Sage Works Press, 1995. (Colleges that emphasize community service opportunities.)

Wilson, Erlene B. *Money for College: A Guide to Financial Aid for African-American Students.* New York: Penguin Books, 1996.

Wilson, Erlene B. *The 100 Best Colleges for African-American Students.* New York: Penguin Books, 1993.

Wolff, Michael., ed. *How to Get Into the School of Your Dreams. Using the Internet and Online Services.* New York: Wolff New Media, 1996.

CULTS

International Cult Education Program (ICEP)
P.O. Box 1232
Gracie Station
New York, New York 10028
212-533-5420

Message Center: 212-249-7693

ICEP, sponsored by the American Family Foundation provides educational forums and materials about cults and psychological manipulation and is a good resource for parents.

Cult Clinic/Hotline
The Jewish Board of Family and Children's Services
120 West 57 St.
New York, New York 10019
212-632-4640

■

On the Internet
http://www.csj.org/

The American Family Foundation Web page offers a wealth of information about cults and resources for families of cult members.

e-mail address: affny@worldnet.att.net

http://www.geocities.com/~cares/

The Cult Awareness RESources (CARES) provides information and resources to the campus community about cult activity.

■

Giambalvo, Carol and Herbert L. Rosedale esq. (editors). *The Boston Movement: Critical Perspectives* Bonita Springs, Florida: American Family Foundation Paperback, 1995. Provides personal accounts, history and analysis of the Boston Church of Christ (also known as the International Churches of Christ.)

Hassan, Steven. *Combatting Cult Mind Control*. Rochester, Vermont: Park Street Press, 1988.

Ross, Joan and Michael D. Langone. *Cults: What Parents Should Know*. Lyle Stuart, 1989.

Rudin, Marcia. *Cults on Campus: Continuing Challenge; Revised Edition*. New York: International Cult Education Program, 1996.

GAYS, LESBIANS, AND BISEXUALS

Borhek, Mary V. *Coming Out to Parents: A Two-Way Survival Guide for Lesbians and Gay Men and Their Parents.* New York: The Pilgrim Press, 1983.

Griffin, Carolyn Welch. *Beyond Acceptance: Parents of Lesbians and Gays Talk About Their Experiences.* New York: St. Martin's, 1990.

HEALTH: PHYSICAL AND EMOTIONAL

Parents may find these resources useful and may want to recommend them to their sons and daughters.

On the Internet

http://www.columbia.edu/cu/healthwise/alice.html

This is an excellent interactive question-and-answer Web site from the Columbia University Health Services. It includes an archive of lively answers to questions commonly asked by college students on many subjects under the headings of general health, sexuality, fitness and nutrition, drugs and alcohol, relationships and emotional well-being.

http://uhs.bsd.uchicago.edu/scrs/vpc/vpc.html/

The Student Counseling Virtual Pamphlet Collection from the University of Chicago provides links to selective on-line pamphlets from counseling centers across the country. The subjects included are: alcohol and substance abuse, anxiety, assertiveness, cults, depression, eating disorders, family issues, relationships, sexual assault, sexual harassment, sexual orientation, sleep, stress, study skills, time management and traumatic events.

http://www.d.umn.edu/hlthserv/counseling/links.html

The University of Minnesota at Duluth Counseling Service has a Web page of General Psychological Links providing links to rich resources ranging from the personal, poetic, and practical to the clinical and academic.

Alcohol and Drug Abuse

On the Internet
http://www.health.org/resref.htm
The National Clearinghouse for Alcohol and Drug Information.

http://www.edc.org/hec/
The Higher Education Center for Alcohol and Other Drug Prevention.

■

Kinney, Jean and Gwen Leaton. *Loosening the Grip: A Handbook of Alcohol Information – 4th edition*. St. Louis, Missouri, Mosby-Yearbook, 1991.

Eating Disorders

American Anorexic/Bulimia Association (AA/BA)
Suite 1 R
293 Central Park West
New York, NY 10024
212–501–8351

National Association of Anorexia Nervosa and Associated Disorders
P.O. Box 7
Highland Park, Illinois 60035
847–831–3438

■

Byrne, Katherine. *A Parent's Guide to Anorexia and Bulimia: Understanding and Helping Self-Starvers and Binge/Purgers*. New York: Schocken Books, 1987.

Siegel, Michelle, Judith Brisman and Margot Weinshel. *Surviving an Eating Disorder: Perspectives and Strategies for Family and Friends*. HarperCollins, 1989.

Depression

Papolos, Demitri and Janice Papolos. *Overcoming Depression (Revised Edition)* New York: HarperPerennial, 1992.

Rosen, Laura Epstein and Xavier Francisco Amador. *When Someone You Love Is Depressed*. New York: Free Press, 1996.

RESPONDING TO TRAUMA

On the Internet
http://www.cs.utk.edu/~bartley/saInfopage.edu
The Sexual Assault Information Page provides a comprehensive collection of resources for male and female victims of sexual assault, abuse, or harassment. Includes links to university resources, rape crises centers, and health and safety information.

■

Ledray, Linda E. *Recovering from Rape*. New York: Henry Holt and Company, 1986.
Parrot, Andrea, ed. *Acquaintance Rape: The Hidden Crime*. New York: John Wiley & Sons, Inc., 1991.

SECURITY AND CRIME PREVENTION

On the Internet
http://www.soconline.org/
Security on Campus, Inc. contains important information for parents and students about campus crime and prevention.

STOPPING OUT/TIME OFF OR TRANSFERRING

These are valuable resources for parents to recommend to students who are considering transferring or taking time off from school.

Dalby, Sidonia and Sally Rubenstone. *The Transfer Student's Guide to Changing Colleges*. New York: Prentice Hall, 1993.
Gilpin Robert, and Caroline Fitzgibbons, *Time Out: Taking a Break from School to Travel, Work, and Study in the U.S. and Abroad*, Fireside, 1992.

Hall, Colin and Ron Lieber. *Taking Time Off* . New York: Noonday
    Press, 1996.

STUDY ABROAD

Parents may want to recommend these supplementary resources to
students whose colleges have limited study abroad information.

Council on International Educational Exchange (CIEE)
205 East 42 St.
New York, New York 10017
212–661–1414
    Provides information about international study, research, and travel
    programs and administers some scholarships.

Institute of International Education (IIE)
U.S. Student Programs Division
809 United Nations Plaza
New York, New York 10017
212–883–8200
    Provides information about international exchange programs and
    funding, study and travel opportunities. Administers Fulbright grants
    for graduate study.

■

On the Internet
http://www.studyabroad.com/
    Listings for the thousands of study abroad programs in more than 100
    countries throughout the world and hundreds of links to study abroad
    home pages, plus other information and resources.

■

Academic Year Abroad, Sara Steen. New York: Institute of International
    Education, 1997
*Peterson's Study Abroad 1997: A Guide to Semester and Year Abroad
    Academic Programs*, (Fourth Ed.) Peterson's Staff.

The Student's Guide to the Best Study Abroad Programs, Greg Tannen and Charley Winkler, (Pocket Books, 1996).

GIFT BOOKS FOR STUDENTS

There are many books written for college students. Here are a few we think would make useful gifts.

Dobkin, Rachel, and Shana Sippy. *Educating Ourselves: The College Woman's Handbook*. New York: Workman Publishing, 1995.

Gardner, John N. and A. Jerome Jewler. *Your College Experience: Strategies for Success*. Belmont, CA., Wadsworth, Inc., 1992.

Hanson, Jennifer, and Friends. *The Real Freshman Handbook: An Irreverent and Totally Honest Guide to Life on Campus*. Boston: Houghton Mifflin, 1996.

Katz, Montana, and Veronica Vieland. *Get Smart! A Woman's Guide to Equality on Campus*. New York: The Feminist Press at The City University of New York, 1988.

Moses, Henry C. *Inside College: New Freedom, New Responsibility*. New York: The College Board.

Otis, Carol L., and Roger Goldingay. *Campus Health Guide: The College Student's Handbook for Healthy Living*. New York: College Board, 1989.

Powell, Elizabeth, M.S., M.A. *Talking Back to Sexual Pressure*. Minneapolis, Minnesota: CompCare Publishers, 1991.

Weinberg, Carol. *The Complete Handbook for College Women*. New York: New York University Press, 1994

CHAPTER TWO

SOME THINGS NEVER CHANGE: THE SEARCH FOR IDENTITY,
INDEPENDENCE, AND INTIMACY

1: Margaret Mahler's pioneering research on the development of young children has provided countless insights into the preverbal period of childhood. Trained as a pediatrician, Mahler later became an eminent child psychoanalyst and researcher. As a result of thirty years of painstaking daily observation of children interacting with their mothers during the first three years of life, Mahler and her associates described a complex developmental sequence, which they named *separation-individuation*. These were seen as two separate but complementary interweaving themes. Separation referred to the young child's emergence from a symbiotic relationship with his or her mother. Through individuation the child develops unique personality characteristics and the ability to retain a consistent mental image of mother and self.

Mahler adopted the biological term *symbiosis* to describe the early bond between mother and infant. She suggested that the first signs of the separation-individuation process are the specific smiles that a baby reserves for its mother at about 4 or 5 months, signs of recognition of her as a separate and special person. Through the next two and a half years, the child goes through the sometimes exhilarating, sometimes painful process of moving away from mother to become a separate person in his or her own right. Mahler described the often contradictory behaviors of the separating child, from the *practicing phase*, when toddlers, who have just learned how to walk, feel all-powerful and in love with the world, to the *rapprochement phase*, when with increasing separation anxiety they become aware of their vulnerability and helplessness. An empathetic and helpful mother responds to her child's natural pull to venture forth with encouragement and support.

By about 3 years of age, healthy children will have the capacity to hold in their mind a loving, positive representation of mother as well as a consistent and clearly separate self-image. This positive *internal mother* image is available for comfort at those difficult times when mother is away or when she is frustrating or disappointing. It is a remarkable and complex achievement for a 3-year-old and one that requires both trust and confidence as well as physical and cognitive maturity.

In recent years, Daniel Stern, a highly respected psychoanalyst and developmental researcher, has challenged Mahler's notion of symbiosis between mother and child, suggesting that infants experience a sense of emergent self from birth. He posits that while separation is going on, at the same time, and of equal importance, children are seeking and creating new ways to connect with their primary caretaker.

2: Psychologist Peter Blos has written extensively about the tumultuous years of adolescence. In his classic work *On Adolescence*, he borrows the term *second individuation* from Mahler to describe this chaotic time, which leads finally to a consolidation of individual identity.

> The oppositional, rebellious, and resistive strivings, the stages of experimentation, the testing of the self by going to excess—all these have a positive usefulness in the process of self-definition. "This is not me" represents an important step in the achievement of individuation and

in the establishment of autonomy; at an earlier age, it is condensed into a single word, "No."

—Peter Blos, *On Adolescence: A Psychoanalytic Interpretation*. New York: Free Press of Glencoe, 1962, 12

3: Psychoanalyst and developmental theorist Erik Erikson points to this critical time as part of the natural evolution of human psychosocial development. His "eight stages of man" extend through the life cycle. Each stage is characterized by a crisis, or turning point, with polar opposite possible resolutions, one leading to growth and the other to difficulties: basic trust versus basic mistrust; autonomy versus shame and doubt; initiative versus guilt; industry versus inferiority; identity versus identity diffusion; intimacy versus isolation; generativity versus stagnation; ego integrity versus despair. At each stage, there is a crossroads, a shifting in perspective, which leads to disequilibrium and vulnerability. The positive resolution of one stage makes moving to the next one possible. The child who has successfully negotiated earlier stages of trust, autonomy, initiative, and industry will have an easier time becoming a confident and self-reliant young adult, discovering the answers to the question "Who am I?"

Erikson's stages are not neatly packaged, clearly defined time periods. Moreover, his clinical observations were based on a male model of development. The more recent research of theorists Nancy Chodorow and Carol Gilligan has pointed to significant differences between identity development for men and women. Whereas men's identity is defined primarily through individual achievement and autonomy, women's identity is formed in the context of relationships. Gilligan's positive acknowledgment of the "woman's voice" of empathy, responsibility, and care adds a provocative dimension to the study of human development, which is only beginning to unfold.

Other theorists are examining the subtleties in the identity formation of specific minority groups. What is it like to be black in a white world? A homosexual in a world that values heterosexuality? A young man or woman from a culture that values close ties and

obligations to extended family living in a Western society that pro-
motes individualism and independence? All pose questions that
challenge or may simply broaden Erikson's original observations.

4: Based on a study in the '50s and '60s involving a series of
interviews with Harvard undergraduates across their college years,
William Perry and his associates postulated a theory of intellectual
and ethical development that has had a far-reaching impact on our
understanding of the college student. Perry's scheme describes how
students think in increasingly complex ways as they move through
their college years. Many educators and researchers have found the
material relevant and useful in tracing the development of critical
thinking in the college student. Perry's research was done on male
subjects. Recently, as an outgrowth of the work of Carol Gilligan,
others have been expanding on Perry's original work to incorporate
"women's ways of knowing."

Perry described nine positions, moving from an early stage of
basic duality, when students see things in black-and-white terms, to
a more complex, relativistic view of the world, and finally to a point
at which they are ready to make personal commitments.

5: According to Erik Erikson, it is essential to develop a solid
sense of identity before moving on to the next task in his developmental scheme, forming intimate relationships. He writes in
Identity: Youth and Crisis:

> It is only when identity formation is well on its way that
> true intimacy—which is really a counterpointing as well as
> a fusing of identities—is possible. Sexual intimacy is only
> part of what I have in mind, for it is obvious that sexual
> intimacies often precede the capacity to develop a true and
> mutual psychosocial intimacy with another person, be it in
> friendship, in erotic encounters or in joint inspiration.

Chodorow and Gilligan challenge Erikson's assumption, claiming
that his linear scheme is not representative of women's experience.

For women, the formation of identity and a capacity for intimacy are much more likely to be intertwined.

CHAPTER THREE
SOME THINGS DO CHANGE: COLLEGE LIFE TODAY

1: Alexander W. Astin, Kenneth C. Green, and William S. Korn, *The American Freshman: Twenty Year Trends, 1966-1985* (Los Angeles: Higher Education Research Institute of UCLA, 1987), 7.

2: Alexander W. Astin, William S. Korn, and Ellyne R. Berz, *The American Freshman: National Norms for Fall 1990* (Los Angeles: Higher Education Research Institute of UCLA, 1990), 4.

3: Helen Lefkowitz Horowitz, *Campus Life* (New York: Alfred A. Knopf, 1987), 289.

4: Joe R. Feagin, Hernán Vera, and Nikitah Imani, *The Agony of Education: Black Students at White Colleges and Universities* (New York: Routledge, 1996), 46.

5: International Cult Education Program, P.O. Box 1232, Gracie Station, New York, NY 10028. Telephone: (212) 533-5420; message center: (212) 249-7693. Marcia R. Rudin, Director.

CHAPTER FIVE
READY, SET, GO: THE DEPARTURE

1: Gail Sheehy, *Spirit of Survival* (New York: William Morrow, 1986), 26.

CHAPTER SIX
ORIENTATION AND DISORIENTATION

1: Ellen Goodman, "When Students Fly from the Empty Nest," *The Philadelphia Inquirer*, September 17, 1986.

CHAPTER SEVEN
THE FRESHMAN YEAR: ACADEMIC LIFE AND THE COLLEGE SCENE

1: David Schoem as quoted in "An Early Start: First Year Seminars" by Leslie Stainton, *LSA Magazine*, University of Michigan, Fall 1996, 12.

CHAPTER EIGHT
IN AND OUT OF YOUR LIFE

1: Robert Arnstein, "The Place of College Health Services in the Prevention of Suicide and Affective Disorders." In *Suicide and Depression Among Adolescents and Young Adults*, ed. Gerald L. Klerman (Washington, DC: American Psychiatric Press, 1986), 350.

CHAPTER NINE
SOPHOMORE SLUMP AND THE YEARS BEYOND

1: Jeff Gordinier, "Sophomore Slump," *Princeton Parents* (February 1987).

2: Kenneth Keniston, "Youth: A 'New' Stage of Life." In *Readings in Adult Psychology: Contemporary Perspectives*, ed. Lawrence R. Allman and Dennis T. Jaffe (New York: Harper & Row, 1977), 133.

3: Richard S. Benner and Susan Tyler Hitchcock, *Life After Liberal Arts* (Charlottesville: University of Virginia, 1986), 10.

BIBLIOGRAPHY

Adler, Joe Anne, with Jennifer Adler Friedman. *Women's Colleges*. New York: Prentice Hall, 1994.

Apter, Terri. *Altered Loves: Mothers and Daughters During Adolescence*. New York: Ballantine Books, 1990.

Arnstein, Robert. "Development Issues for College Students." *Psychiatric Annals* 14 (September 1984): 9.

——"The Place of College Health Services in the Prevention of Suicide and Affective Disorders." In *Suicide and Depression Among Adolescents and Young Adults*, ed. Gerald L. Klerman. Washington, DC: American Psychiatric Press, 1986.

Ascher, Carol. "Ensuring a Rainbow After the Storm: Recent Initiatives to Institutionalize Pluralism on Predominantly White Campuses." *Review* (Higher Education Extension Service at Yale University and ERIC Clearinghouse on Urban Education, Teachers College, Columbia) (Spring, 1991): 1–11.

Astin, Alexander W. *What Matters in College?* San Francisco: Jossey-Bass Publishers, 1993.

Astin, Alexander W., Kenneth C. Green, William S. Korn. *The American Freshman: Twenty Year Trends, 1966–1985*. Los Angeles: Higher Education Research Institute of UCLA, 1987.

Astin, Alexander W., William Korn, and Ellyne R. Berz. *The American Freshman: National Norms for Fall 1990*. Los Angeles: Higher Education Research Institute of UCLA, 1990.

Astin, Alexander W., Linda J. Sax, William S. Korn, and Kathryn M. Mahoney. *The American Freshman: National Norms for Fall 1995*. Los Angeles: Higher Education Research Institute of UCLA, 1995.

Baxter Magolda, M.B. *Knowing and Reasoning in College: Gender-Related Patterns in Students' Intellectual Development*. San Francisco: Jossey-Bass Publishers, 1992.

Beadle, Sandy J. "The Triumphs of Teaching with Technology." *LSA Magazine*, University of Michigan (Fall 1996): 15–20.

Beckham, Barry, ed. *The Black Student's Guide to Scholarships*. Lanham, MD: Madison Books, 1996.

Belenky, Mary F., Blythe M. Clinchy, Nancy Rule Goldberger, and Jill M. Tarule. *Women's Ways of Knowing*. New York: Basic Books, 1986.

Benner, Richard S., and Susan Tyler Hitchcock. *Life After Liberal Arts: Information and Advice for Students from the University of Virginia's College of Arts and Sciences Alumni Career Survey*. Charlottesville: University of Virginia, 1986.

Berent, Polly Dittmer. *Getting Ready for College*. Seymour, IN: Moonshadow Press, 1996.

Bloom, Allen. *The Closing of the American Mind*. New York: Simon & Schuster, 1987.

Bloom, Michael V. *Adolescent Parental Separation*. New York: Gardner Press, 1980.

Blos, Peter. *On Adolescence: A Psychoanalytic Interpretation*. New York: Free Press of Glencoe, 1962.

——*The Adolescent Passage*. New York: International Universities Press, 1979.

Borden, Marian Edelman, Mary Anne Burlinson, and Elsie R. Kearns. *In Addition to Tuition: The Parents' Survival Guide to Freshman Year in College*. New York: Facts on File, 1995.

Bordin, Edward S. "The Role of Alienation in Identity Formation in College Students." In *Counseling for the Liberal Arts Campus: The Albion Symposium*, ed. Jos. C. Heston and Willard B. Frick. Yellow Springs, Ohio: Antioch Press, 1968.

Borhek, Mary V. *Coming Out to Parents: A Two-Way Survival Guide for Lesbians and Gay Men and Their Parents*. New York: Pilgrim Press, 1983.

Boyer, Ernest L. *Campus Life: In Search of Community*. Princeton, NJ: Carnegie Foundation for the Advancement of Teaching, 1990.

——*College: The Undergraduate Experience in America*. New York: Harper & Row, 1987.

——*The Condition of the Professoriate: Attitudes and Trends*. Princeton, NJ: Carnegie Foundation for the Advancement of Teaching, 1989.

Boyer, Ernest L., and Paul Boyer. *Smart Parents Guide to College*. Princeton, NJ: Peterson's, 1996.

Brans, J. *Mother, I Have Something to Tell You*. Garden City, NY: Doubleday, 1987.

Brown, John Seely, and Paul Duguid. "Universities in the Digital Age." *Change* (July/August 1996): 11–18.

Bunzel, John H. *Race Relations on Campus*. Stanford, CA: Stanford Alumni Association, 1992.

Cernea, Ruth Fredman, ed. *Hillel Guide to Jewish Life on Campus*. New York: Random House, 1995.

Chodorow, Nancy. *The Reproduction of Mothering: Psychoanalysis and the Sociology of Gender*. Berkeley: University of California Press, 1978.

Clark, Andy, and Amy Clark. *Athletic Scholarships*. New York: Facts on File, 1994.

Cohen, Robert D., ed. *Working with the Parents of College Students*. San Francisco: Jossey-Bass, 1985.

Colarusso, Calvin, and Robert Nemiroff. *Adult Development*. New York: Plenum Press, 1981.

Colt, George Howe. "Suicide." *Harvard Magazine* (September/October 1983): 47–66.

Dalby, Sidonia, and Sally Rubenstone. *The Transfer Student's Guide to Changing Colleges*. New York: Prentice Hall, 1993.

Dalby, Sidonia, Sally Rubenstone, and Emily Harrison Weir. *The International Student's Guide to Going to College in America*. New York: Macmillan, 1996.

DeBuono, B. A., S. H. Zinner, M. Daamen, and W. M. McCormack. "Sexual Behavior of College Women in 1975, 1986, and 1989." *The New England Journal of Medicine* (March 22, 1990): 821–5.

Dobkin, Rachel, and Shana Sippy. *Educating Ourselves: The College Woman's Handbook*. New York: Workman Publishing, 1995.

Dolber, Roslyn. *College and Career Success for Students with Learning Disabilities*. Lincolnwood, IL: NTC Publishing Group, 1996.

D'Souza, Dinesh. *Illiberal Education: The Politics of Sex and Race on Campus*. New York: Free Press, 1991.

Dublin, Thomas, ed. *Becoming American, Becoming Ethnic: College Students Explore Their Roots*. Philadelphia: Temple University Press, 1996.

Edgerton, Russ, and Barbara Leigh Smith. "Learning, Technology, and the Way We Work." *The American Association for Higher Education Bulletin* (September 1996): 7–9.

Edward, Joyce, Nathene Ruskin, and Patsy Turrini. *Separation-Individuation Theory and Application*. New York: Gardner Press, 1981.

Ehrhart, Julie K., and Bernice R. Sandler. *Campus Gang Rape: Party Games?* Washington, DC: Project on the Status and Education of Women, Association of American Colleges, 1985.

Eichenbaum, Luise, and Susie Orbach. *Understanding Women: A Feminist Psychoanalytic Approach*. New York: Basic Books, 1983.

El-Khawas, Elaine. "Campus Trends, 1986." *Higher Education Panel Report Number 73*. Washington, DC: American Council on Education, August 1986.

Erikson, Erik H. *Childhood and Society*. 2d ed. New York: W. W. Norton, 1963.

——*Identity and the Life Cycle*. New York: W. W. Norton, 1980.

——*Identity: Youth and Crisis*. New York: W. W. Norton, 1968.

——"Youth: Fidelity and Diversity." In *Youth and Culture: A Human-Development Approach*, ed. Hazel V. Kraemer. Monterey, CA: Brooks/Cole Publishing, 1974.

Feagin, Joe R., Hernán Vera, and Nikitah Imani. *The Agony Of Education: Black Students at White Colleges and Universities*. New York: Routledge, 1996.

Fiske, Edward B. *The Fiske Guide to Colleges*. New York: Times Books, Random House, 1997.

Fleming, Jacqueline. *Blacks in College: A Comparative Study of Students' Success in Black and White Institutions*. San Francisco: Jossey Bass, 1984.

Gilbert, Steven W. "Technology and the Changing Academy." *Change* (September/October 1995): 58–62.

Gilligan, Carol. *In a Different Voice: Psychological Theory and Women's Development*. Cambridge: Harvard University Press, 1982.

Goethals, George W., and Dennis S. Klos. *Experiencing Youth: First Person Accounts*. 2d ed. Boston: Little, Brown, 1976.

Goodman, Ellen. "When Students Fly from the Empty Nest." *The Philadelphia Inquirer*, September 17, 1986.

Gordinier, Jeff. "Sophomore Slump." *Princeton Parents*, February 1987.

Green, Kenneth C., and Steven W. Gilbert. "Great Expectations: Content, Communications, Productivity, and the Role of Information Technology in Higher Education." *Change* (March/April 1995): 8–18.

Green, Madeleine F., ed. *Minorities on Campus: A Handbook for Enhancing Diversity*. Washington, DC: American Council on Education, 1989.

Griffin, Carolyn Welch. *Beyond Acceptance: Parents of Lesbians and Gays Talk About Their Experiences*. New York: St. Martin's, 1990.

Hafner, Katie. "Wiring the Ivy Tower." *Newsweek* (January 30, 1995):62–66.

Hanson, Jennifer, and Friends. *The Real Freshman Handbook: An Irreverent and Totally Honest Guide to Life on Campus*. Boston: Houghton Mifflin, 1996.

Hassan, Steven. *Combatting Cult Mind Control*. Rochester, VT: Park Street Press, 1988.

Historically Black Colleges and Universities. Wintergreen/Orchard House, Inc., New York: Arco Publications, 1995.

Horowitz, Helen Lefkowitz. *Campus Life*. New York: Alfred A. Knopf, 1987.

Hughes, Jean O'Gorman, and Bernice Sandler. "Friends Raping Friends: Could It Happen to You?" Washington, DC: Project on the Status and Education of Women, Association of American Colleges, April 1987.

The Insider's Guide to the Colleges. New York: St. Martin's Griffin, 1997.

Johnston, Lloyd D., Jerald F. Bachman, and Patrick O'Malley. *Monitoring the Future: A Continuing Study of the Lifestyles and Values of Youth*. Ann Arbor: University of Michigan Institute for Social Research, 1991.

Jones, Thomas B., ed. *The Educated Person: A Collection of Contemporary American Essays*. St. Paul, MN: Metropolitan State University, 1983.

Josselson, Ruthellen. *Finding Herself: Pathways to Identity Development in Women*. San Francisco: Jossey-Bass, 1990.

Kaplan, Louise. *Adolescence: The Farewell to Childhood*. New York: Simon & Schuster, 1984.

——*Oneness and Separateness: From Infant to Individual*. New York: Simon & Schuster, 1978.

Katz, Montana, and Veronica Vieland. *Get Smart! A Woman's Guide to Equality on Campus*. New York: Feminist Press at the City University of New York, 1988.

Keniston, Kenneth. "Youth: A 'New' Stage of Life." In *Readings in Adult Psychology: Contemporary Perspectives*, ed. Lawrence R. Allman and Dennis T. Jaffe. New York: Harper & Row, 1977.

Koehler, Michael. *Advising Student Athletes through the College Recruitment Process: A Complete Guide for Counselors, Coaches and Parents*. Englewood Cliffs, NJ: Prentice Hall, 1996.

Kuh, George D., John H. Schuh, Elizabeth J Whitt, and Associates. *Involving Colleges*. San Francisco: Jossey-Bass, 1991.

Ledray, Linda E. *Recovering from Rape*. New York: Henry Holt, 1986.

Levine, Arthur. "Hearts and Minds: The Freshman Challenge." *American Association of Higher Education Bulletin*, 1986:3 6.

MacGowan, Sandra F., and Sarah M. McGinty. *50 College Admissions Directors Speak to Parents*. San Diego: Harcourt Brace Jovanich, 1988.

Mahler, Margaret S., Fred Pine, and Anni Bergman. *The Psychological Birth of the Human Infant*. New York: Basic Books, 1975.

Mitchell, Robert. *The Multicultural Student's Guide to Colleges: What Every African-American, Asian-American, Hispanic and Native American Applicant Needs to Know about America's Top Schools*. New York: Noonday Press, 1996.

Money Guide: Your Best College Buys Now. From the editors of *Money* magazine. 1996 edition.

Offer, Daniel, and Judith Baskin Offer. *From Teenage to Young Manhood*. New York: Basic Books, 1975.

Otis, Carol L., and Roger Goldingay. *Campus Health Guide: The College Student's Handbook for Healthy Living*. New York: College Board, 1989.

Parrot, Andrea, ed. *Acquaintance Rape: The Hidden Crime*. New York: John Wiley & Sons, 1991.

Pascarella, Ernest T., and Patrick T. Terenzini. *How College Affects Students*. San Francisco: Jossey-Bass, 1991.

Pearson, Carol S., Donna L. Shavlik, and Judith G. Touchton. *Educating the Majority: Women Challenge Tradition in Higher Education*. New York: American Council on Education/Macmillan, 1989.

Perry, William G., Jr. *Forms of Intellectual and Ethical Development in the College Years*. New York: Holt, Rinehart & Winston, 1968.

Peterson's Study Abroad 1997: A Guide to Semester & Year Abroad Academic Programs. Princeton, NJ: Peterson's, 1997.

Powell, Elizabeth. *Talking Back to Sexual Pressure*. Minneapolis: CompCare Publishers, 1991.

Reese, Deborah Frankel. "The Children Are Gone." Letter to the Editor. *The New York Times*, December 1985.

Reschke, Wayne, and Karen H. Knierim. "How Parents Influence Career Choice." *Journal of Career Planning and Employment* (Spring 1987).

Ross, Joan and Michael D. Langone. *Cults: What Parents Should Know*. Seacaucus, NJ: Lyle Stuart, Inc., 1989.

Rudin, Marcia. *Cults on Campus: Continuing Challenge*. Rev. ed. New York: International Cult Education Program, 1996.

Sacks, Peter. *Generation X Goes to College*. Chicago: Carus Publishing, 1996.

Sanford, Nevitt. *The American College*. New York: John Wiley & Sons, 1962.

——*Where Colleges Fail*. San Francisco: Jossey-Bass, 1967.

Sheehy, Gail. *Spirit of Survival*. New York: William Morrow, 1986.

Siegel, Dorothy. *Campuses Respond to Violent Tragedy*. Phoenix, AZ: American Council on Education/Oryx Press, 1994.

Singer, Margaret Thaler, with Janja Lalich. *Cults in Our Midst: The Hidden Menace in Our Everyday Lives*. San Francisco: Jossey-Bass, 1995.

Smith, Barbara Leigh. "On Learning, Technology and the Way We Work." *American Association of Higher Education Bulletin*, September 1997: 8.

Smith, Michael Clay, and Margaret D. Smith. *Wide Awake: A Guide to Safe Campus Living in the 90s*. Princeton, NJ: Peterson's Guides, 1990.

Steen, Sara. *Academic Year Abroad*, New York: Institute of International Education, 1997.

Stern, Daniel N. *The Interpersonal World of the Infant.* New York: Basic Books, 1985.

Sweet, Ellen. "Date Rape: The Story of an Epidemic and Those Who Deny It." *Ms/Campus Times* (October 1985): 56–85.

Tannen, Greg, and Charley Winkler. *The Student's Guide to the Best Study Abroad Programs.* New York: Pocket Books, 1996.

Toth, Susan Allen. *Ivy Days: Making My Way Out East.* New York: Ballantine Books, 1984.

Upcraft, M. Lee, John N. Gardner, and Associates. *The Freshman Year Experience.* San Francisco: Jossey-Bass, 1990.

Viorst, Judith. *Necessary Losses.* New York: Simon & Schuster, 1986.

Wallerstein, Judith, and Sandra Blakeslee. *Second Chances: Men, Women, and Children a Decade After Divorce.* New York: Ticknor & Fields, 1990.

Warshaw, Robin. *I Never Called It Rape: The Ms. Report on Recognizing, Fighting and Surviving Date Rape.* New York: HarperCollins Publishers, 1989.

Wechsler, Henry. "Alcohol and the American College Campus: A Report from the Harvard School of Public Health." *Change* (July/August 1996):20–25, 60.

Weinberg, Carol. *The Complete Handbook for College Women.* New York: New York University Press, 1994.

Weinstein, Miriam. *Making a Difference College Guide.* San Raphael, CA: Sage Works Press, 1995.

Whiteley, John. *Character Development in College Students: The Freshman Year.* Vol I. Schenectady, NY: Character Research Press, 1982.

Willimon, William H., and Thomas H. Naylor. *The Abandoned Generation: Rethinking Higher Education.* Grand Rapids, MI: William B. Eerdmans, 1995.

Wilson, Erlene B. *Money for College: A Guide to Financial Aid for African-American Students.* New York: Penguin Books, 1996.

——*The 100 Best Colleges for African-American Students.* New York: Penguin Books, 1993.

Wolensky, Robert. "College Students in the Fifties: The Silent Generation Revisited." In *Adolescent Psychiatry: Developmental and Clinical Studies,* ed. Sherman C. Feinstein and Peter Giovacchini. Vol V. New York: Jason Aronson, 1977.

Wolff, Michael, ed. *How to Get into the School of Your Dreams Using the Internet and Online Services*. New York: Wolff New Media, 1996.

Zikopoulos, Marianthi, ed. *Open Doors 1989/90: Report on International Educational Exchange*. New York: Institute of International Education, 1990.

I N D E X

NOTES

This is a place for you to record your own stories and notes. If you would like to share any of these with the authors, you can contact them via the Harper-Collins Web site at: http://www.harpercollins.com.

NOTES

NOTES

NOTES

NOTES

NOTES

NOTES